Deepest Practice, Deepest Wisdom

Deepest Practice, Deepest Wisdom

Three Fascicles from *Shōbōgenzō*
with Commentaries

KŌSHŌ UCHIYAMA

Translated by DAITSŪ TOM WRIGHT
and SHŌHAKU OKUMURA

Wisdom

Wisdom Publications
199 Elm Street
Somerville, MA 02144 USA
wisdompubs.org

Library of Congress Cataloging-in-Publication Data
Names: Dōgen, 1200–1253, author. | Uchiyama, Kōshō, 1912–1998, writer of added commentary. | Wright, Thomas, 1944– translator. | Okumura, Shōhaku, 1948– translator.
Title: Deepest practice, deepest wisdom: three fascicles from *Shōbōgenzō* with commentaries / Kōshō Uchiyama; translated by Daitsū Tom Wright and Shōhaku Okumura.
Description: Somerville, MA: Wisdom Publications, 2018. | Includes bibliographical references and index. |
Identifiers: LCCN 2017018055 (print) | LCCN 2017020908 (ebook) | ISBN 9781614293392 (ebook) | ISBN 1614293392 (ebook) | ISBN 9781614293026 (paperback) | ISBN 1614293023 (paperback)
Subjects: LCSH: Sōtōshū—Doctrines—Early works to 1800. | BISAC: RELIGION / Buddhism / Zen (see also PHILOSOPHY / Zen). | RELIGION / Buddhism / Sacred Writings. | PHILOSOPHY / Zen.
Classification: LCC BQ9449.D654 (ebook) | LCC BQ9449.D654 S53213 2018 (print) | DDC 294.3/85—dc23
LC record available at https://lccn.loc.gov/2017018055

ISBN 978-1-61429-302-6   ebook ISBN 978-1-61429-339-2

22 21 20 19 18   5 4 3 2 1

The cover art is a painting by Ch'i Pai-shih: "Chrysanthemums and Mantis" (hanging scroll). Courtesy of Heritage Image Partnership Ltd / Alamy Stock Photo. Cover design by Phil Pascuzzo.

The sumi-e paintings on pages 1, 61, 185, and 261 are courtesy of Michael Hofmann, http://www.michaeldhofmann.com/. Interior design by Michael Russem. Set in Diacritical Garamond Pro 11/16.

Wisdom Publications' books are printed on acid-free paper and meet the guidelines for permanence and durability of the Production Guidelines for Book Longevity of the Council on Library Resources.

♻ This book was produced with environmental mindfulness. For more information, please visit wisdompubs.org/wisdom-environment.

Printed in the United States of America.

Please visit fscus.org.

Contents

Introduction

Interest in Buddhist thought and practice has grown immensely during the past thirty or forty years. Zen Buddhism in particular has caught the eye of scholars in Western philosophy and ethics and also of ordinary people (nonspecialists), young and old alike. Among exponents of Zen thought, enthusiasm has centered on the writings of the great thirteenth-century Japanese Zen master Eihei Dōgen (道元). Dōgen was not the first to talk about Zen in Japan, but his complete devotion to explicating the teachings of the Buddha and putting those teachings into action left a most impressive legacy for many generations following. Dōgen also coined many expressions and wrote in a style that has had a lasting influence on the Japanese language. Dōgen's ideas were revolutionary, fresh, and thoroughly rooted in the Buddha's teachings.

Today, more and more translations of Dōgen's works are emerging, as well as commentaries on the depth of his teachings. If scholars find this book helpful, that is fine, but if this book were only for scholars, then the audience would indeed be a small one. It is my sincere hope that this book will be most helpful to anyone who raises the questions "Who am I?" or "What is all of this around me?" or "How can we be free of suffering?"

A Brief History of Dōgen's Life

Eihei Dōgen lived during the Kamakura period (鎌倉時代, 1185–1333) in Japan. Only fifteen years prior to Dōgen's birth, the emperor was overthrown and a military government called the *bakufu* took over. The military government controlled most or all of Japan for the next several hundred years with frequent conflicts and battles between clans and classes. Dōgen's father died when he was three years old, and his mother died when he was seven. So he was orphaned as a child and lost several relatives due to military conflict. Thus, it was in no ideal state of calm and peace that Dōgen surely carried within himself the questions of "Who am I?" "What is all this?" and "How can we be free from suffering?"

At thirteen years of age, young Dōgen was ordained as a novice priest on Mt. Hiei in the Tendai tradition. At Mt. Hiei, he studied the *Lotus Sūtra* extensively, which led to the question *if we are already enlightened, why do we have to practice?* Dōgen's teachers were unable to answer him and advised him to visit Eisai Zenji, abbot of Kenninji monastery in the capital, Miyako. Eisai had returned from China a few years earlier and had brought the Zen teaching with him to Japan. Whether Dōgen actually met Eisai Zenji or not[1] no one really knows, but it is certain that Dōgen stayed at Kenninji for several years before taking the very hazardous journey to China, together with Myōzen, Eisai's first disciple, in 1223. Dōgen spent the first two years visiting various teachers in Sung China, but he became rather disillusioned at the quality of the practice there. Before returning to Japan, however, he heard that a new abbot had been installed at Keitokuji Monastery on Tendōzan and decided to see for himself. Dōgen was very impressed with the new abbot, Tendō Nyojō,[2] and was invited to visit the abbot's room at any time.

On one occasion at the monastery, Dōgen presented his dilemma to Nyojō, who had now become his teacher. If we are all enlightened, as is written in the *Lotus Sūtra*, why do we need to practice? Nyojō's reply turned Dōgen's life around. He said that practice is a manifestation of enlightenment. In other words, the practice of zazen was not something one did in order to gain enlightenment; rather, sitting itself fully manifests enlightenment and the Buddha's teaching.

---

1. It appears that Eisai had died or was on his deathbed around the time Dōgen visited Kenninji.

2. Tendō Nyojō (天童如淨, Chi. Tiantong Rujing; 1163–1228).

Dōgen returned from China in 1227 or 1228 and reentered Kenninji Monastery, where he lived for three more years. But, from a few brief statements among his writings, we understand that he was very disappointed in the collapse of the practice there and left.

Dōgen then lived in a small hermitage southeast of Miyako, present-day Kyoto. Finally, in 1233, Dōgen was able to found his first temple, Kannon-dōri Kōshō Hōrinji in Fukakusa, a district south of the city of Kyoto. This is not the same Kōshōji monastery that is today located on the north side of the Uji River across from Byōdō-in Temple in the city of Uji. The former burned down after Dōgen moved to Echizen, in today's Fukui Prefecture, and was rebuilt in Uji in the seventeenth century.

As *kōan* practice was gaining in strength and popularity in Miyako, and as increasing criticism came from Mt. Hiei, Dōgen decided to leave the area of the capital completely and move to the countryside. So, in 1243, Dōgen left Kōshōji and made the arduous journey to the province of Echizen. The following year, he moved into Daibutsuji Monastery. Later, Daibutsuji was renamed Eiheiji, and it was there that Dōgen spent his final ten years of teaching. In 1253, Dōgen fell ill and decided to seek treatment in Miyako. When he left Eiheiji, Koun Ejō (孤雲懐奘) became the next abbot. After his arrival in the capital and a brief stay at the home of a lay follower, Dōgen passed away.

Dōgen's Writing Style

Dōgen wrote in a Japanese as far removed from the present-day language as Chaucer's work is from modern English. His writing style is incisive and also very poetic. He used metaphors and hyperbole, as well as Zen *mondo* or kōans in his writings. Dōgen often quoted from various scriptures, many times tweaking them with his own turn of phrase. He also coined many new words to express his vision of Buddhadharma. It takes several readings to even begin to grasp the connection of Dōgen's writing to our practice, but the effort is worth it; every reading deepens one's understanding. As Alexander Pope says: "A little learning is a dangerous thing, drink deeply, or taste not the Pierian spring, for shallow draughts intoxicate the brain, and drinking largely sobers us again." In fact, even having much knowledge about something is incomplete unless it can come to function in our day-to-day life through wisdom. And the way to begin to unfold the many layers of the teaching of Buddhadharma as wisdom is to practice it.

Context for the Chapters

Each part in this book will begin with a fascicle from Dōgen Zenji's *Shōbōgenzō*. Next, there will be a commentary by Kōshō Uchiyama Rōshi. The fourth section of the book is comprised of comments from the translators.

All of Uchiyama Rōshi's remarks were derived from Dharma talks he gave at Sōsenji Temple in Kyoto at the monthly zazen gatherings there between 1978 and 1988, after Uchiyama Rōshi's retirement as abbot of Antaiji Monastery in 1975. The talks were at the invitation of then-abbot Hosokawa Yūhō Rōshi and recorded and later transcribed by Ishiguro Bunichi. The transcriptions were then edited and published by Hakujusha Publishers, Tokyo, in the volumes *Shōbōgenzō: Appreciating Makahannya-Haramitsu, Ikka no Myōju, and Sokushin Zebutsu* (正法眼蔵：摩訶般若波羅蜜／一顆の明珠／即心是仏を味わう) in 1982 and in 1984 *Shōbōgenzō: Appreciating Uji and Shoaku Makusa* (正法眼蔵：有時／諸悪莫作を味わう).

The first fascicle in this book is "Maka Hannya Haramitsu" (摩訶般若波羅蜜, "Practicing Deepest Wisdom"), Dōgen's commentary or teaching on the *Heart Sūtra*. Presented to the assembly during the first practice period in the summer of 1233, "Maka Hannya Haramitsu" was one of the first of Dōgen's writings that were later put together and became known as *Shōbōgenzō*.

The second fascicle from *Shōbōgenzō* in this book takes up the problem of the relationship of good and evil to our lives and is entitled "Shoaku

Makusa" (諸悪莫作, or, in English, depending on the context, "Refraining from Evil" or "Evil Refrained From"). This fascicle was presented to the resident monks living with Dōgen at Kōshōji in Uji of Yamashiro Province, on July 16, 1240. Ejō copied the writing in his quarters in 1243.

The final fascicle, "Uji" (有時, "Living Time"), takes up the problem of time and connection to the life force. ("Uji," the name of the third fascicle in the book, should not be confused with the name of the district Uji 宇治 or the Uji River, along which the Kōshōji Monastery of today is located.) "Uji" was written in November, at the start of the winter of 1240, while Dōgen was still at Kōshōji Temple, and was later copied by Ejō in his quarters in 1243, during the summer practice period, called *ge-ango* (夏安居). Today, there are two *ango* a year, one in the summer and one in the winter, called *tō-ango* (冬安居) or winter practice period, but in Dōgen's time, it appears there was only one per year.

Brief Background of Uchiyama Rōshi's Life

Before being ordained by Kōdō Sawaki Rōshi (興道沢木老師) at the outset of the Pacific War in 1941, Kōshō Uchiyama was Hideo Uchiyama. Hideo, born in 1912, lived with his parents and an older brother in the district of Hongo in Tokyo. In 1923, during the Great Kanto Earthquake, Hideo's family all survived, but their home was totally destroyed. Young Hideo's father, Mitsuhiro, was well known for his *kirigami* and *kamonori*, different styles of origami. Hideo, however, preferred the origami that he had learned meticulously from his grandmother and later in life would become well known for it, publishing several books systematizing all the origami folds. He used to humorously call himself the "Kamisama of Origami," or "god of origami"; in Japanese, the word *kami* can mean "god" or "paper," so Rōshi was making a Japanese pun.

After high school, Hideo entered Waseda University in the spring of 1930 and graduated from the Bungakubu (Faculty of the Humanities and Social Sciences, Department of Philosophy), in the spring of 1935. While at Waseda, he majored in Western philosophy, specializing in Kant. He continued on at Waseda in the graduate school for two more years, and in the spring of 1938, he took a position as instructor at Miyazaki Kōkyō Shin Gakkō (at the time, a Catholic junior and senior high school). While he was still an undergraduate at Waseda, young Hideo had met his first love, and they were together during those years. After four years, however, his wife contracted and soon after died of tuberculosis, which was not uncommon in Japan at that time.

Perhaps to take his mind off his grief at the loss of his wife at such a young age, the distraught Hideo signed on to teach mathematics at a Catholic school and seminary in Miyazaki. While he was there, he decided to learn about Christianity and began studying with the priests at the school. After only half a year, he became disillusioned, quit, and returned to Tokyo, where another young woman he had known from childhood was waiting. Hideo married again. But, again, misfortune struck; his new bride died in childbirth, along with the baby. After consulting with his father, it was decided that it would be good for him to meet Kōdō Sawaki Rōshi. Shortly after listening to Sawaki Rōshi give a Dharma talk, Hideo realized that the only way he could possibly understand Buddhadharma would be to become a monk and practice it. So, on December 7, 1941, Hideo Uchiyama was ordained as Kōshō Uchiyama, novice priest.

During the war, Sawaki Rōshi, knowing that Kōshō was not physically strong and would certainly be unfit to serve in the military, sent him to various places. In tucked-away, rural Shimane Prefecture, Kōshō spent his time making charcoal to survive. Later, he spent some time in Shizuoka Prefecture making salt. One week prior to the end of the war, Kōshō was drafted into the army. However, as the war was soon over, he never had to go into training.

When the war ended, Sawaki Rōshi sent Kōshō to Jippōji Monastery in Hyogo Prefecture, where he stayed for about three years. In 1949, Sawaki Rōshi became the new abbot of Antaiji Monastery in Kyoto and called all his disciples to join him there. At the time, Japan was still suffering from the ravages of war, and the temple had been occupied by squatters. When Sawaki Rōshi took over the temple and established a routine of daily zazen and study, most of those residing there left.

Kōshō Uchiyama stayed at Antaiji from this point until his retirement in 1975. Sawaki Rōshi was a very severe teacher, which can be seen by the fact that Uchiyama was the only disciple to stay with him from 1949 until his death in 1965. Other than for the regular monthly sesshins, Sawaki Rōshi was rarely at Antaiji. He traveled all over the country conducting sesshin—several days or, sometimes, weeks, concentrating on just sitting zazen—at various temples and giving Dharma talks. Just before his death, Sawaki Rōshi told his disciple Kōshō that he knew he would not have enough money to pay for a fancy funeral, so he should donate his corpse to Kyoto University Hospital and have them use it for their research. The significance of this is that in the Japanese Buddhist tradition once a body has been cut up, a funeral can no longer be held. Kōshō did exactly as he was told and, in lieu of a funeral, held a forty-nine-day sesshin at Antaiji. Anyone who wanted to pay their respects to Sawaki Rōshi could do so by going up to the *zendō* and sitting zazen with Uchiyama.

At the same time, Kōshō's own father was quite ill and hospitalized with throat cancer. Kōshō's mother had died in 1955, and his father finally passed away in 1967, two years after Sawaki Rōshi's death.

After his teacher's death, Kōshō Uchiyama became abbot of Antaiji and, for the first time, was addressed as Rōshi. He often joked about how he had been a novice monk (*shami*) until old age. When Sawaki Rōshi died, Uchiyama Rōshi vowed to stay at Antaiji for ten more years to write texts for ordinary people and to raise young people to face the twenty-first century.

Rōshi retired from Antaiji in 1975, and he and his third wife and ardent disciple, Keiko, moved to Ōgaki, in Nagano Prefecture, where they lived for two years. Then, in 1977, he returned to Kansai, living at a small hermitage, Nōke-in, in Kohata, a district in southern Kyoto Prefecture.

During Rōshi's final years, he often spent several months of the year in bed with a type of tuberculosis; his wife looked after him with great care in order that he might continue to write texts for the next generation for as long as possible. Finally, on the evening of March 13, 1998, just after his evening walk, Rōshi passed away quietly at Nōke-in.

Uchiyama Rōshi often said that he felt that the twenty-first century would become the century of true religion. He defined the word *religion* quite differently from most people; Rōshi felt religion was to "develop the most refined and distilled life attitude." And I believe that is what he did.

Uchiyama Rōshi's Style

Many years ago, Uchiyama Rōshi stated that his aim as a teacher was to produce texts for people to read and study and to nurture young practitioners in their practice. He did both. Despite being very busy preparing his talks on the Dharma teachings (*teishō*, 提唱), writing books, meeting with the many guests who visited Antaiji, and of course, sitting the bimonthly sesshins, Rōshi always found time after meals to be with all of those who resided in the monastery.

As difficult as Dōgen's thinking and writings are to penetrate, Uchiyama refused to explain these matters using Buddhist jargon or philosophical discourse. Rather, he chose to talk about Buddhadharma in everyday language. For this reason, his style may be somewhat deceptive, because on first reading, it may appear that he is being too simplistic. I think that is why it is necessary to read through his commentaries again and again.

One more thing about Rōshi that will gradually become apparent to readers is that he never said, "Do as I say, not as I do." He never hesitated to show through personal example how he himself had made plenty of mistakes before and during his many years of practice; he never tried to cover them up. And quite often he told us that he was serving as a model to others, but whether he was a good one or bad one was up to us. If there is something to emulate, then go ahead, if not, then discard it.

My Relationship with Uchiyama Rōshi

In December 1968, I hitchhiked my way from Sapporo, Hokkaido, down to Kyoto. It took me two days. When I arrived at Antaiji, the day before the sesshin for that month was to begin, I was ushered into Rōshi's room to speak with him and give him a letter of introduction written by Kawamura Kōyu Rōshi, who was at the time abbot of his own temple in Hokkaido. Kawamura Rōshi had finished reading Uchiyama Rōshi's *How to Cook Your Life* (*Jinsei Ryori no Hon*) and was very impressed with the regimen of zazen that was available at Antaiji. Somehow, from my very first visit, even though my Japanese was still very basic, Rōshi made me feel as though I were fluent in the language. His warmth and directness left a deep impression on me, and I was eager to return the next day to begin the sesshin.

I arrived at the temple just after dinner and was assigned a room and given some bedding. The room was cold, and it took some time for me to fall asleep; even in my futon, I remained cold for several hours. Then, at 4:00 A.M.—BOOM CLANG, BOOM CLANG, BOOM CLANG CLANG CLANG—the wake-up call! Up to the zendō, find a cushion, and sit still. The time passed so slowly I thought I was going to die after the first period. I lived, though, and the sesshin continued minute after minute, hour after hour, slow day after slow day. After three and half days, I became sick from the cold and had to rest for the remainder of that day. Somehow, I managed to get through the final day, and the sesshin ended. When I left Antaiji, I thought I would never, ever return to that *refrigerator* again.

However, during the ensuing days and months, I put the experience behind me; January soon became March, which soon became July. By August, it was blazing hot when I hitchhiked down to Kyoto once more in order to visit Antaiji and wait for a friend who was to join me later that month. The plan was that our next stop would be India, in order to find a guru.

When I arrived at Antaiji this time, I was again ushered in to see Uchiyama Rōshi, who graciously invited me to stay for as long as I wished. He also asked me something that rather startled me: "Did you bring your Bible?" A bit shocked, I inquired, "Isn't this a Buddhist monastery?" Rōshi replied, "Yes, of course, it is. But you have come from a very different culture and tradition. So, while you're at Antaiji, it would be good for you to reread your Bible while practicing zazen and find out the wonderful things that Jesus had to say." Well, this time I stayed three months at Antaiji, after which I moved into a tiny apartment just across the road from the temple. And for the next three years, I commuted to the temple in the mornings and evenings for zazen and survived by teaching English part-time wherever I could find work.

The long hours of zazen were never easy for me. My legs were like two stiff boards, but with the support of the other monks living there and the many other American and European practitioners who came and went from Antaiji, I somehow managed to continue. The daily schedule at Antaiji consisted of three hours of zazen in the mornings and two more hours in the evenings. Besides the monthly sesshins of five days, we also had mid-monthly sesshins of three days. There were also several months of the year when we sat not five hours daily, but nine.

Besides the zazen schedule, there were two other "pillars" of the practice there—work and study. Work consisted of laboring in the fields growing a few vegetables, while study meant finding and reading whatever books on Buddhism in English I could. As Antaiji had no parishioners, we had to go out on mendicant begging called *takuhatsu* (托鉢) several times a month. Takuhatsu was, in a sense, the fourth pillar of our practice.

Little by little, I also continued my study of Japanese so I could read and eventually translate Uchiyama Rōshi's books. During these years, besides sitting the sesshins with everyone, Rōshi was working on his own writings to explain Buddhadharma to us and preparing for his Dharma talks. There was also an endless trail of guests to and from his room. It's a wonder he was able to study at all! Nevertheless, Rōshi always managed to find time to listen to and speak with his disciples. After meals, he would often sit on the porch at Antaiji and talk informally with us while he smoked three of the four cigarettes he allowed himself every day.

One day I went in to see Rōshi to ask him a question about something I had read in *Shōbōgenzō Zuimonki* (正法眼蔵 随聞記), a compilation of notes taken down by Dōgen Zenji's disciple Koun Ejō. Coincidentally, Rōshi had a copy of the book open on his desk. He showed it to me, and I couldn't help but sense how old the copy was, because it was all beaten up and every page was filled with notes in the margins. I kidded him that it must be about time to buy a new copy. Silently, he lifted his hand and pointed his finger at the bookshelf behind me. When I found the shelf he was pointing to, he said to take a look at the books there. In all, I counted fourteen copies of the same *Zuimonki* and every one of them was as raggedy as the next. And all of them had many lines underlined with notes in all the margins. I asked Rōshi what changes when you read the same book so many times. His reply was quite interesting. He said that "the lines you underline change." What he meant was that when first reading a book like that, you might be impressed by some idea of Dōgen's and think that it is very important. But after you read the book again and again, what is truly important changes. What had seemed important on first reading seems less so in the context of several hundred readings. And what you hadn't noticed in earlier readings begins to stand out.

After I'd been at Antaiji for some time, Rōshi would ask me to translate for him when he had foreign guests. One day he had a visitor from the Middle East, and I was called on to interpret. The young man began by saying that he was already enlightened but simply came to Antaiji to get his enlightenment confirmed by Uchiyama Rōshi. I prefaced my translation to Rōshi by saying that I think this fellow is serious and what he wants to ask you seems ridiculous but please don't laugh. Rōshi understood immediately and inquired of the man as to why he felt he was now enlightened. The young man said, "Well, when I sit down to eat a bowl of noodles at a noodle shop, I can eat the noodles, tap my foot, and listen to the music on the radio simultaneously." Rōshi thought about that for a minute and replied in all seriousness to his visitor, "Well, if doing things simultaneously is a sign of enlightenment, wouldn't the jugglers in a circus be the most enlightened?" The young visitor didn't seem to get the point, and I suspect went home somewhat disillusioned.

Even when I wasn't living in Antaiji, I would visit (pester) Rōshi regularly to ask him a question or two. After I asked the question and Rōshi had thought about it, he would give his reply. I would thank him and then leave. Each time, Rōshi's reply would cover what I had asked, but there was also always a portion of his reply that I didn't immediately understand. Then, during the next few days or weeks (or months), I would be someplace and realize, "Oh, what Rōshi said applies here." And at another time, "Oh, and it applies here, too!" Eventually, when I realized fully what Rōshi had said, I would be satisfied for a while before another question would arise. I would see Rōshi again, and the same thing would happen again: his reply would cover more than my question. Over the years, I understood what Rōshi was doing. He was slowly but purposefully trying to get me to ask bigger, more comprehensive questions. If he had replied with some super-duper universal answer to my first narrow questions, I would have drowned. Besides, it wasn't his replies that were important for me, but rather learning how to ask bigger questions.

One day in an early spring when Rōshi was often sick and in bed, I took the train down to Kohata to visit him and his wife at Nōke-in to cheer him up. When I arrived, Keiko greeted me as usual and invited me in. When I went into his room, Rōshi was lying in his futon. After I told him what it was like outside and inquired about how he was feeling, he propped himself up on one elbow and began to talk. After a while, he sat up straight in bed, seemingly feeling a bit energized. On that particular day, he showed me a poem he had recently written and explained it to me. After about thirty minutes, not wanting to tire him out, I left and returned to the station. And on the way back into town, a question occurred to me: which one of us was sicker? Despite going to cheer *him* up, *I* was the one who walked away full of energy and enthusiasm. The one who was to be comforted wound up being the comforter. That was what he was like—a truly fully alive human being.

During his time at Antaiji, and also in many of his Dharma talks at Sōsenji, Rōshi often quoted Sekitō Kisen on the gist of Buddhadharma. Sekitō said: "The vast sky never impedes the drifting white clouds." Sawaki Rōshi made a calligraphy of this quote that was hung in the dining hall at Antaiji. At the time, it didn't occur to me, but after Rōshi retired and often took long walks along the banks of the Uji River, he frequently talked about how he would just look up at the sky in wonder as the clouds drifted by.

Now, the Uji River itself is not good for swimming in as it has many whirlpools that form here and there. In fact the name of the river comes from the word *uzu*, meaning "whirlpool." I think that looking at those eddies and whirlpools as the river flowed along and looking at the clouds taking different shapes and colors as they drifted by must have made a deep impression on Rōshi. And he used these natural happenings as a metaphor to talk about the "secretions of the brain," which we normally call thoughts of the human mind. Just as various clouds drift through the open sky—sometimes large fluffy ones, sometimes dark menacing ones—or as whirlpools of resistance appear in our mind, when we sit zazen, letting go of whatever it is that has come up in our head, eventually all of them just appear out of nowhere and eventually drift apart or fall away. I think that Rōshi must have felt that the sky and the river were teaching him about the depths of Buddhadharma as a life teaching.

In fact, during one of my visits to Nōke-in to see Rōshi just after his eighty-first birthday, he remarked, "You know, at eighty-one, I'm finally beginning to understand just a little about the depth of Buddhadharma."

In the late afternoon of March 13, 1998, Rōshi went for his usual walk along the river. When he returned, however, Keiko noticed something peculiar in his walk, and when he entered Nōke-in, Rōshi collapsed in the entryway. His wife soon called the doctor, who came immediately. Just a few hours later, as Keiko was holding his head, Rōshi looked up at her and smiled, saying, "Today I finished my poem 'Ogamu.'" Those were his last words, and below is the poem he was referring to, translated as "Just Holding Precious," along with one other poem, "Undivided Life," which he composed during the final two years of his life. Another poem, "The Expansive Sky," written around the same time, features in his commentary to "Shoaku Makusa."

Undivided Life:
The Final Resting Place for a *Jiko*
That Has Clarified All That Is to Be Clarified

At the end of aging
We can see that
Lifedeath is one Life
Not life *and* death
Lifedeath is one undivided
Lightness and darkness
One vast blue sky
Is like the depth of
One Lifedeath is
The depth of Life—
Encountering right now
That depth-ful Life
While holding it precious

To revere that depth
Walking toward that Lifedepth

To divide, classify, separate
Letting go of the hand of thought
Just holding precious
Undivided Life
Life as it is.

Just Holding Precious

Meeting right hand with left hand—just holding precious
God and Buddha becoming one—just holding precious
Everything encountered becoming one—just holding precious
All things coming together as one—just holding precious
Life becoming life—just holding precious

In closing, I would like to dedicate this book to my teacher and friend, Kōshō Uchiyama Rōshi. His life will always be an inspiration to me and serve as a model for one way to live in a vibrant and alive way. I had the good fortune to meet both Uchiyama the practitioner and bodhisattva and also Uchiyama the man.

DAITSŪ TOM WRIGHT

Part I. Practicing Deepest Wisdom

1. Maka Hannya Haramitsu
Practicing Deepest Wisdom[3]

摩訶般若波羅蜜

EIHEI DŌGEN ZENJI

Translated by SHŌHAKU OKUMURA

The time of Avalokiteśvara Bodhisattva practicing profound *pra-jñāpāramitā* is the whole body clearly seeing the emptiness of all five aggregates.[4] The five aggregates are forms, sensations, perceptions, predilections, and consciousness; this is the fivefold prajñā. Clear seeing is itself prajñā. To unfold and manifest this essential truth, the *Heart Sūtra* states that "form is emptiness; emptiness is form." Form is nothing but form; emptiness is nothing but emptiness. Hence, there are the hundred blades of grass, the ten thousand things.

The twelve sense-fields are twelve instances of prajñāpāramitā.[5] Also, there are eighteen instances of prajñā: eye, ear, nose, tongue, body, mind;

3. "Maka Hannya Haramitsu" (摩訶般若波羅蜜): in Sanskrit, "Mahāprajñāpāramitā," or "Practicing Deepest Wisdom." *Pāramitā* (in Japanese, *haramitsu* or 波羅蜜) refers to the perfecting or practicing of *prajñā* (*hannya*) or deepest wisdom. Deepest wisdom, in this case, means the wisdom to cut through the roots of our selfish greed, ignorance, and anger.

4. The aggregates (Skt: *skandhas*; Jpn: *goun*, 五蘊) are the five elements of existence. In the case of human beings, form is the physical body and the four elements are mental.

5. The twelve sense-fields (Skt: *dvādaśa-āyatana*) are the six sense-organs and their objects. These are the first twelve of the eighteen dhatus (Skt: *aṣṭādaśa-dhātavaḥ*) mentioned in the next sentence.

form, sound, smell, taste, touch, objects of mind; as well as the consciousnesses of eye, ear, nose, tongue, body, and mind.

Further, there are four examples of prajñā: suffering, its cause, its cessation, and the path [to cessation].[6] Moreover, there are six instances of prajñā: generosity, pure precepts, calm patience, diligence, quiet meditation, and wisdom.[7] There is also a single instance of prajñāpāramitā manifesting itself right now—unsurpassable complete, perfect awakening.[8]

Also there are three instances of prajñāpāramitā: past, present, and future. And there are six instances of prajñā: earth, water, fire, wind, space, and consciousness.[9] Also four instances of prajñā are going on daily: walking, standing, sitting, and lying down.

There was a monk in the assembly of Śākyamuni Tathāgata. He thought to himself, "I should venerate and make prostrations to this most profound prajñāpāramitā. Although prajñāpāramitā teaches that within all things there is neither arising nor extinguishing, there are practical approaches such as the skandhas of maintaining the precepts of body, mouth, and mind, of quietly meditating, of enacting wisdom and emancipation, and of the insight resulting from emancipation.[10] Also there are the practical approaches consisting of the ranks of those entering the stream, the once-returners, those who will no longer return, and

6. These are the four noble truths, which are considered to be the Buddha's first teaching.

7. These are the six *pāramitās*, which are the basic points of bodhisattva practice. The Prajñāpāramitā sūtras assert that prajñā (wisdom) is the most essential among the six points.

8. In Sanskrit, *anuttarā samyak-sambodhi*. This is the same "the one supreme living and enlightened reality" referred to in "Shoaku Makusa."

9. These are the six elements of all existence. To the original four of Theravādan Buddhism, Mahāyāna added space, and Vajrayana added consciousness.

10. These are called five merits of the Dharma-body (Jpn: *gobun-hosshin*, 五分法身).

the arhats.[11] Self-awakening is also a practical approach.[12] Unsurpassable perfect awakening is yet another practical approach. The [Triple] Treasures of Buddha, Dharma, and Sangha are also a practical approach. Turning the wondrous Dharma wheel, saving various sentient beings, is also a practical approach."

The Buddha, knowing the monk's thoughts, said, "So it is! So it is! The most profound prajñāpāramitā is indeed subtle and difficult to fathom."

The monk realizes now that by venerating and making prostrations to all things, he is venerating and making prostrations to prajñā, which teaches that even though there is neither arising nor extinguishing, there is arising and extinguishing. In this very moment of veneration and prostration, prajñā manifests itself in practical approaches such as keeping the precepts, quietly meditating, manifesting wisdom, and so forth, and saving various sentient beings. This [moment of veneration] is called nothingness. The approaches to nothingness thus become practical. This [veneration] is the most profound prajñāpāramitā, subtle and difficult to fathom.

Indra asked the Elder Subhūti, "Venerable one, when bodhisattva-mahāsattvas want to study the most profound prajñāpāramitā, how should they do it?" Subhūti replied; "Kausika,[13] when bodhisattva-mahāsattvas want to study the most profound prajñāpāramitā, they should study it as empty space."[14]

---

11. These are the four ranks of śrāvaka, which means those who listened to the Buddha's voice: (1) stream-enterers (Skt: *srota-āpatti-phala*; Jpn: *yoruka*, 預流果), (2) once-returners (Skt: *sakṛd-āgāmi-phala*; Jpn: *ichiraika*, 一来果), (3) nonreturners (Skt: *anāgāmi-phala*; Jpn: *fugenka*, 不還果), and (4) arhats (Skt: *arhat-phala*; Jpn: *arakanka*, 阿羅漢果).

12. This refers to *pratyekabuddhas*, who practiced by themselves, attained enlightenment without a teacher, and did not teach others. The path of pratyekabuddhas and *śrāvakas* were called the "two small vehicles" by Mahāyāna (greater vehicle) Buddhists.

13. Indra is a guardian god of Buddhadharma; Kausika was his name when he was a human being before he became a god.

14. This refers to Mahāyāna practitioners. Literally *bodhisattva* means one who has aroused a Way-seeking mind (道心), and *mahāsattva* refers to a great being.

Therefore, to study prajñā is itself empty space. Empty space is studying prajñā.[15]

Indra spoke again to the Buddha, "World-honored one, when good men and women accept and keep, read and recite, ponder in accord with reality, and expound to others this profound prajñāpāramitā [which you have just] presented, how can I protect them? World-honored one, I simply wish that you bestow your compassion and teach me."

At that time, the Elder Subhūti said to Indra, "Kausika, do you see a Dharma that can be protected, or not?"

Indra replied, "No! Venerable one, I don't see any Dharma that I can protect."

Subhūti said, "Kausika, when good men and women speak as you have, the most profound prajñāpāramitā is itself protection. If good men and women act as you said they do, they are never separate from the most profound prajñāpāramitā. You should know that, even if all human and nonhuman beings wanted to harm them, it would not be possible to do so. Kausika, if you want to protect them, you should do as you said. Wanting to protect the most profound prajñāpāramitā and all bodhisattvas is not different from wanting to protect empty space."

You should know that accepting and keeping, reading and reciting, pondering in accord with reality, is nothing other than protecting prajñā. The desire to protect is accepting and keeping, reading and reciting, and so on.

My late master, the ancient buddha, said:

The whole body [of the wind bell] is like a mouth hanging in
    empty space—
Without distinguishing the winds from east, west, south, or
    north
Together expressing prajñā equally to all beings—
Di ding dong liao di ding dong.[16]

15. To study prajñā is to study things just as they are, in their ungraspable nature.
16. Dōgen's teacher Tendō Nyojō wrote this poem about a wind bell hanging under

This is how prajñā has been expressed authentically through the buddhas and ancestors. The whole body is prajñā. All others [which include the self] are prajñā. The whole self [which includes others] is prajñā. The entire universe—east, west, south, and north—is prajñā.

Śākyamuni Buddha said, "Shariputra, all these sentient beings should make offerings and prostrations to prajñāpāramitā as they do to a living buddha. They should contemplate prajñāpāramitā just as they make offerings and prostrations to a *buddha-bhagavat*.[17] What is the reason? Prajñāpāramitā is not different from a buddha-bhagavat. A buddha-bhagavat is not different from prajñāpāramitā. Prajñāpāramitā is itself a buddha-bhagavat. A buddha-bhagavat is itself prajñāpāramitā. What is

---

the temple roof. In the *Hōkyō-ki* (寶慶記), Dōgen recorded his conversation with Nyojō about this poem.

Dōgen made one hundred prostrations and said, "In your poem about the wind bell, I read in the first line, 'The whole body [of the wind bell] is like a mouth hanging in empty space' and in the third line, 'Together expressing prajñā equally to all beings.' Is the empty space referred to one of the form [*rūpa*] elements? Skeptical people may think empty space is one of the form elements. Students today don't understand Buddhadharma clearly and consider the blue sky as the empty space. I feel sorry for them."

Nyojō replied with compassion, "This empty space is prajñā. It is not one of the form elements. The empty space neither obstructs nor unobstructs. Therefore, this is neither simple emptiness nor truth relative to falsehood. Various masters haven't understood even what the form is, much less emptiness. This is due to the decline of Buddhadharma in this country."

Dōgen remarked, "This poem is the utmost in excellence. Even if they practice forever, the masters in all corners of the world would not be able to match it. Every one of the monks appreciates it. Having come from a far-off land, and being inexperienced, as I unroll the sayings of other masters in various texts, I have not yet come across anything like this poem. How fortunate I am to be able to learn it!

"As I read it, I am filled with joy and tears moisten my robe and I am moved to prostration because this poem is direct and also lyrical."

When Nyojō was about to ride on a sedan-chair, he said with a smile, "What you say is profound and has the mark of greatness. I composed this poem while I was at Chingliang monastery. Although people praised it, no one has ever penetrated it as you do. I acknowledge that you have the Eye. You must compose poems in this way."

17. *Bhagavat* is one of the ten epithets of a buddha, which is usually translated as "World-Honored One."

the reason? Shariputra! This is because all supreme awakened tathāgatas issue from prajñāpāramitā. Shariputra! This is because all bodhisattva-mahāsattvas, pratyekabuddhas, arhats, nonreturners, once-returners, stream-enterers, and so on issue from prajñāpāramitā. Shariputra! This is because the way of the ten good deeds in the world, the four quiet meditations, the four formless samadhis, and the five divine powers all issue from prajñāpāramitā."[18]

Therefore, a buddha-bhagavat is itself prajñāpāramitā. Prajñāpāramitā is nothing other than all beings. All these beings are empty in form, without arising or extinguishing, neither defiled nor pure, without increasing or decreasing. Actualizing this prajñāpāramitā is to actualize buddha-bhagavat. Inquire into it! Practice it! Making offerings and prostrations [to prajñāpāramitā] is attending and serving buddha-bhagavat. Attending and serving [all beings] is itself buddha-bhagavat.

> Expounded to the assembly at Kannon-dōri-in [Monastery],
> on a day of the summer practice period in the first year of Tenpuku [1233].
> Copied by Ejō while serving at the attendants office [jisharyo] of the
> Yoshimine Monastery on the twenty-first day of the third month,
> spring of the second year of Kangen (1243).

18. The ten good deeds are (1) not killing living beings, (2) not stealing what is not given, (3) not committing sexual misconduct, (4) not telling lies, (5) not uttering harsh words, (6) not uttering words that cause disharmony between two or more persons, (7) not engaging in idle talk, (8) not being greedy, (9) not giving in to anger, and (10) not having mistaken views.

The four quiet meditations refer to the four steps of meditation in the realm of form (Skt: rūpadhātu). The four formless samadhis are the four stages of meditation in the realm of no-form (arūpadhātu).

In India people thought a practitioner could attain five super-human powers by the practice of meditation: (1) the ability to go anywhere at will and to transform oneself or objects at will, (2) the ability to see anything at any distance, (3) the ability to hear any sound at any distance, (4) the ability to read another's mind, and (5) the ability to know one's and others' former lives.

2. Commentary on "Maka Hannya Haramitsu"

KŌSHŌ UCHIYAMA

Translated by SHŌHAKU OKUMURA

Reality is prior to comparison.

Dōgen Zenji always sets forth his comments about the most significant points in the opening of his writings. It would be easier for me to give a talk on Dōgen Zenji's writings if he began with a light story and gradually introduced important points after people became interested and were ready to listen. But in the case of "Maka Hannya Haramitsu" ("Practicing Deepest Wisdom"), the title itself is one of the most essential matters in Buddhadharma.

Let us turn the ignition key and warm up the engine to prepare for listening. The first part of the title, *maka* in Japanese (摩訶) or *mahā* in Sanskrit ("great" or "greatness"), itself expresses the Buddhadharma as a whole. In the *Awakening of Faith in the Mahāyāna*, we read, "Generally speaking, Mahāyāna is to be expounded from two points of view. One is the principle [Dharma], and the other is the significance."[19] A common Japanese expression is *makafushigi* (摩訶不思議), meaning

---

19. The *Awakening of Faith in the Mahāyāna* (Jpn: *Daijō Kishin-ron*, 大乗起信論) is attributed to Aśvaghoṣa (80–150). Yoshito S. Hakeda, trans., *The Awakening of Faith* (New York: Columbia University Press, 1967), 28. I have taken the liberty to insert the word "Dharma" here because the Dharma that Uchiyama Rōshi talks about in the latter part refers to this.

"very mysterious or profound." In Sanskrit, *mahā* can mean "large," "many," or "superior." As it is difficult to translate *mahā* into Chinese or Japanese, *maka* is used as a transliteration, as in the title of Dōgen's fascicle. The difficulty is that this word is not an adjective. Generally, *large*, *many*, and *superior* are adjectives, but in Buddhadharma, *mahā* is a noun that indicates the whole of Buddhadharma itself. *Mahāyāna* in the *Awakening of Faith in the Mahāyāna* also expresses Buddhadharma as a whole.

What does *mahā* mean as a noun? As I often say, it means "Buddhadharma beyond comparison." Comparatively speaking, when we inquire in detail, it is impossible to judge whether something is big or small. For instance, we think a flea's testicles are small. But there must be some viruses that are parasitic on a flea's testicles, and for those viruses, a flea's testicles must be immeasurably vast.

With our very sophisticated microscopes and telescopes, it is very hard to distinguish what is big and what is small. For instance, one light year is the distance that light travels in one year. On the basis of our usual sense of distance, we cannot imagine how far a hundred billion light years is. When we compare human beings with such an extraordinary distance, we feel ourselves to be very small, almost as nothing. Yet when we take a look at it from a different angle, we can recognize the vastness of the universe only in our own life experience as a human being, which is as small as nothing. Without the life experience of the self as a basis, there is no comparative reality of a vast space of a hundred billion light years.

We cannot perceive such reality through our comparisons. The vital point is that such life experience itself is beyond comparison. In living our lives as an individual self, we experience vast and small things. That is our reality. With this life experience of the self that is beyond comparison, we are born and live, and when we die, we die together with all such life experiences. This is the incomparable reality of our lives in which each one of us lives and dies. The Dharma points to this reality of life. In the *Awakening of Faith in the Mahāyāna*, we read, "So-called Dharma is the mind of living beings."[20] The world in which all of us carry out our life experience is Dharma. In a Buddhist context, *mind* sometimes implies human psychology, but more often it means life. It can be understood as the mind of all living beings, or one-mind. In short, mind is life that includes all beings, or *jin issai seimei* (尽一切生命).

Also, since all beings exist as the life experience of the self, mind can be understood as the self that is one with all beings, *jin issai jiko* (尽一切自己). The basis of all beings is the fact that this self is alive. There is no reality beside this.

In the *Awakening of Faith in the Mahāyāna*, we find the following: "This mind includes all dharmas [beings] in this world and outside this world. This Dharma and one-mind are the Buddhadharma."[21] Such insight into Buddhadharma is entirely different from the usual Western, scholastic, or scientific way of thinking. *Mahā*, in Buddhadharma, includes all beings and is beyond comparison. In other words, mahā is the reality of life itself.

In the beginning of *Bendōwa*, we read, "All buddha-tathāgatas together have been simply transmitting wondrous Dharma and actualizing incomparable awakening for which there is an unsurpassable, unfabricated, wondrous method. This wondrous Dharma, which has been transmitted only from buddha to buddha without deviation, has as its criterion *jijuyū zanmai* [the samadhi of freely receiving and functioning]."[22] The wondrous Dharma is called *mahā* here.

The significance of *Mahāyāna*, or "greater vehicle" in the *Awakening of Faith in the Mahāyāna* is that all buddhas ride on this vehicle of mahā and all bodhisattvas reach buddhahood riding this Dharma, or mahā. The *Awakening of Faith in the Mahāyāna* discusses the body, form, and function of mahā. Here, the function of mahā is called "prajñā." Mahā

20. Ibid.
21. Ibid.
22. Kōshō Uchiyama, *The Wholehearted Way: A Translation of Eihei Dōgen's Bendōwa*, trans. Shōhaku Okumura and Taigen Daniel Leighton (Tuttle, 1970), 19.

is body. In *Bendōwa*, the same function of reality is called an "unsurpassable, unfabricated, wondrous method."[23] In short, it is zazen.

All Buddhist teachings are ultimately the same. They are not difficult to understand. Yet, if you don't clarify the fundamental expressions, they are ungraspable. Once you make it clear, you will know that "Mahāyāna," "one-mind," "wondrous Dharma," and other expressions in Buddhist literature indicate only one reality. The one reality is mahā. Prajñā, Mahāyāna, or jijuyū zanmai work on the basis of mahā.

Therefore, first we must understand mahā, then actually practice zazen. As a result, mahā-prajñā will begin to function.

Traditionally, in Japanese Buddhism, the most significant terms such as "mahā," "Dharma," "wondrous Dharma," "mind of living beings," "one-mind," and so forth have not been translated into the Japanese vernacular. Japanese Buddhist priests have been using them simply as technical Buddhist terms. They've preserved them like canned foods. From ancient times, Buddhist scriptures have been stored away in the treasuries of Buddhist temples. Cans are a convenient way to preserve or carry food, but unless we open the can and eat the food, just carrying it around is meaningless. We cannot appreciate the taste.

What I am attempting now is to open these canned Buddhist terms, taste them myself first, and if they taste good, recommend them to you. This is why I named our gathering *midokkai* (味読会): a gathering for reading and "tasting" or appreciating *Shōbōgenzō*.

Now, I would like to explain the deeper meaning of *mahā*. *Mahā* refers to the reality of life itself. I want to examine our lives on the basis of this reality. I will take a simple example. Each one of us was born of a woman. We can understand the reality of life when we carefully observe a newborn baby. About one week after birth, a baby begins to perceive things visually. All beings in the world are reflected on the baby's retinas. Yet

---

23. Ibid.

because of its immaturity, the baby doesn't see things clearly or recognize things as independent entities. The same face regularly appears in front of the infant's eyes. The figure speaks and puts her nipple into the baby's mouth. Gradually, in the baby's brain, images of mama and nipple are formed. In other words, the baby starts to grasp things as concepts after abstracting them from the reality of life. Later we obtain the ability to abstract things by using words.

Within a few years, the young child begins to differentiate using words when she/he comes across something like a dog or a pig. If the child is male, he eventually questions why a female friend does not have a penis, and he begins to understand the distinction between male and female. The concept of "I" is being gradually formed. He understands that "I" belongs to one specific group of people (males, Japanese, etc.) and then to a larger group of all humankind.

Thus when someone comprehends his- or herself as part of a group, we think he or she has become an individual adult. Therefore, in the usual process of human growth, every person develops the habit of viewing his- or herself as a separate human being among humans. Consequently, one loses sight of a self that can be understood as all-over-all (all/all), that all beings are the self as the true form that is the reality of life.

Buddhadharma always teaches about the reality of life. So, isn't the world that is created by discrimination through the use of abstract words also the reality of life? Yes, it is. The power to conceptualize, that is, to grasp things using categories resulting from abstraction, is nothing other than the reality of life.

This is a very difficult point. If there were a clear distinction between one side of the world where we grasp things by abstract concepts and the other side where we see the reality of life prior to any such abstraction, then this dimension of the reality of life would be rather easy to understand. However, such a clear distinction is not the case.

Although we think that we are looking at the same cup, the reality of life is that each one of us looks at this cup with their own retinas, with their own feelings, and from their own particular angle. The most understandable example is money. A one-thousand yen bill for a penniless person is totally different in value as well as in actual feeling than it would be for a millionaire. The same is true for an item of clothing or a drop of water. Each of us lives within our own world.

Nevertheless, since childhood we have been trained to abstract reality by using words. We do so by habit and then we come to believe that all of us share the same social world in which we express everything in words. For instance, now I am speaking and you are listening. It seems we understand each other. But it is questionable whether each one of you understands my words completely and in the same way. These days we trust instruments to measure brain waves. Even when we measure our brain waves by computers, it is questionable whether the result coincides completely with the reality of the person. I think it strange that science encourages the assumption that under the same conditions, no matter how many times we repeat certain experiments, we will get the same results. For example, if I push this cup with the same force, it moves this far. Each time I repeat the same action, if conditions are the same, the cup moves exactly the same distance. People think this is an objective truth. Repeated measurements confirm this. But this is merely belief in the world of science.

The reality of life, however, is that the same thing never occurs twice. The world of reality is always flowing moment by moment. We casually believe that spring, summer, fall, and winter repeat in the same way every year. But does the same thing really happen every year? No, never. On the same date of any year, the weather will be different. In any one year, we say that we had an exceptionally hot summer or an unusually cool summer compared to last year. It varies. The temperatures we have for this year are never exactly the same as the temperatures for an average year. If we do, it is really exceptional. We do have four seasons every year in the same order. Roughly speaking, the same things repeat. But, as a matter of fact, the same events never occur again. We must realize that to consider natural science as an exact study is actually to think very loosely. We cannot understand our lives with such a loose way of seeing things. Life itself is not so simple a matter that it can be dealt with by mere measurement of brain waves.

The reality of life as we are actually living it here is truly subtle. This moment lives with no comparison to past and future.

That which created the natural science that I am criticizing now is also a part of the reality of life. We cannot say that natural science is outside of life. This is a very difficult point. *The Awakening of Faith in the Mahāyāna* points to this when it says "the mind of living beings includes all dharmas both within the world and beyond the world." The loose way of seeing things scientifically and the subtler way of seeing are both included in the one-mind. The abstracted world and the world beyond abstraction are both within this life—that is the mind of living beings, Dharma, mahā.

Usually we each see things as if we were one of all myriad beings (one/all). In Buddhadharma, *mahā* means all/all. Dharma and one-mind are like this. Infinity divided by infinity (∞/∞) is 1, even in mathematics. But this one is different from the 1 in mathematics. All-divided-by-all, all-inclusive reality is entirely impermanence itself. There is nothing fixed. This is why it is said in the *Xinxin Ming*, "Do not cling even to the oneness."[24]

People often say that Christianity is a monotheistic religion, that God is only one. This common view is a mistake. God is one and God is simultaneously all beings. In the book of Exodus, God said, "I am who I am." The Christian God must be one and, at the same time, all beings. Such an idea is conveyed in Buddhism with expressions such as "one is everything, everything is one" (*ichi soku issai, issai soku ichi*; 一即一切、一切即一). On this point, Buddhism and Christianity are not different.

---

24. *Xinxin Ming* (信心銘; Jpn: *Shinjinmei*) or *On Faith in Mind* or *Clarifying Mind* was written by the Third Ancestor, Kanchi Sōsan (鑑智僧璨; Chi: Jianzhi Sengcan; ?–606).

There are many scholars who insist that Christianity is monotheistic and Buddhism is pantheistic. Such scholars' heads are too loose.

Next, *prajñā* means "wisdom," or in Japanese *chie* (智慧). In Buddhist terminology *chi* and *e* have different connotations. As for the fundamental definition of the word, *chi* means making selections, and *e* means making distinctions.

All Christian theological terms have been largely defined since the Middle Ages. In the same way, almost all Buddhist terms were defined in the *Abhidharmakośabhāṣya* written by the Indian master Vasubandhu in the fourth–fifth century CE. This definition of wisdom is mentioned there.

When we buy something, we compare this thing and that thing and choose the most appropriate one. This comparing and making distinctions is *e*. The choosing and selecting is *chi*. In our daily lives, we compare this with that, right with left, good with bad, like with dislike. In any situation, we make choices, judge, select one thing, and reject another. Our life is a continuum of this kind of choosing. There are some people who say of themselves that they are just coasting along. Such people choose coasting. These days it seems that everybody wants to buy a house. Buying a house is the largest purchase most people will make in their lifetime. Some people have been badly taken in by real estate brokers and have lost all their money and property. Making a choice is a very significant matter for us. Yet, if every time we need to make a choice we think too much about choosing one thing over another, we might become neurotic. Even in our daily affairs, making a choice can be pretty difficult.

In Buddhism, wisdom, prajñā, is neither intelligence in such worldly matters, nor is it scientific knowledge. By prajñā, the reality of life itself, mahā, starts to work. Mahā is the foundation from which we make choices. In other words, each time we make a choice, we are to make it from the perspective of universal life (all things being equal and interconnected).

We commonly think: "I should do this or that." "I want to get a good deal." "I don't want to lose anything." We worry, going back and forth in our minds. With prajñā, we don't think according to our personal desires, but make choices on the basis of all-inclusive life. This is the way we function as the self of universal life. Whatever the situation, each one of us is actually living out universal life. Realizing this fact, I live out the life of my self no matter what happens. Consequently, we are not hung up by conventional ideas of good/bad or win/lose. Neither do we just coast along without judging right or wrong. This is a most critical point.

A long time ago, the famous tea master Sen Rikyu (千利休, 1521–91) asked a carpenter to put a nail on an alcove post to be used for hanging a ladle. After discussing where the best place would be, the carpenter made a tiny mark at a spot indicated by Rikyu. If he had hammered a nail right away, they wouldn't have had a problem. But, after taking a short break, the carpenter couldn't find the mark. He asked Rikyu again to select a location. When Rikyu pointed to a spot, the carpenter found the small mark he had made the first time. This story means that even though we can put a nail anywhere on a post, if it is for a particular use, then there must be one best particular spot. This possibly made-up story is nevertheless quite interesting. Sawaki Rōshi often said, "You can go in any direction—east, west, south, or north. Wherever you go, you are the self that is only the self." Herein lies true peace of mind. Yet peacefulness is not enough. Within that peace of mind we have to aim at the best spot. This is prajñā, wisdom.

Further, in the *Shinjinmei,* we read, "There is no difficulty in the Supreme Way, but picking and rejecting are not in accord with it." Picking and rejecting mean making choices based on the judgments of our small mind. The true Way is not difficult; it does not involve making choices based on our preferences. This is wisdom. We only choose to dislike choices based on our egocentricity.

There's a proverb that goes, "A poor chess player's thinking is the same as taking a nap." Acting on a poor player's thinking is not a good idea.

Stop doing it, and instead make choices based on the vivid reality of life. In other words, having the wisdom that is prajñā means not being controlled by our thoughts, but letting decisions of right and wrong arise naturally from the life that permeates all beings. Herein, mahā functions in a very vigorous way.

Reality embodies limitless profundity.

Pāramitā is translated into Chinese as *duo* (度, *do* in Japanese), which means to cross over. In Mahāyāna Buddhism this means to cross over from the shore of delusion to the shore of enlightenment—and not only to ferry oneself across, but also to ferry all others across as well.

Pāramitā also means "perfection." Sawaki Rōshi expressed these dual meanings of pāramitā as "a way of life in which we have reached the point we have to reach." All of us without exception are self as the life that permeates all beings. Wherever we go, we live out our own self. Instead of living in comparison with others, I live my own life. This is prajñāpāramitā, perfection of wisdom.

The first of the six pāramitās, *dāna pāramitā*, or perfect or unconditional giving, does not mean to give something to others that ends up belonging to us. In reality, we are living out the self that is only the self. The "you" in front of my eyes is a part of my self. If you are there in need of something and I am here with some extra of it, since fundamentally there are no personal possessions, I just move it a little bit from here to there. This is dāna pāramitā. It is completed within the self that is only the self. There is no separation between my self and others. There is no private property in the all-inclusive self.

If I take some money from my wallet and give it to someone, thinking that I am giving away something of mine, this is not unconditional giving. In true giving, you and I are completely connected and permeate each other, so I am happy to help you. In the practice of dāna pāramitā, I become completely the self that is only the self.

This is also true for *śīla pāramitā*, perfect keeping of the precepts. Through observation of the precepts, the self that permeates all beings as total life is manifested. Therefore we cannot in truth say, "I am good because I keep the precepts, and you are not good because you don't keep the precepts." If we say so, we are violating the precepts. In an old scripture we read, "Neither having evil desires nor clinging to the proper forms of precepts—this is called keeping the pure precepts." The precepts are truly maintained when we live out our lives according to them, but without clinging to them. We just live out our lives in a straightforward way. Through this practice the self as inclusive of all beings is being completed.

Kṣānti pāramitā, the perfection of patience, does not mean that I put up with meanness. If we try to be patient in our relationships with someone we perceive to be outside of rather than within us, anger can accumulate until we think we cannot stand it anymore, and the anger bursts forth. We must practice the patience of *jiko*, or self that is only and wholly self.[25]

Vīrya pāramitā, the perfection of diligence, means to be diligent in genuinely living out all-inclusive life and continuing to courageously practice good deeds and cut off bad deeds. That's it. Diligence is to pour our whole self into each moment and each activity, animated by our life force. Some people try hard to avoid work. I think such people suffer instead. Since the life force works naturally, we're at peace when we work in harmony with our own life force. This is the perfection of diligence.

25. I haven't been consistent in translating the Buddhist term *jiko* (自己) in order to suggest various ways to look at the term. "Self before individuation" would be another legitimate way to look at it. In other words, in Buddhism, *jiko* includes two aspects; self as an individual, separate from other people and things (separate, of course, not intrinsically but by our thoughts, which by their own nature create a thought-dichotomy between self and other), and self that is actually the whole universe itself. Uchiyama Rōshi goes into more detail on this in chapters 3 through 6 of his book *Jiko: Religion without Sects* (自己——宗派でない宗教), which was first published by Hakujusha Publishers in 1965 and later republished by Daihorin-kaku Publishers as *Jiko: The Spiritual Travels of a Zen Monk* in 2004.

Dhyāna pāramitā, the perfection of meditation, is the reality of life settling into the reality of life itself.

Prajñāpāramitā, the perfection of wisdom, is choosing the reality of life as reality.

In summary, *pāramitā* means this: The true self manifests the true self and completely lives out that self.

The time of Avalokiteśvara Bodhisattva practicing profound pra-jñāpāramitā is the whole body clearly seeing the emptiness of all five aggregates.

In this first sentence of the text, we have to examine the Japanese names for two different Chinese translations of the Sanskrit name Avalokiteś-vara Bodhisattva—Kanjizai Bosatsu (観自在菩薩) and Kanzeon Bosatsu (観世音菩薩)—and we have to examine the meaning of *kan* (観) in those names. Kanjizai Bosatsu is a translation by Genjō,[26] and Kanzeon Bosatsu is an earlier translation by Kumārajīva. Often *kan* is used as a compound with *shi* (止) as *shikan* (止観). In this case, *shi* is a translation of the San-skrit term *śamatha* (single-pointed concentration), and *kan* is a transla-tion of the Sanskrit term *vipaśyanā* (insight). In the Tendai[27] school, for instance, there are two texts on meditation, one called *Makashikan* (摩 訶止観) or *Larger Śamatha-Vipaśyanā*, and the other called *Shoshikan* (小止観) or *Shorter Śamatha-Vipaśyanā*. Here, *shikan* refers to zazen.

In a little more detail, *shi* means to stop doing everything. In my own expression, this is "letting go of thought" or "opening the hand of thought." We always grasp things with our thoughts. When we stop doing that, we let go of thoughts, and what we have been grasping falls away—though the thoughts do spring up again repeatedly. Thoughts are secretions of the brain, which is of course also a part of our life. To see

26. Genjō (玄奘; Chi: Xuan-zang; 602–64).
27. Tendai (天台; Chi: Tientai).

that these secretions are nothing other than secretions is kan—insight. Usually, we act basing our actions on those thoughts. We live, so to speak, for the sake of these secretions of the brain. Many people say that they live for the sake of seeking happiness, as if they know what happiness is.

But what is happiness? Happiness is nothing more than what we feel when we have joy or pleasure in our mind. What we call happiness is merely the condition in which our desire for self-satisfaction is fulfilled. This is the root of our confusion: what do we human beings live for? Until recently, there were quite a few people in the East who thought they lived for the sake of Buddhadharma and people in the West who lived for the sake of following God's will. Such people saw God or Buddha as the absolute supreme value in their lives. However, these days, people have begun to think that God or Buddha exists only in the world of myths and fairy tales. Not many people find value in God or Buddha. So, ultimately, people live for the sake of their own happiness. Human beings these days can be motivated only if we can convince them that something will improve their standard of living and will fulfill their desire for self-satisfaction.

Nevertheless, "happiness," "a better standard of living," or "a prosperous society" are concepts, just secretions of the brain. We are living upside down if we find the meaning of our lives solely in fulfilling desires that are based only on secretions. Kan is to understand this well and see thoughts just as thoughts. See secretion simply as secretion, neither more nor less than that. See everything as reality of life just as it is. This is kan.

The meaning of the name Kanjizai Bosatsu is that, as the reality of life, we clearly see self as all beings as it is and we actually live out that self. To be a Kanjizai Bosatsu is to see (*kan*) the true reality (*zai*) of the self (*ji*) as life.

Kanjizai Bosatsu is not someone outside us. Each one of us must be Kanjizai Bosatsu. All of us, without exception, are actually living out the self that is only the self. This is the only possible way of life, and yet we mistakenly chase after secretions of the brain and live as if we are separated from the self that is only the self. We live, just floating around.

Each one of us is originally Kanjizai Bosatsu. We have to apply what Dōgen Zenji is saying to our own lives because Kanjizai Bosatsu is not someone other than ourselves.

"To practice profound prajñāpāramitā" means to actually do it, to carry out the perfection of wisdom in our lives. We often take the phrase only as words without putting it into practice. Right now I am talking about prajñā or wisdom, not practicing it. But isn't this talk a practice? Yes, it is. I am practicing by talking wholeheartedly about prajñā. It is not so easy to distinguish what is practice from what is not practice. In short, to practice means to actually live out the life of Kanjizai Bosatsu in its true meaning.

The word *jin* (深) or "profundity" in the opening line ("practicing profound prajñāpāramitā") is, as with mahā, not a matter of comparison between shallowness and depth. It means to thoroughly penetrate reality. Reality is infinitely profound.

The whole body.

The five aggregates are forms, sensations, perceptions, predilections, and consciousness; this is the fivefold prajñā. Clear seeing is itself prajñā.

Whole body, in Japanese *konshin* (渾身), means that there is no separation between subject and object. Since each of us is life-as-all-beings, there is no separation between the seer and things seen. The seer is also seen. Things seen also see. For example, when we talk about the sun, we see everything as if we are the sun itself. We emit the light, and so see all beings. This is what I mean when I say that the sun sees us. Although we imagine the sun is vast, it is not something vast in comparison to ourselves. As the reality of life, the sun is just an aspect of ourselves. Because we illuminate the sun with our own light as life-as-all-beings, it is possible for us to see the sun as the sun.

Since I illuminate all beings with the light of my life force, I can see all beings. This is what *shōken* (照見), or "clear seeing," means. Right now

I am talking to you, and while I am talking, I am looking at the faces reflected on my retinas. There are some faces that seem to understand what I am saying, and others that look a bit sleepy. I wholeheartedly try to make those faces show understanding if possible. But actually, self is speaking to self. Seeing self speaking to self is clear seeing—shōken.

The five aggregates of forms, sensations, perceptions, predilections, and consciousness make up a well-known Buddhist concept. The Japanese term for "forms," *shiki* (色), refers to material elements, and a different character, also read *shiki* (識), refers to elements of the mind or consciousness. But Buddhism doesn't divide everything into just mind and matter, but into these five categories. The other three categories are between mind and matter. The definition of *rūpa*, the Sanskrit term for "form," is things, which change and obstruct each other. Material things constantly change between the time of arising and passing away, and two things cannot be in one place at the same time. Consciousness (Skt: *vijñāna*; Jpn: *shiki*, 識) is mind itself that recognizes and differentiates between objects.

Matter and mind already include all beings, but in Buddhism, phenomena are categorized into impersonal elements to help us let go of the idea of ego and overcome deluded desires. The other three elements— sensations, perceptions, predilections—are the psychological functioning that arise between matter and mind.

Sensation (Skt: *vedanā*; Jpn: *ju*, 受) refers to receiving stimulation from objects when we encounter them and accepting them into our mind. *Perception* (Skt: *saṃjñā*; Jpn: *sō*, 想) refers to labeling sensations and creating images of the objects. *Predilection* (Skt: *saṃskāra*; Jpn: *gyō*, 行) means "fabrication" and "flowing." For instance, when we see a cup, we not only create an image but also add previous associations from our mind. We may think, "I like the shape of this cup," or "I want to touch it." We entertain those kinds of thoughts. In other words, predilections include all the psychological functions except sensation and perception, and encompass all conditioned beings except materials. To think that the cup has a good shape or that I want to touch it is a kind of psychological function. When we think further, such as, "How much does it cost?" this is not only a psychological function but also has something to do with numbers and is therefore a mental function. These are all included in predilection in Buddhist Abhidharma.

The oldest Buddhist sūtras are called the Āgama Sūtras. *Āgama* is not the name of a single sūtra, but rather a collection of sūtras categorized into four groups in the Chinese translation (five categories in the Pāli Tripiṭaka). Among the four, the most fundamental is called *Zōagon-kyō* (雑阿含経), or *Shorter Āgama Sūtras*. Within the first section of *Zōagon-kyō*, there is a sūtra called the *Sūtra of Impermanence* in which Śākyamuni Buddha's basic teaching about the five aggregates is recorded. The Buddha said, "You must see that rūpa, material form, is impermanent." And, "To see things this way is the right way of seeing." Then he continued, "A person who correctly sees forms arouses the mind of departure [from attachment to material objects]. A person who arouses the mind of departure extinguishes greed and pleasure. A person who extinguishes greed and pleasure liberates his/her mind. Thus, you should see that sensation, perception, predilection, and consciousness are also impermanent."

All things change. Their nature is impermanence. Sensations of objects, perceptions of them, predilections or volition of like and dislike, and consciousness are all impermanent. Observing things in this way is the right way of seeing. When we see things in this way, we can be liberated. This is the basic teaching about the five aggregates in the Āgamas.

However, in the Prajñāpāramitā sūtras or Perfection of Wisdom Sūtras of the Mahāyāna tradition, it is said that impermanence is also impermanent. This is called *emptiness*, "without fixed permanent nature." In the ninth chapter, "Arising and Perishing," of the *Larger Prajñā Sūtra*, it is written, "Bodhisattva-Mahāsattvas, if you want to practice prajñā-pāramitā, do not attach yourselves to the view that form resides in impermanence. Do not be caught up in the view that sensation, perception, predilection, and consciousness reside in impermanence. Why? Because impermanence is empty. Since impermanence is empty, it cannot be called impermanence. There is no impermanence apart from emptiness. Impermanence is emptiness. Emptiness is impermanence." We should not take for granted that the five aggregates are impermanent. Impermanence is also impermanent. Since everything is impermanent, without exception, we cannot grasp anything at all. So: emptiness.

I take a walk along the Uji River every evening, but I have never seen people swimming in it. Once I asked a friend of mine who lives near my house and who used to be a marine, "You can swim in this river, can't you?" He replied, "It is dangerous to swim here because of the eddies and whirlpools." We saw big whirlpools here and there in the river. The five aggregates are the same as the whirlpools. Each one of the five aggregates is life connected with everything. They turn around endlessly without stagnation. It is like seeing the whole life of a person in a short time-lapse movie. A newborn baby grows bigger and bigger in a twinkling of an eye and then begins to age and pass away. Not only human beings, but all beings, are like this. Everything is like a whirlpool.

Therefore, in the *Diamond Sūtra*, we read; "All conditioned beings are like dreams, phantoms, bubbles, shadows, drops of dew, flashes of lightning. We should see things in this way." And yet, is it possible for us to always see that all five aggregates are empty?

True enlightenment is not an enlightenment that can be acquired.

> To unfold and manifest this essential truth, the *Heart Sūtra* states that "form is emptiness; emptiness is form." Form is nothing but form; emptiness is nothing but emptiness. Hence, there are the hundred blades of grass, the ten thousand things.

"Form is emptiness; emptiness is form." These well-known phrases express the realm of the reality of life. As the reality of life, "all empty things" means all things, everything.

As I quoted from the *Zōagon-kyō*, Śākyamuni Buddha taught that we should see that form is impermanent. It seems that for Indian people during the Buddha's time, sexual desire was thought to be the biggest problem. People today in Japan and North America do not consider it to be a problem in the same way; if a novelist describes sexual activities, it isn't usually considered indecent. However, at the time of Buddha, Indian society was much stricter, and talking even a little about sex was considered immoral. Even today, movie audiences in India become excited when they see the hero and heroine merely holding hands with each other at the end of the movie. It was probably this attitude that made it important to teach monks that a beautiful woman becomes an old woman, and when she dies, her body is abandoned in the mountains, eaten by birds or animals, and finally becomes white bones. Because forms are impermanent, monks should detach themselves from them. They shouldn't be greedy for pleasure from forms, and they should never hold on to sexual desires. In the Āgamas, this stage or state of mind was referred to as liberated mind.

However, in the *Zōagon-kyō*, we find the following story. Several decades after Śākyamuni Buddha passed away, the monk Channa visited many elders in the sangha and asked how he could see the Dharma truth. The elders told him that the five aggregates are impermanent and egoless. And yet he still had a question and said to himself, "I have heard more than enough about the teaching that form, sensation, perception, predilection, and consciousness are impermanent. I understand that, but still I am not liberated from attachments to the five aggregates. What prevents me from seeing reality as it is? Isn't there someone who could give me an expression that better hits home?" Someone suggested to him to visit Venerable Ānanda who had been Śākyamuni's attendant for a long time. Since Venerable Ānanda had practiced with Śākyamuni, he must have been very old at the time.

The monk Channa went to the Venerable Ānanda and asked, "Isn't there a teaching of Buddha that would touch me more deeply?"

The Venerable Ānanda started to speak. "A long time ago, the Buddha said to one of his ten prominent disciples, whose name was Kātyāyana (Jpn: Kasennen, 迦旃延), 'The Tathāgata teaches the Middle Way, which is free from the extreme views of being [existence] and nonbeing [nonexistence]. Why? A person who sees correctly the arising of things as they are does not arouse the view of nonbeing. A person who sees correctly the perishing of things as they are does not arouse the view of being. This is right view.'"

This sūtra shows that the same teaching of reality, the same Buddhadharma, has been maintained from the very beginning of Buddhism. All beings fade and perish into nonbeing. There is no substance that will not be destroyed. But this does not mean nothing exists. Things are always arising and perishing. Conceptually, this is not easy to grasp. From the temporary collections of causes and conditions, everything arises and perishes the same as a whirlpool in a river or clouds in the wide-open sky. Clouds are collections of drops of water. Although they seem to exist as fixed entities, they gradually disappear.

Human beings constantly fight over power and money. Sawaki Rōshi said such struggles are like a tug of war over clouds. As ordinary human beings, we take for granted that money, social status, and power surely exist as something we can win through competition. But we're just playing tug of war. Everything is a result of temporary collections of causes and conditions. Nothing is substantial, just like clouds. From the beginning of Mahāyāna Buddhism, this reality has been called *emptiness* (Skt: śūnyatā; Jpn: *kū*, 空). We should understand emptiness in this way.

In chapter 35 of the *Mahāprajñāpāramitā Śāstra*,[28] we read, "Since all things are born of collections of causes and conditions, they lack self-

---

28. The *Treatise on the Great Perfection of Wisdom* (Jpn: *Daichidoron*, 大智度論; Chi: *Ta-chih-tu-lun*), a commentary on the *Mahāprajñāpāramitā Sūtra*, is said to have been written by Nāgārjuna (龍樹, c. 150–c. 250 CE) in the third century and later translated into Chinese in the fourth century by Kumārajīva.

nature.[29] Since all have no self-nature, they are ultimately empty." And in chapter 6 of *Mahāprajñāpāramitā Śāstra*, it is written: "All things born of causes and conditions, we declare them to be empty. Also all things are called by expedient names. These two truths—emptiness and expedient names—together are called the Middle Way." This last sentence also appears in Nāgārjuna's *Mūlamadhyamakakārikā* (*Fundamental Verses on the Middle Way*).

The Middle Way means that since all things neither exist nor do not exist, we see them as they are, in the same way we see whirlpools just as whirlpools, clouds as clouds. We cannot say clouds or whirlpools don't exist, but since they don't have a fixed self-nature, we cannot say they do exist. Although we cannot grasp them as entities with fixed self-nature, we cannot say they don't exist. This is the reality of life. This reality is expressed as "Form is emptiness; emptiness is form." A newborn baby grows quickly and becomes a beautiful woman. And the next moment, she becomes a middle-aged woman. Then age lines her face, her body starts to shrink, and she is old. Finally, she dies. This is truly the reality of our life. Form is emptiness and emptiness is form. Intellectually, we can understand that everything is empty. However, in our actual lives, it is not so easy to arouse the mind of departure and become free of greed for pleasure from objects simply by understanding the theory of emptiness of all beings.

A charming person is still attractive. We still try to grasp forms as fixed entities. A biology teacher taught a class: "Eighty percent of the human body is water. The power that maintains the shape of the human body is the same as the surface tension of water." A student was deeply impressed with this fact. When he left the class, he saw a good-looking woman walking down the street. He admired her and said to himself, "What charming surface tension!" We see things only on their "surface tension" and act accordingly.

---

29. The Japanese term is *mujishō* (無自性), literally meaning "no self nature," although a further interpretive translation might be "having no independent self."

The other day, a young woman visited me and talked about her life. She seemed very kindhearted. She had felt taking care of sick people was her calling and had become a nurse. In the beginning, she completely devoted herself to her work. However, after she got accustomed to her job, she noticed one day that she was thinking about where she wanted to go on her next vacation right in front of a patient who was suffering with pain from cancer. She was shocked to discover this aspect of herself. She thought she could not be qualified to be a nurse because of her egocentricity and lack of compassion toward the person in front of her. So she quit her job.

As I was listening to her story, I thought she was a very gentle and sincere person, but if nurses had to live up to her ideal image, I don't think anyone in the world could qualify as a nurse. The most important practice is to see that thoughts springing up in our minds are merely secretions and then, here and now, wholeheartedly take care of the sick person. Although various thoughts come up in our minds, if we're not caught up in them, we are able to care single-mindedly for someone who is ill—and we can be good nurses.

This is the same in the case of a husband and wife. I don't think there are many men who are never attracted to other beautiful women, even men who are faithful and care deeply about their wives. Reflecting upon myself, I really think this is true. If a man with such a tendency ought not marry, then no man but a saint could marry. We are fickle-minded beings. But an important point is to see that such fickle-mindedness is merely a secretion of our brain and let go of it. Men who see this point care for their wives and put themselves in the place of their wives in their daily lives. If both husband and wife have this attitude, they can be a wonderfully married couple.

Practitioners of Buddhadharma are the same. A community of practitioners traditionally is called a "pure and clean, great ocean of people."[30] Don't defiled thoughts arise at all in their minds? Yes, they do!

30. *Shōjōtaikaishū* (清浄大海衆), the assembly of a practicing sangha. The implication is

In fact, because monks live in a quiet setting without moving around so much, they actually have more random thoughts that are difficult to deal with. Even though various thoughts can be as powerful as a typhoon, an important point of practice is to remain unmoved by them. While they may very well have various mental or emotional problems, monks in a monastery just keep practicing quietly. By doing this, they truly understand that thoughts are merely the brain's secretions. This is the reality of practice in a monastery.

It is off the mark to think that delusive thoughts and desires will be eliminated as a result of practice. Mahāyāna Buddhists criticized a certain early Buddhist attitude as being *hīnayāna* ("small vehicle"), partly because monks with that attitude thought they could gradually reduce delusive thoughts and desires and finally attain arhathood when they eliminated them.

Practice is not something like vacuuming a room when it is dusty. As human beings, even if we clean ourselves up, dust and rubbish appear repeatedly according to causes and conditions. We should thoroughly understand that thoughts are merely temporary collections of causes and conditions as secretions from our brains, and we should keep practicing wholeheartedly whatever it is that we have to practice. Dōgen Zenji expressed this in *Gakudō Yōjinshū* (学道用心集), *Points to Watch in Practicing the Way*, as "Practice within delusion and attain realization before enlightenment." We mustn't wait to practice until after we have cleaned up all delusive desires. Rather, we must keep carrying on our practice as a practice in the midst of delusions that are hard to deal with. This is called "buddha practicing within delusion." If we think that we practice in order to gradually reduce delusive thoughts and desires and that after we have finished cleaning up all the rubbish we can be true practitioners, we will become completely confused. Delusive thoughts

---

that, once ordained, all secular names and ethnic and racial identities are finished. Hence, the community is undefiled and pure, free from the three poisons and other shackles.

and desires that we think we have gotten rid of raise their heads again and again when we meet with certain causes and conditions. It is natural to question why we are practicing. Without meddling with our delusions, we just carry on our practice. This is what Dōgen Zenji meant when he said "Form is nothing but form. Emptiness is nothing but emptiness." The thought that connects form and emptiness as "form is emptiness, emptiness is form" is already just a secretion of the brain.

I wrote in *Opening the Hand of Thought*:

What Dōgen Zenji meant by the phrase "practice and enlightenment are one," Shakyamuni Buddha called precepts, or *prātimokṣa* (Sanskrit). In the Sutra of the Last Discourses,[31] which was Shakyamuni Buddha's final teaching just before his death, there is a passage that reads:

Monks, after my death, respect and follow the *prātimokṣa*. If you do, you will be like a person who has been given a light in the dark, or like a pauper who acquires a great treasure.

These are Shakyamuni Buddha's last words. He said his disciples should respect and follow the precepts. *Prātimokṣa* has been translated into Japanese not just simply as "precepts" but also as "emancipation through the observance of the precepts" (*shosho gedatsu* or *betsubetsu gedatsu*). Each precept that is kept liberates us from its corresponding evil. Where we observe a particular precept, there we are immediately emancipated.

I think this idea of *prātimokṣa* is the origin of Dōgen Zenji's "practice and enlightenment are one." *Betsubetsu gedatsu* means that if we uphold a certain precept, we will be emancipated to the extent of that precept. If we open the hand of thought right here,

31. The *Sūtra of the Last Discourses* (Jpn: *Yuikyōgyō*, 遺教経) was translated from Sanskrit by Kumārajīva.

right now, and experience reality, that is true enlightenment. Dōgen expressed the spirit of Shakyamuni Buddha in his own words when he said "practice and enlightenment are one."[32]

Even when various idle thoughts arise in our mind, reality is only *gyō* (practice or action) on the ground of the reality of life. In *Shōbōgenzō* "Genjō Kōan," Dōgen Zenji writes, "When a person carries out practice/enlightenment in the Buddha Way, as the person realizes one Dharma, the person permeates that Dharma; as the person encounters one practice, the person [fully] practices that practice." Just wholeheartedly do whatever you are encountering right now. I think Dōgen Zenji wrote this fascicle "Maka Hannya Haramitsu" because he wanted to clarify this point. In the *Heart Sūtra*, this point is not yet clear. To say, "Form is emptiness; emptiness is form" is not enough. Since he wanted to show us the reality of our actual practice, he had to say further that form is form and emptiness is emptiness.

Tōzan Ryōkai[33] is an important Zen master in our lineage; Dōgen Zenji called him *kōso*, or "great ancestor." When Tōzan was leaving his master Ungan Donjō,[34] he asked, "A hundred years after your death, if someone asks me, 'What was the face of your master?' what should I say?" Ungan said, "This, just this." After Tōzan left Ungan, he traveled, keeping Ungan's words in mind. Once, when he was crossing a river, he saw his face reflected on the water, and he suddenly understood what Ungan meant. His insight immediately gave rise to a verse:

Never seek outside myself
    Or I will be far from me.

---

32. Kōshō Uchiyama, *Opening the Hand of Thought* (Boston: Wisdom Publications, 2015), 144–45.

33. Tōzan Ryōkai (洞山良价; Chi: Dongshan Liangjie; 807–69).

34. Ungan Donjō (雲厳曇晟; Chi: Yunyan Tansheng; 782–841), studied and practiced under Hyakujō Ekai (百丈懐海; Chi: Baizhang Huaihai; 720–814) and Yakusan Igen (薬山惟厳; Chi: Yaoshan Weiyan; 745–828), who was a disciple of Sekitō Kisen (石頭 希遷; Chi: Shitou Xiqian; 700–790).

Now I go only by myself.
    Everywhere I meet my reflection—
Now, he is surely me,
    But I am not him.
Seeing in this way
    I will act in accord with whatever comes.

"This, just this" is a precise expression of the reality of "Form is emptiness. Emptiness is form."

Dōgen Zenji expresses the same reality when he says, "Form is nothing but form; emptiness is nothing but emptiness. Hence, there are the
hundred blades of grass, the ten thousand things." From babyhood, we
memorize the names of things, such as "mama," "nipple," "doggy," etc.
Eventually we begin to think that the things we have named are individual, concrete existences outside ourselves. That is a cup. That is a water
pitcher. That is a pair of glasses. We think they are truly there, just as
we have abstracted them. However, the reality of life occurs before such
abstraction, and yet, includes the ability of abstraction. It excludes nothing. "Hence, there are the one hundred blades of grass, the ten thousand
things." Each thing is only itself. Or, as Ungan said, "This, just this."
Within the world of the reality of life, just "form is form and emptiness
is emptiness."

Usually I don't have much social contact. I don't watch TV. So I don't
have an abundant source of topics for conversation. I often talk about
walking. Walking and sky-watching are the only topics I can talk about.
Recently, I wrote a poem:

Big sky is just doing big sky;
White clouds are just doing white clouds;
Fall is here.

Perhaps the poem appears a bit pretentious, but this is my actual feeling. Big sky is always just big sky. White clouds are only white clouds.

Already it is fall. Fall is just doing fall. This is the meaning of "the one hundred blades of grass and the ten thousand things."

> The twelve sense-fields are twelve instances of prajñāpāramitā. Also, there are eighteen instances of prajñā: eye, ear, nose, tongue, body, mind; form, sound, smell, taste, touch, objects of mind; as well as the consciousnesses of eye, ear, nose, tongue, body, and mind.

The twelve sense-fields are the so-called six sense organs and their six objects. The eighteen instances refer to these twelve sense-fields and the six consciousnesses. The six sense organs are eyes, ears, nose, tongue, body, and mind. These organs are part of the makeup of our bodies. The six objects are forms (colors and shapes), sound, smell, taste, touch, and objects of mind. These are in the external world. The six sense organs meet with the six objects in the external world and are reflected onto our minds, producing the six consciousnesses: eye-consciousness, ear-consciousness, nose-consciousness, tongue-consciousness, body-consciousness, and mind-consciousness. The six sense organs, the six objects, and the six consciousnesses together are called the eighteen instances. Dōgen Zenji says that these are all prajñāpāramitā.

What is seeing? How can we see? It's truly a mystery! Scientists may explain the function of retinal cells, optic nerves, and so forth, but no matter how much explanation is given, we cannot understand the most crucial point. Eyes are eyes, and things are things, but how does the consciousness of seeing arise? This is really mysterious and beyond our comprehensive thought. The root of this wondrous phenomenon can only be called "life." Even if we put all the various parts of the human body together, such as head, chest, or legs, and connect them, we still cannot create a human being. Only if life functions there, is there a living human being. The ground such wondrous life is rooted in is prajñāpāramitā.

> Further, there are four instances of prajñā: suffering, its cause, its cessation, and the path [to cessation].

Suffering, the cause of suffering, the cessation of suffering, and the way leading to the cessation of suffering are the Four Noble Truths, a formulation of Śākyamuni's teachings. The first truth is that everything is suffering. The second truth is that the source of suffering is our tendency to collect various elements in our minds and become attached to them. In other words, as we assemble and categorize various elements, clinging or possessive yearnings arise. The third truth is that it is possible to reach cessation of such desires and suffering. The fourth truth is that there is a path leading to the cessation of desires. Dōgen Zenji says that these four truths are all prajñā. Ordinarily people may think that the first and the second are not prajñā, that only the third and the fourth are prajñā. But this is not the case. Suffering, as it is, is prajñāpāramitā, the perfection of wisdom. The covetous desires that cause suffering are as they are prajñāpāramitā. Suffering is a condition in which problems come toward us and we feel uneasy. Suffering is just suffering. We just suffer. People may think that they can be released from mental suffering through Buddhist practice, but they cannot be released from physical pain, no matter how much they practice.

I had an experience in 1952, five or six years after the end of World War II. At the time, many Japanese people suffered extreme poverty. Since even ordinary people might feel the need to beg, it was very hard to go out on takuhatsu, or mendicant begging. I mostly received five-sen bills or ten-sen bills. One sen was one hundredth of one yen. Since the bus fare was twelve or thirteen yen, I was not able to ride a bus. Day after day, I walked in the city of Kyoto on takuhatsu and came back to Antaiji, trudging exhaustedly up the long slope of Takagamine. One day in November, I stumbled on the slope and slightly injured the big toe of my right foot, probably because I stepped on a piece of glass or something. As soon as I arrived at the temple, I washed my feet with cold water. My injury did not seem serious, so I continued my daily takuhatsu. Several days later, it started to rain during takuhatsu, and I was completely wet when I returned to the temple. By then, the injury was closed, but it must have become infected. Gradually, it became swollen and painful and was accompanied by a high fever. It was all I could do just to bear the pain. Obviously, I didn't have money to go to a doctor, so I didn't know exactly what I should do. If it were an extremely acute infection, I might have died. If it were gangrene, they might have had to cut off my foot. I writhed in agony. But, since I couldn't see a doctor, there was no use in struggling with it. In despair, I said to myself, "If I have to die, I will die." I folded my futon and leaned against it for three days and three nights. Since it was November, it was quite cold, but the right half of my body was hot with fever. I covered only the left side of my body with another futon. The pain in my big toe echoed even to my head. On the third day, I was completely exhausted. As soon as I fell asleep, the pain would wake me up. At the time, I wondered how I would persevere in this pain if I had parents or a wife to help me. Fortunately or unfortunately, I had no one to rely on. I couldn't do anything but just endure the terrible pain. When I reached that conclusion, I felt that the foundation of suffering was taken away, and I wrote this poem:

Suffering a Foot Injury[35]

If I had a wife to care for me,
If my parents were near,
If I had money,
I wouldn't have suffered
In my dust-covered room
Lying on ragged quilts
Recalling Job—
"I can bear this hard pain"—
I am grateful.
People worry—
"What if I become ill?

---

35. Quoted from Kōshō Uchiyama, *How to Cook Your Life: From the Zen Kitchen to Enlightenment*, trans. by Thomas Wright (Boston: Shambhala Publications, 2005), 80.

Lose my job?"
Always framing their thoughts in
"What if. . . ."
They're afraid, though their fears
Are groundless.
Though I'm ill,
Without savings
Or income,
Unable to eat,
Even if I starved
I wouldn't think it strange,
And, just for that,
I feel grateful.

This kind of liberation certainly happens. But it is a big mistake to think that, once we have this kind of experience, we will necessarily be able to endure a painful situation next time. Since everything is impermanent, the next time is the next time. When there is pain, just be with the pain. When there is suffering, just face the suffering. "This, just this." We can do nothing else.

Mental agony is the same. As long as we are living as human beings, we will have various thoughts. They well up constantly and with irresistible force. Contrary to what is commonly thought about the condition of our minds in zazen, there is no time when we have "no thought, no mind." Following conditions such as temperature, humidity, and nutrition, various thoughts arise. Troubles come from taking actions based on such thoughts. Rather, what we can do is "this, just this."

For six months I lived and taught at a Catholic monastery and had a chance to see close up the lives of Catholic priests. I thought they ate too much rich food. On Fridays, they ate fried fish or something other than meat, but for the rest of the week they ate amazing amounts of meat. I supposed that because they ate too much rich food, various problems arose in their minds, and that must have been why they went to the statue of the Holy Mother Mary and prayed for mercy.

In whatever situation, if we are "this, just this," every instance of suffering is prajñāpāramitā. The third truth, cessation, means to be in serenity. The fourth truth, the path, signals the entrance into serenity. There is profound meaning in Dōgen's statement that all four truths, including suffering and the cause of suffering, are prajñā.

> Moreover, there are six instances of prajñā: generosity, pure precepts, calm patience, diligence, quiet meditation, and wisdom.

This refers to the six points of bodhisattva practice. When we practice offering (*dāna*, or generosity), we just offer. Sometimes laypeople complain, "Although I made such a large donation, the priest chanted only a short sūtra for the memorial service. He is a mean-spirited priest." If we have such an attitude, our donation is not dāna pāramitā. This is true not only for donations to priests. Sawaki Rōshi said, "Giving is to treat *public* things as *public* things." Within this world as reality, there is no private property about which we can claim, "This is my possession." Including our own selves, all things are public things. Since we only own public things temporarily, when someone is in need, I return those things to the public. This is what is meant by the phrase "Treat public things as public things." Unconditionally, gainlessly, without expecting reward, we just offer. This is offering as the practice of pāramitā.

As for the practice of maintaining the precepts, we can say that we are observing the precepts only when we keep the precepts. If we say that we are celibate to be in accordance with the precepts and then criticize others for having a family, we are taking a small-vehicle, or narrow, attitude toward the precepts. This is a violation of the precepts in the Mahāyāna sense.

Ordinarily, *patience* means to endure something. We might say to someone, "I was patient for a long time, but the person didn't understand me. I could not stand it anymore." This attitude cannot be called patience as a practice of pāramitā. Within practicing patience, we have to be calm. Calm patience means to be just patient.

Diligence is the same. It is dangerous to say, "I am working hard," because later we may say, "I am tired of it. I'll quit." Unconditionally, without expecting rewards, without gaining something, we just keep making an effort. This is true diligence as the practice of pāramitā.

Quiet meditation refers to the practice of zazen. We just sit.

The last instance of pāramitā is wisdom. This is the most important point. Prajñāpāramitā, perfection of the deepest wisdom, is the foundation of Buddhism.

> There is also a single instance of prajñāpāramitā manifesting itself right now—unsurpassable complete, perfect awakening.

Unsurpassable complete, perfect awakening is *anuttarā samyaksaṃbodhi*. This is different from a half-baked understanding of enlightenment—such as when someone says, "I have attained enlightenment." Rather, it is enlightenment actualized by just doing without attainment. In the *Diamond Sūtra*, Śākyamuni Buddha said, "Since *anuttarā samyaksaṃbodhi* is not something to attain, Dīpaṃkara Buddha predicted my future attainment of buddhahood." After all, true enlightenment is not graspable. Śākyamuni Buddha's enlightenment is like this. There is nothing we can name as our enlightenment. The *Diamond Sūtra* is very clear about this.

> Also, there are three instances of prajñāpāramitā: past, present, and future. And there are six instances of prajñā: earth, water, fire, wind, space, and consciousness. Also, four instances of prajñā are going on daily: walking, standing, sitting, and lying down.

Past, present, and future; earth, water, fire, wind, space, and consciousness; walking, standing, sitting, and lying down are all just as they are—just doing.

The boundless vast universe is nothing
but one scene of my own life experience.

> There was a monk in the assembly of Śākyamuni Tathāgata. He thought to
> himself, "I should venerate and make prostrations to this most profound
> prajñāpāramitā. Although prajñāpāramitā teaches that within all things
> there is neither arising nor extinguishing, there are practical approaches
> such as the skandhas of maintaining the precepts of body, mouth, and
> mind, of quietly meditating, of enacting wisdom and emancipation, and
> of the insight resulting from emancipation. Also, there are the practical
> approaches consisting of the ranks of those entering the stream, the
> once-returners, those who will no longer return, and the arhats. Self-
> awakening is also a practical approach. Unsurpassable perfect awakening
> is yet another practical approach.

It seems Indian people had a tendency to categorize by counting (they
even categorized different types of sneezing). Sūtras were written like
this, full of categories called Dharma numbers, or *hossū* (法数). Buddhist
scholars treat Dharma numbers seriously and argue over their significance. Such arguing makes no sense. If we eliminate the numbers when
we read the sūtras, we can better understand Buddhadharma. It is impossible to understand the Indian sūtras as they are written, even if we study
them our whole lives. So many things are repeated so many times, and
the style is so complicated. Therefore, when I read sūtras, I read them
by ignoring the numbers and ranks. Creating hierarchical stages in our
zazen is rather odd.

"Self-awakening is also a practical approach" refers to practitioners
who were not Buddha's disciples, but who, living in the midst of nature,
realized the reality of life by seeing, for instance, leaves falling or flowers
scattering. Buddhism is not something Śākyamuni Buddha fabricated
himself. The reality of life in nature is Buddhadharma when we see truly.
Therefore, it is not strange that there were some people who realized the
reality of life before Buddha's time.

> The [Triple] Treasures of Buddha, Dharma, and Sangha are also a practical
> approach. Turning the wondrous Dharma wheel, saving various sentient
> beings, is also a practical approach.
>
> The Buddha knowing the monk's thoughts, said, "So it is! So it is! The
> most profound prajñāpāramitā is indeed subtle and difficult to fathom."

The Buddha expounded the Buddhadharma and saved sentient beings.
Although there is no incoming and no outgoing, no gain and no loss,
there are still practical approaches. We cannot say there are no such
things. Even within emptiness, there are practical approaches; this is
the most important characteristic of prajñā. The monk resolved to pay
homage to such profound prajñā.

Sawaki Rōshi spoke of prajñāpāramitā with the word *yūsui*, meaning
limitless profundity. Within just doing, there is limitless profundity.
We cannot say that we attain enlightenment to this or that extent; there
are no such stages. Buddhadharma should just be practiced. Within the
reality of no-classification and no-steps, there is boundless profundity.
This is the world of the reality of life.

> The monk realizes now that by venerating and making prostrations to all
> things, he is venerating and making prostrations to prajñā, which teaches
> that even though there is neither arising nor extinguishing, there is arising
> and extinguishing.

Venerating in this context is an expression of our system of values. People who become materially minded put the highest value on money;
living a wealthy lifestyle is most desirable for them. Such people put
their values on worthless things, but in Buddhadharma it is different.
We put fundamental value on all-pervading life. The total interpenetrating reality of life itself is the absolute value, so we respect and pay
homage to it. Since it is absolute and interpenetrating, there is no arising
or perishing. And yet, we venerate this reality of life and make prostrations to it unconditionally, without expecting any reward or gain. This

is the way we pay homage. The world of Buddhadharma is the world of profundity.

I wrote this poem for a New Year's greeting card:

Life of the self that lives and dies
    is all/all—
Opening the hand of thought,
    just live out the life that so variously manifests itself.

All-pervading life that manifests itself as our lives, living and dying, is all/all. Ordinarily people think only of life without death. When we think only of life as separate from death, money becomes the most important thing. However, if we realize that life includes being born, living, and dying, we can see clearly that money is not so valuable at all. No matter how much money, social status, and power we have, when we are dying, we have to let go of them all. When we die, we have to leave happiness and abundance behind. If we live on the basis of measuring happiness materially, we will be at the bottom of our unhappiness when we are dying. This is very understandable, isn't it?

Truly, this life of the self that lives and dies is all/all. As I say repeatedly, each one of us is born simultaneously with their own world and dies simultaneously with that world. The world of total interpenetrating life is all/all; myriad dharmas appear there. We venerate them. Because everything appearing in front of our eyes is our life, we pay homage to all of it. Everything I encounter is my life.

> In this very moment of veneration and prostration, prajñā manifests itself
> in practical approaches such as keeping the precepts, quietly meditating,
> manifesting wisdom, and so forth, and saving various sentient beings.

Although practical ways are conceptual fabrications, we cannot say that there are no such things. "Practical ways" are the phenomena right in front of us; all of these ways are nothing but our lives. Therefore, all practical approaches are manifestations of prajñāpāramitā.

> This [moment of veneration] is called nothingness. The approaches to nothingness thus become practical.

Since everything is ungraspable and unattainable, everything is nothingness, *mu* (無). All our practice is without gain and unattainable, yet our practice is guided by the teaching of *no gain*, in itself a practical approach. It is a mistake to say that there are no such things as practical approaches.

> This [veneration] is the most profound prajñāpāramitā, subtle and difficult to fathom.

This is the Buddhadharma with limitless profundity.

In the beginning, I talked about what *mahāprajñāpāramitā* means, but since it is very significant, I will repeat it.

Mahā is usually translated as "great." But this suggests comparison and, as a Buddhist term, *mahā* cannot be used for comparison. If something is compared with something else, no matter how big it might be, it is still obviously small. True greatness is beyond comparison. *Mahā* is greatness beyond comparison.

When someone said to me, "The universe is amazingly big. It is said the diameter of the universe is one hundred billion light years," I said, "Tiny, tiny!" One hundred billion light years is smaller than infinity. Is infinity the biggest? If infinity is compared with the finite, then it is still small. In Christianity, it is said that God is infinity, who created finite human beings. If God does not include human beings, such a god is still small. A god who is separate from limited creatures is small.

True greatness includes both the infinite and the finite: all/all, or total, interpenetrating life. We cannot pick out one special entity and call it God. Total interpenetrating life is all-inclusive. All divided by all equals one. This oneness is total, interpenetrating life, what Dōgen Zenji called total, interpenetrating self. Although you and I are finite individuals, the self, or jiko, is as vast and boundless as the reality of life.

It is said that we can see things that are billions of light years away. Such a phenomenon exists because of the life experience of the seer. Even the universe that has a diameter of one hundred billion light years is only a part of the life experience of the total, interpenetrating self.

First of all, I think that one hundred billion light years is an unconvincing number. When I was a student, it was said that the diameter of the universe was about nine billion light years. Sooner or later the number will change again. Theories in science change constantly. It is too simple to believe that science is absolutely reliable.

It is through the experience of life that we can say that the diameter of the universe is one hundred billion light years or that it is getting bigger and bigger. In other words, the world we see exists as reality only because we experience life. Nothing exists without the experience of life. On the other hand, in experiencing life, we also think certain things do not exist. For example, there are expressions such as "turtle's hair" and "rabbit's horns." Although we don't think "turtle's hair" or "rabbit's horns" exist, we still think that to not exist is a form of existence because this "thinking" is also a part of the total experience of life. Turtle's hair or rabbit's horns "exist" in the form of our thinking that such things "don't exist." Although this is a complicated way of speaking, what I want to say is that all things exist as reality only within our own experience of life. When I say "all-divided-by-all" or "total, interpenetrating self," I refer to the self that experiences all things as reality. Truly each and every one of us without exception is living out the self as "all-divided-by-all" (all/all) or "total, interpenetrating self," but we are often unaware of this fact and we instead think of ourselves as "one divided by all" (one/all).

Why don't we awaken to this reality? As I have said before, each one of us sees a cup in a different way. Each of us has our own experience of life. We think words can be communicated universally among people.

It seems that the words I am speaking now are understood by all of you, but that is uncertain. Although you are listening to me, you may not understand the raw truth of my words, or each of you may understand my words differently. Ultimately, I am living in my own world and each of you is living within your own world. While I am talking, your faces are reflected in my eyes. I am looking at your faces and making an effort to speak in a way that, by the looks on your faces, you seem to understand. So, as I speak to you, I am really speaking to myself; I convince myself that you understand. The communication between you and me is completely the self that is only the self. As you listen to me, you are also listening to yourself. You listen with your own life experience, with the self that is only the self. There is in fact no transaction with others. This is what *mahā* means. I talk repeatedly to convey that this is a most significant point.

Usually we think that when we are born, we enter into the world, which already exists, and when we die, we exit from this world. As reality, this is not true. When I am born, I am born together with my own world. When I die, my world dies with me. This is called total, interpenetrating self. Since it is completely interpenetrating with all beings, this self is never born and never dies. There is no incoming or outgoing. Although we fear dying, or we sometimes think that we have to carry our regrets beyond the grave, when we actually die we die together with such emotions and thoughts. On the level of reality beyond thoughts, there is no incoming or outgoing. But as long as we think we were born, we will die. Grasped by thoughts, people usually think only of living and put a lid on dying in order not to see it; they don't understand true life. When we uncover the lid and see that life includes death, we can see true life clearly. As the reality of life, we are born and die within the total, interpenetrating self that has no birth and death. This is mahā—great, boundless vastness.

Prajñā is wisdom, or chie. The character *chi*, 智, means to make a decision, while *e*, 慧, means to distinguish. The two characters together form the term *chie*, 智慧, meaning to distinguish between things and choose the better one. We live by making choices. If, when walking down the street, we come face to face with a bicycle, we go either right or left to avoid a crash. Moment by moment, we constantly have to make such decisions. Wisdom in Buddhism, however, is different from common sense or scientific knowledge. Wisdom in Buddhism is about making choices on the grounds that everything we encounter without any exception is our life. There is no discrimination at all. There is nothing that is not my life. We make choices on the basis of the self that is only the self. This is discrimination based on nondiscrimination. We can also say that wisdom is nondiscrimination on the basis of discrimination.

Pāramitā means crossing over to the other shore—and to already be where we are going. This is the most refined way of life as a human being. Sawaki Rōshi often said, in one breath, "halfway, incomplete, insufficient, and evasive," in order to describe people's misguided attitude toward life. For instance, he was in the habit of saying things like this: "In the world, people say, 'Congratulations!' when a man and a woman, neither of whom really understands what life is, have a wedding. And when the couple has a baby, still without any understanding about life, people say, 'Congratulations!' again. Now what is all this congratulating about? I don't understand at all. All this congratulating is a halfway, incomplete, insufficient, evasive way of life." Buddhadharma is entirely different from this halfway, incomplete, insufficient, evasive way of thinking. In order to understand Buddhadharma, we must hear it repeatedly.

I am not just explaining the meanings of words and phrases in *Shōbōgenzō*. Rather, using *Shōbōgenzō* as a text, I would like to inspire people with a way of viewing things and of thinking that is based on the reality of life. Therefore, I repeatedly say the same things, blistering your ears. Please understand this.

No matter how hard we practice, there is no reaction—
we just act.

> Indra asked the Elder Subhūti, "Venerable one, when bodhisattva-
> mahāsattvas want to study the most profound prajñāpāramitā, how should
> they do it?" Subhūti replied, "Kausika, when bodhisattva-mahāsattvas
> want to study the most profound prajñāpāramitā, they should study it
> as empty space."
>
> Therefore, to study prajñā is itself empty space. Empty space is study-
> ing prajñā.

"Venerable" refers to a person who is endowed with Dharma life, a monk who has received the complete precepts. Indra, a god who protects this world, asked Subhūti, a monk, how to study prajñāpāramitā.

Subhūti said that prajñāpāramitā should be studied like empty space. The problem here is what empty space is. Old Japanese martial arts storybooks used the expression "falling down grasping empty space" to describe someone being killed by a sword. But there is nothing to grasp; we grasp empty space. In the reality of life, as well, there is nothing we can grasp—despite how much we want to. This is empty space. This is why Buddhist thought coined expressions like *fukatoku* (不可得), nothing to attain, or *mushotoku* (無所得), nothing to gain.

In our day-to-day lives we always have something in front of us to grasp. We have business connections. We live in a world of calculated give-and-take, and we become too familiar with it. But, like sliding back the beads of an abacus, when we clear out worldly calculations, the reality of life is present. This is what "empty space" means.

For example, conventionally speaking, if we walk on the sidewalk, we aren't likely to have a traffic accident. However, Rev. Gentai Nishikawa was once in an accident when two cars crashed on the roadway and one of them jumped onto the sidewalk. As long as we are living in this world, as reality, there is no knowing, no calculating, what may happen.

In the Bible, it is said that God can do anything. Some Zen priests say that they don't have any hardships because they have attained enlightenment. I think such an attitude defies God. On the ground of the reality of life, it is no wonder that we can have bitter experiences at any time, anywhere—because God can do anything. Some people say that we become sick because we live an unhealthy life. They think we don't take responsibility for our health because if we lived a wholesome life, we would never get sick. However, no matter how healthily we live, in reality, we sometimes become sick. To say that one has to be responsible for one's sickness can be a very cold-hearted comment. Only a person who has never experienced sickness could utter such a thing. We have to be ready to suffer from sickness at any time, anywhere, and when we encounter people who suffer from illness, we should care for them wholeheartedly. That is life.

The same thing can be said about our practice, study, or work. Takuboku Ishikawa (1886–1912) wrote the following poem:

No matter how hard I work
My living doesn't become easy
I watch my hands without words

We often find that no matter how hard we try, we do not succeed. In only one period in my life did I receive a salary. That was for about six months when I was a teacher at a theological school. During that time, I had a student from Saipan, an island in the Mariana Islands, which was a Japanese colony at the time. His name was Bisente. He had difficulty especially in mathematics. There was a Japanese student, Tokita, who had the same difficulty. For example, they just could not understand the concept of fractions. I gave the two students supplementary lessons for about a month. I did my best, but I couldn't bring the knowledge home to their hearts. When I felt totally exhausted, I had to give up. But somehow, at the next math exam, both of them received perfect scores.

Since other students knew that I was making an effort to teach them, they praised me and said I was a good teacher. At the time, I felt that this was all very strange.

When we try to nurture living beings, making a wholehearted effort, we do not always get good results. And yet, just when we are tired and give up, they sometimes start to grow remarkably. In my experience, there is not a simple cause-and-effect relationship, such as a teacher's effort, that perfectly enables students to grow. Rather, the teacher's effort is just the teacher's effort. Or, "this, just this." The student's growth is just the student's growth. This, just this.

In Buddhism there is the expression "cause and effect are self-evident." I think this is true. We cannot ignore it. However, the relationships between causes and effects function in a much broader and deeper way than we can understand with our small intellects. We think that if we push the power switch, then, as a result, the TV will come on, but causation in our lives is not so simple. It has a much, much broader and deeper interdependent relationship with all times and all beings.

For example, when a man lives a self-indulgent life filled with drinking, gambling, and pursuing women, it is only natural that he will have hardships in his life. I don't think it would be possible for a man like this to clarify what human life is in the midst of such degenerate living. It is better, without question, to stop licentious living and practice something like zazen instead. But is it certain that if we stop our self-indulgence that our lives will become more pleasant? Not really. Is it assured that we can attain deep insight about human life if we start to practice? No. The true self-evidence of the cause-and-effect relationship lies beyond our expectation and understanding. Therefore, all we can do is to be "this, just this."

In zazen we sit being "this, just this." We never seek enlightenment as a reward after accumulating the merits of zazen. The practice of zazen would be more understandable if it were like playing pachinko. If you can get the metal balls to go into certain holes, you get lots of balls back and all sorts of bells start going off. One may think that if you sit in a certain posture for a certain period of time, you attain sudden and fascinating enlightenment. This is not the case. We just sit, being beyond such expectation. This zazen is itself enlightenment. It is what is meant when Dōgen Zenji says, "The approaches to nothingness thus become practical."

This attitude is called "form is emptiness, emptiness is form," or "form is form, emptiness is emptiness." It is also called "undefiled practice-enlightenment."

In *Shōbōgenzō* "Shoaku Makusa," there is a famous *gāthā*, or poem:

Refraining from committing various evils
Carrying out all sorts of good actions
Personally clarifying this mind
This is the essential teaching of all the buddhas.

In short, refraining from committing bad deeds is the basis of Buddhism. However, with even a slight misunderstanding, the gāthā from which this line comes takes on a completely different meaning. People often say, "Good actions bring about good results. Bad actions bring about bad results. Good actions in a family will bring unexpected happiness. Lack of good actions in a family will bring misfortune." If we understand the poem above with such an attitude of calculated expectation, our understanding has nothing to do with Buddha's teaching.

Some religions shallowly teach people to expect good when they do good and to expect bad when they do bad. With these expectations, there will surely be a time when one's faith collapses. Even if we work hard and honestly, sometimes we still become sick, get into a traffic accident, receive a bad check, or become unable to collect from our credit customers. Consequently, we say, "There is no God or Buddha! Throw the family altar away!"

Refraining from evil and practicing good in terms of Buddhist teaching are not like this. There are no such deals and no one to make such deals with. It is the same as "studying empty space." We refrain from doing evil and practice doing good within the framework of jiko—a self that is only the self and all/all. Many people living in the world today have a different attitude. When they do something good, they do so with the attitude that they are giving someone credit; they carry out this "good" action for the sake of getting back what they lent. When they take care of others, they do so because inwardly they expect some reward. On the other hand, when these same people commit some misdeed, they try to hide it in order to avoid meeting the bill collector.

I lived in Ōgaki for about two years. I heard that Ōgaki used to be called "the City of Water" because it had abundant water resources. In each house, spring water welled up constantly. In summer, people cooled arrowroot starch cakes in the water and enjoyed them. These days, however, there are only one or two artesian wells there. Evidently, many factories were built, and they pumped up huge amounts of water.

Our life is the same. When we do good just for the sake of doing good, we find a limitless vein of water. When we try to pump up more and more water, the vein dries up. It is the same in the case of our household finances. In a housekeeping account book, there are columns for income and expenditures. In Japan, most housewives think it is better to have more income and fewer expenditures. And yet, in order to earn income, husbands usually have to work somewhere outside the family. This is a kind of expenditure and a significant one at that. In addition, in usual bookkeeping, borrowing is a form of income, and lending is a form of expenditure. But I think lending is more important than income.

The other day I talked about this with someone. Later I heard that the person used to be the vice president of the Bank of Japan, and I felt a touch of embarrassment. However, I don't think what I am saying is mistaken. Sawaki Rōshi often said that losing is enlightenment and gaining is delusion. In the ordinary world, the principle is that if expenditures keep increasing, we'll eventually go bankrupt. In Buddhadharma, we have to become comfortable with the attitude that even if we are bankrupt and live in poverty, we should keep increasing expenditures. Unless we really accept such an attitude, we'll never live a truly wealthy life. In other words, if you want to be rich, first of all be poor. In human life, it is very difficult to lower our standard of living once we have enjoyed a materially rich life. So, we should not try to raise our standard of living; rather we should try to train ourselves to settle in poverty. This is the wealthiest way of life.

In my case, my standard of living has become a little bit higher than it was during World War II, since I don't suffer from malnutrition these days. But in my day-to-day life, I try to keep my standard of living on the same level as during the war. Then I feel more lighthearted; because I don't need to worry about money, I can spend each day deliberately. I think this is a wealthy life, and I learned it from my life in the monastery.

In *Instructions to the Cook*, Dōgen Zenji said, "Do not overlook one drop in the ocean of virtue [by entrusting the work to others]. Cultivate a spirit which strives to increase the source of goodness upon the mountain of goodness." Although water in the ocean of virtues is limitless, we should be careful not to lose even one drop. No matter how much we have accumulated good deeds, we should continually try to add even a tiny speck more. Unless we have this spirit, we cannot practice at a monastery.

I practiced in various monasteries for more than twenty-five years. The reason I could keep practicing without too much trouble was that I tried to avoid taking only the good parts of monastic life. In a monastery, some positions are difficult and some are easy; some are readily appreciated and others are thankless. If we only wanted to take the easy jobs and avoid the difficult ones, we would not be accepted by the community for very long. On the other hand, if we were always willing to take the hard and thankless jobs, even a physically weak and inept person like myself would be able to continue practicing.

In everyday society, it is the same. If we only look for personal profit and try to take only what is good, even if we might have good fortune for a while, in the long run we will have to drop out of the rat race. On the contrary, if we try to do beneficial things for society, even if they are small things, a peaceful world will naturally open in front of us. We should just carry out good things silently, without advertisement and without expectation. Each day we refrain from doing bad and just practice doing good, an upright character naturally develops. If we are always looking for personal gain, even our face will come to resemble that of a pickpocket. The essential point here is living with an attitude of just doing, without expecting some sort of gain—no business deals, no one to do business with. This is called "studying empty space." Therein, a boundless and peaceful world will open. This is what Dōgen Zenji means when he writes that within no arising and no perishing, there are practical approaches to nothingness; that to study prajñā is itself empty space; that empty space is studying prajñā.

As I always say, jiko, in whatever situation, is all-divided-by-all; jiko is the total, interpenetrating self, self that is only the self. There is nothing that is not jiko. Therefore, wherever we are, in the same way we value our own lives, we try to help other people and contribute to society. We live out our lives with the attitude that we do our best whenever we can be helpful to others. As I wrote in my first book, titled *Jiko* (*Whole Self*), I had a very hard time when I stayed at a temple in Nagano for a year in 1947–48. Although I practiced wholeheartedly, no one recognized my efforts. Rather I was used like a servant by an old woman at the temple. I felt miserable! At the time, I wrote a poem titled "How Hard the Way of a Monk." I always felt that I was throwing stones into a bottomless ravine. I didn't have even the slightest response from others about my activities. Empty space is like this. No matter how hard we practice, there is no response. And yet we just keep practicing. This is the point: we have to practice.

Living with reverence within the emptiness of all things.

Indra spoke again to the Buddha, "World-honored one, when good men and women accept and keep, read and recite, ponder in accord with reality, and expound to others this profound prajñāpāramitā [which you have just] presented, how can I protect them? World-honored one, I simply wish that you bestow your compassion and teach me."

At that time, the Elder Subhūti said to Indra, "Kausika, do you see a Dharma that can be protected, or not?"

Indra replied, "No! Venerable one, I don't see any Dharma that I can protect."

Subhūti said, "Kausika, when good men and women speak as you have, the most profound prajñāpāramitā is itself protection."

Fathers and mothers want to protect their children. I want to protect my disciples from misfortune. In the same way, Indra wanted to protect practitioners who recited sūtras or expounded prajñāpāramitā and asked how he could protect such people. Subhūti asked whether Indra found any Dharma that could be protected. Indra replied that he did not.

Since prajñāpāramitā, the perfection of wisdom, is emptiness of all things, in an ordinary way of thinking there is no way to protect prajñāpāramitā. This pair of glasses can be protected from breaking by putting them in a case. But how can we protect empty space?

In the dialogue, Subhūti says, "When good men and women speak as you have, the most profound prajñāpāramitā is itself protection." To "speak as you have" means to clarify ungraspability and gainlessness. There is no way to grasp. To see that there is no way to protect prajñāpāramitā is to protect it.

Parents these days overprotect their children, and consequently, they prevent their children from growing up. In my case, too, if I want to protect my disciples, I should refrain from interfering and allow them to grow by themselves.

The self that is only the self just venerates all beings. Since all things are my life, I value all of them. Keeping this attitude toward life is the only thing I can do to protect my disciples. If parents want to protect their children, parents need to venerate all beings and value and take care of their own lives. Seeing such parental examples, children will flourish.

Otherwise, if parents try to raise children based upon their own desires, they prevent their children from maturing.

> "If good men and women act as you said they do, they are never separate from the most profound prajñāpāramitā. You should know that, even if all human and nonhuman beings wanted to harm them, it would not be possible to do so."

When we live with an attitude of no grasping, no gaining, no business deals, no one to do business with, we can receive and maintain prajñāpāramitā.

"Nonhuman beings" in this passage means the eight kinds of demons who harm Buddhadharma as opposed to the eight kinds of guardians of Buddhadharma. Even if those demons want to harm practitioners, they cannot actually do any harm if the practitioners have nothing to grasp and no desire to gain. If we grasp something, thinking that we have to protect it, there is a time when we will lose it. In other words, if we have something to lose, demons will take advantage of this, but if we have nothing to lose, demons cannot do any harm. No matter what happens, we are the self that is only the self, all/all. If so, there is no way to harm us.

> "Kausika, if you want to protect them, you should do as you said. Wanting to protect the most profound prajñāpāramitā and all bodhisattvas is not different from wanting to protect empty space."
> You should know that accepting and keeping, reading and reciting, pondering in accord with reality, is nothing other than protecting prajñā. The desire to protect is accepting and keeping, reading and reciting and so on.

When we want to protect something, we should do so with the idea that there is nothing we can protect. Without any objects to protect, we just maintain an attitude of protection. And an attitude toward life as empty space—no grasping and no gaining—is the basis of the teachings as Buddhadharma.

> My late master, the ancient buddha, said;
>
>> The whole body [of the wind bell] is like a mouth hanging in empty space—
>> Without distinguishing the winds from east, west, south, or north
>> Together expressing prajñā equally to all beings—
>> Di ding dong liao di ding dong.[36]
>
> This is how prajñā has been expressed authentically through buddhas and ancestors. The whole body is prajñā. All others [which include the self] are prajñā. The whole self [which includes others] is prajñā. The entire universe—east, west, south, and north—is prajñā.

Japanese wind bells are small, often made of glass, and hang under eaves. So, the sound they make is something like "tinkle-tinkle." However, Chinese wind bells hang under the eaves of much larger temple buildings, such as Buddha halls or five-story pagodas. They are much bigger than Japanese bells and are made of copper. It is not surprising that Chinese bells do not make light sounds like "tinkle-tinkle" but, rather, much heavier sounds.

The more I read this poem, the more I appreciate its profundity. "The whole body is like a mouth, hanging in empty space" is a marvelous line. Not distinguishing the winds from east, west, south, or north, the bell does not discriminate. It does not reject wind from any direction. The whole body is prajñā. All others are prajñā. Self includes others. Self and others are one; self is only self. The whole self is prajñā. Since the

36. In Menzan Zuihō Zenji's commentary on *Shōbōgenzō* entitled *Monge* (聞解), this was pronounced as *chichin-tsunran-chichin-tsun*. Sawaki Rōshi had a question about the sound and asked a Chinese person about it when he visited China. He was told that in Chinese, it is pronounced *tenten-tonryan-tenten-ton*.

self totally interpenetrates all things and is all-divided-by-all, the entire universe—east, west, south, and north—is prajñā. The universal reality of life is prajñā.

In 1947 or '48, when I was troubled with questions about the Dharma, I wrote a letter to Sawaki Rōshi. He sent me the following poem by Dōgen Zenji:

Forgetting all adoption and rejection, my mind is at peace.
All things simultaneously manifest themselves.
Within Buddhadharma, from now on, [discriminating] mind is
Completely extinguished. I follow the conditions of all things.[37]

When we give up the mind that grasps and rejects, the mind that discriminates, our own minds become flexible and things appear as they are. "[Discriminating] mind is completely extinguished" refers to letting go of thought. We don't do anything based on our preferences. So, what shall we do? Just live following the conditions of all things. Since everything we encounter is our life, there is nothing we have to do in a fixed way. We venerate and make prostrations to whatever we meet. We pay homage to all things and put the highest value on them. Following the conditions of all things—this is an important point. We live out the life of the self that penetrates the whole universe and contains all others.

---

37. The Japanese reads: 取捨を隻忘して思い翛然　万物同時現在前　仏法今より心既に尽く身儀向後しばらく縁に従う. This poem appears in volume 10 of Dōgen Zenji's *Eiheikōroku*. An alternate translation of the poem can be found in *Dōgen's Extensive Record*, trans. Taigen Dan Leighton and Shōhaku Okumura (Boston: Wisdom Publications, 2010), 626:
> Though settled, no longer picking up or discarding,
> At the same time before me myriad things appear.
> [Within] Buddha Dharma, from now on [seeking] mind's abandoned.
> After this my activity will just follow conditions.

Śākyamuni Buddha said, "Shariputra, all these sentient beings should make offerings and prostrations to prajñāpāramitā as they do to a living buddha. They should contemplate prajñāpāramitā just as they make offerings and prostrations to a *buddha-bhagavat*. What is the reason? Prajñāpāramitā is not different from a buddha-bhagavat. A buddha-bhagavat is not different from prajñāpāramitā. Prajñāpāramitā is itself a buddha-bhagavat. A buddha-bhagavat is itself prajñāpāramitā.

The sūtra Dōgen cites says that prajñāpāramitā is itself Buddha-bhagavat. *Bhagavat* means "world-honored one," that is, one of the epithets of a buddha. Buddha is nothing other than prajñāpāramitā. To serve, venerate, and contemplate bhagavat means to put the highest value on buddha and prajñāpāramitā. In other words, we esteem the reality of life that is the total interpenetrating self.

More than fifty years ago, when I was a middle school student, a book titled *How to Live on Twenty-Four Hours a Day*, which was originally written in English by a British author, became a bestseller in Japan. Every bookstore had tall stacks of this book. The author showed how to work most efficiently every hour of the day. When I read it, I thought the idea was ridiculous. However, at that time, I couldn't clearly understand what was ridiculous about such an attitude. Now I can point it out.

Many people are not interested in the question "what is most precious in life?" Without thinking, they work relentlessly simply to meet a higher and higher standard of living. It seems that Westerners were the same way back then. Subsequently, the United States became the most prosperous country in the world. And yet, did this prosperity make Americans happy?

The most significant thing is to understand what is most valuable in human life, what we should put the highest value on, rather than on how to use the twenty-four hours in a day most efficiently. We should consider this seriously. The most important thing is not to become rich, but to live out an attitude of awakening to the self that is only self in any situation; we should put the highest value on that self. This attitude is prajñāpāramitā and Buddha.

"What is the reason? Shariputra! This is because all supreme awakened tathāgatas issue from prajñāpāramitā. Shariputra! This is because all bodhisattva-mahāsattvas, pratyekabuddhas, arhats, nonreturners, once-returners, stream-enterers, and so on issue from prajñāpāramitā. Shariputra! This is because the way of the ten good deeds in the world, the four quiet meditations, the four formless samadhis, and the five divine powers all issue from prajñāpāramitā."

These are Buddhist technical terms that are not important unless you are a Buddhist scholar, so I won't explain them now. They all come from prajñāpāramitā.

Therefore, a buddha-bhagavat is itself prajñāpāramitā. Prajñāpāramitā is nothing other than all beings. All these beings are empty in form, without arising or extinguishing, neither defiled nor pure, without increasing or decreasing.

Buddhas are prajñāpāramitā. Prajñāpāramitā is all beings. Although I call it the life of the self or all/all, the reality of life does not exist as a fixed entity, rather it appears as all different things within the life experience of the self. As Dōgen Zenji said, prajñāpāramitā is nothing other than various beings. My world is all the things I experience. Therefore, I have to value and take care of even this tiny glass as I value and take care of my own life. We should cherish our own possessions. To meet a person is to meet my life. I often have visitors, and I meet with them as I meet with myself. I hold them as valuable as my own life. All these beings are empty in form, without arising or extinguishing, neither defiled nor pure, without increasing or decreasing.

The life of my self that is only the self manifests itself as various forms. These various forms are not separate from me. I meet people as my own life, not as business partners. When we encounter people, we often calculate how much we can get from them. We need to completely let go of these various forms since they are empty forms. There is neither incoming nor outgoing. All forms neither arise nor perish. They are all universal. We do not attain enlightenment as a result of practice in the way a room becomes clean as a result of sweeping. Therefore, there is neither defilement nor purification. I don't become a great person. Nothing increases or decreases.

> Actualizing this prajñāpāramitā is to actualize buddha-bhagavat. Inquire into it! Practice it! Making offerings and prostrations [to prajñāpāramitā] is attending and serving buddha-bhagavat. Attending and serving [all beings] is itself buddha-bhagavat.

When we just actualize total interpenetrating life, we actualize buddha. Although prajñāpāramitā is the wisdom to see the emptiness of all things, this is not license to negate cause and effect and do whatever we want. We have to inquire into prajñāpāramitā and practice it. We should make offerings and prostrations to prajñāpāramitā. We should attend and serve buddha-bhagavat.

The reason Dōgen Zenji emphasizes attending and serving is that there must have been many Zen practitioners who, because of their clinging to the emptiness of all things, were self-indulgent and did whatever they wanted. Today, this kind of Zen is called "wild fox Zen." We should practice continuously in a reverential attitude as though we are attending and serving buddhas. We should live with thanks and respect for all beings. In the end, I think Dōgen Zenji wrote this fascicle to point this out.

Part II. Refraining from Evil

3. Shoaku Makusa
Refraining from Evil

諸悪莫作

EIHEI DŌGEN ZENJI

Translated by DAITSŪ TOM WRIGHT

I.

A gāthā of the ancient buddhas says:

> Refraining from committing various evils
> Carrying out all sorts of good actions
> Personally clarifying this mind
> This is the essential teaching of all the buddhas.[38]

We find this teaching to be held in common by the first seven buddhas[39] and, subsequently, by our ancestors as well. These teachings were trans-

---

38. In Japanese, this gāthā is referred to as "The Gāthā of the Commonly Held Precepts of the Seven Buddhas" ("Shichi Butsu Tsūkai (no) Ge," 七仏通戒の偈). It is common to all Buddhists regardless of the school: Zen or Pure Land, Mahāyāna or Theravāda. It appears first in the *Dhammapada*. It can also be found in the *Zōagōn-kyō*, and also the *Nehan-gyō* or *Nirvana Sūtra*.

39. The "first seven buddhas" refers to Bibashibutsu (in Pāli, Vipassī) Daiosho, Shikibutsu (Sikhī) Daiosho, Bishafubutsu (Vessabhū) Daiosho, Kurusonbutsu (Kakusandha) Daiosho, Kunagonmunibutsu (Koṇāgamana) Daiosho, Kashobutsu (Kassapa) Daiosho, and Shakyamunibutsu (Gautama) Daiosho. The first three buddhas lived in previous *kalpas* (ancient times) and the latter four buddhas lived in the current *kalpa* of time.

mitted from the earlier buddhas to their successors and were received directly by the latter from their predecessors. This holds true not only for the first seven buddhas; this is the teaching common to all buddhas.[40] We must ardently practice and carefully examine these universal truths.

The actual Dharma teaching and Way of practice[41] of the seven buddhas necessarily include the transmission and reception of that reality and of that practice. Further, it is the internal and direct transmission of how all things are,[42] and it is held in common by all the buddhas. It is without exception the totality of the teaching of the various buddhas. Moreover, this is the teaching, the practice, and the actualization of the entire myriad of buddhas.

The "various evils" here refer to one of the three qualities of all things/ actions—those three characteristics being good, evil, or unmarked.[43] The nature of the various evils precedes conscious effort, and this holds true for good and unmarked things/actions as well. Though they are not sullied[44] by human judgment and are truly how they appear, the qualities

---

40. That is, it is common to all Buddhists, regardless of the school.

41. *Hōdō* (法道), a combination of the terms *Buppō* (仏法) and *butsudō* (仏道), "Dharma truths" and "Buddha Path" or "Way (of practice)."

42. *Kori no tsūshōsoku* (箇裏の通消息). Uchiyama Rōshi interprets this as the "internal structure of *jiko* or our universal identity." In her footnote to this expression Mizuno Yaoko translates it as "the appearance of reality within the truth of *jiko*, our whole self." Mizuno Yaoko 水野弥穂子, trans., *Shōbōgenzō* 正法眼蔵 (Tokyo: Iwanami Shoten, 1993), 2: 230.

43. "Unmarked" (Jpn: *muki* 無記; Skt: *avyakrta*) has two basic meanings.

The first meaning is dharmas that cannot be definitively explained as being either good or not good. This definition is found in *Abidatsuma Kusharon* (倶舎論; Skt: *Abhidharma-kośa Śāstra*), one of the oldest writings on Buddhist terms. However, readers interested in going deeper into the term might be advised to read the writings of the Yogācāra school of Buddhism.

The second meaning of *muki* is in regard to the Buddha's response to questions that are unanswerable.

44. *Muro* (無漏). Literally, "to leak." In Buddhism, it refers to the "pollution" of things by human greed, ideas, thoughts, judgments, etc.

of all actions are revealed through the myriad dharmas.[45] In different societies, that which is considered evil or unwholesome sometimes appears to be the same, sometimes it does not. In former and later times, sometimes evil appears to be identical, sometimes it does not. Evils in the heavenly realm may or may not be the same as evils in the human realm. Much less, looking at the Way of the buddhas and the ways of the conventional world, there are enormous differences concerning what is good, evil, or unmarked. Good and evil occur in time, although time is neither good nor evil. Good and evil take the form of dharmas, although the dharmas are not of themselves good or evil. Since all dharmas are held equally, all evils are held equally. In the same manner, because all dharmas are viewed equally, all sorts of good are also seen impartially.[46]

Nevertheless, in cultivating the one supreme living and enlightened reality—*anuttarā samyak-saṃbodhi*—we hear the teaching, practice it, and bear the awakened fruit of that practice. This Way is profound beyond measure; it is all-inclusive, all-encompassing; it is subtle, and it is deep.

We can hear and understand this unsurpassable enlightenment from experienced teachers or learn about it from reading the sūtras; one of the first things we hear from those who have practiced for a long time is the teaching on refraining from various evils. If we are not told about refraining from various evils, then our instruction is not the same as that of the buddhas' true teaching; it is nothing other than some malevolent casuistry. Make no mistake: learning "various evils refrained from" is the

45. "Myriad of dharmas" is Dōgen Zenji's way of referring to the activities of day-to-day life.

46. Rather than simply saying good and evil are dharmas, I expressed this as I did, supported by Uchiyama Rōshi's definition of dharmas as meaning "taking a form." And, since the lines must be understood as defining or expressing verbally the scenery of zazen, in the succeeding line as well, rather than to say that the dharmas are equal, which would be a literal translation, I have understood this passage as saying that all dharmas, both evil and good, are held or viewed equally. In this case, *equally* implies impartially, that is, without emotion or sentimentality. And from the actual sitting practice, this makes sense.

true teaching of the buddhas. "Refraining from various evils" is not to be identified with that which people ordinarily conjure up in their minds.[47] Hearing the teaching of "awakening to the living reality" is the same as hearing the one on refraining from various evils. They sound the same, because both are the words of awakening to the one living reality. In fact, they are totally awakening words. For that reason, the words themselves are fully living [awakening] words. For the words to be heard as the teaching of the one living reality, and to be moved by them, we vow to hold dear the teaching on refraining from various evils and to practice it. Where various evils can no longer be created,[48] there the virtue of practice manifests directly.[49] This living actualization does so in all lands and all worlds, as all times and all dharmas. This vivid actualization of the entire universe is the parameter of various evils refrained from.[50]

II.

When a rare person actualizes this very time[51]—even when living in, or

47. Ordinarily, people are apt to think that "refraining from various evils" simply means not doing bad or unwholesome things. Here, Dōgen is referring to the ethics and moral injunctions that have been created and evolved in various societies and among various peoples around the world.

48. This is the aim or direction of our practice.

49. The Japanese word *tachimachi* (忽) means "at once," "directly," "simultaneously," or "right away." That is, the influence or virtue of practice functions at a level or dimension in our day-to-day lives, beyond our imagination or conscious awareness, beyond any creation of our minds.

50. That is, "refraining from various evils" transcends the narrow boundaries or limitations of what is good or evil that are imposed or established by individual societies or cultures. Here, Dōgen is taking the discussion beyond the limiting morality or ethics of any one society.

51. The beginning of this passage is premised on the previous paragraph in which Dōgen says, "Where various forms of evil can no longer be created, then the virtue of practice manifests directly. Uchiyama Rōshi explains this passage, which in Chinese reads "正当恁麼時の正当恁麼人 (*shōtō immoji no shōtō immojin*)," as "when this truly alive person actualizes this truly living time, . . ." The *Zengaku Daijiten* paraphrases this as "truth

only coming from or going to, a place where evil might be expected to abound; or when encountering occasions when carrying out evil deeds would seem only natural; or when keeping company with those who seem to act in evil ways—no evil is ever committed. Since it is the functioning and power of *refraining from* that is being entirely revealed, we cannot say definitively that various evils are necessarily evil; not even a weapon can be said to be intrinsically evil! It is a matter of picking up and putting down.[52]

When we thoroughly live out truly living time, it becomes clear and utterly natural that evil does not break the person and that the person can't destroy evil.[53] By the time we gather our wits and physically begin to practice, the lion's share [of that practice] has already been accomplished.

---

itself." There is a strong implication here of an image of one actualizing, in Uchiyama Rōshi's words, "opening the hand of thought," because when we let go of the fetters of preconceived notions and biased opinions, etc., then we live where nothing is fixed and there are no boundaries. Simply put, when we are truly living in the present and fully meeting the present encounter.

Mistakes arise on this point, however, when one merely *thinks* that he or she is living where nothing is fixed and where there are no boundaries and, therefore, can do whatever he or she selfishly wants. It is living with the mistaken or arrogant sense that one is beyond good or evil.

52. Here, Dōgen uses a weapon as an extreme example of how such a thing is not in itself intrinsically evil, but depends on how it is used. Broadly speaking, he is referring to how the various things in our day-to-day life are used—picked up and put down. Today, we might think of a nuclear bomb as being inherently evil, because its purpose is to kill indiscriminately. But, if there is any evil to be found, it is in how such a thing is actually put into operation by human beings, not in the thing itself.

53. If there is nothing inherently evil, how can it be destroyed in the first place? A classic example of this mistaken thinking is the logic of racism that arose in the nineteenth and early twentieth centuries in the West. Even Christian anti-Semitic polemics insisted that Jews could not be good—even those who had converted to Christianity could not be "true" converts—that all Jews not only committed evil deeds but actually were the embodiment of evil. This idea led to the eliminationist policy of Nazi Germany—the "Final Solution." Similar thinking can be found in the myriad examples of so-called ethnic cleansing being carried out in various parts of the world today.

This is the quick of *refraining from*.[54] We practice, bringing into play the totality of body and mind.[55] And we who practice physically and mentally do so substantively—with the full power of the four elements and the five constituents that comprise our body and mind. This fuller body does not contaminate our true self, our jiko. It is always in this very present that our whole body naturally practices. The power of the

54. In Japanese, Dōgen uses the expression *nōkō no makusa* (脳後). *Nōkō* literally means "behind the head" or "in back of the head"; in Zen it refers to the crux or heart or core of a matter. In this case, the "matter" is the matter of refraining, and 80 percent or 90 percent of it has already been accomplished by the time we get to the cushion. This is the living quick of refraining.

55. Here, Dōgen uses the traditional Buddhist term for body and mind, *shidai goun* (四大五蘊) or the four elements and five constituents. According to Nakamura Gen's *Bukkyōgo Daijiten*, in the *Mumonkan,* this highly technical term is referred to simply as *shintai* (身体) or body (Nakamura Gen 中村元, Bukkyōgo Daijiten 仏教語大辞典 [東京書籍, 1983]). So, it would be good to point out here that when "body and mind" are used in Zen texts, it is with an understanding of the original term and the much broader, more inclusive definition of the words "body" and "mind."

Actually, not only modern teachers of Zen like Kōdō Sawaki, Suzuki Shunryu, or Kōshō Uchiyama, but historical teachers as well have steered away from just repeating the technical terms that have been passed down and instead have passionately tried to put those terms into the idiom of everyday life. While we usually conceive of our body in a limited sense, in Buddhism it is understood that our body doesn't stop with the contours of our skin. Everything in our environment as well—gravity, moisture, warmth, movement, vegetables riddled with herbicides, noxious air, polluted water—all of these things go into the composition of our body and mind. It is said by scientists that the atoms that make up our body came from an exploding star.

Traditionally, *shidai* (四大) refers to the four elements, earth, water, fire, and, in this case, wind. (Here, the (大) refers to elements and not its usual meaning of large or magnanimous. *Chidai* (地大), represents solidity and support, *suidai* (水大) moisture and containment, *kadai* (火大) warmth that matures things, and *fūdai* (風大) that which causes movement. In this case, these elements are the elements of the environment and, therefore, contribute to the composition of our body. *Goun* or *goon* (五蘊) refers more specifically to the material and spiritual elements of the body. *Shikiun* (色蘊) refers to matter or form, *juun* (受蘊) perception, *sōun* (想蘊) conception, *gyōun* (行蘊) volition, and *shikiun* (識蘊) consciousness.

whole body and mind that we are practicing right now brings the body and mind of previous times into the practice. And just as our practice enables the mountains and rivers, the earth, the sun and moon and stars all to practice, they, in turn, bring us to practice. This is not merely a one-time realization; it is the vibrant attitude in all times. Because it is the living vision of each and every moment of time, it induces all the buddhas and ancestors to practice, it induces them to listen to the teaching, and it induces them to carry out the fruit of their learning.[56] The buddhas and ancestors have never vitiated the teaching, practice, or realization; hence, these things have not been an encumbrance to the buddhas and ancestors.[57] Consequently, in being brought to practice, no buddha or ancestor has ever tried to circumvent the facts of the past or to take flight into the future. Acting as an ordinary sentient being or as a buddha poses no obstacle to what is widely thought of as a "buddha" or "ancestor." Still, we need to consider constantly and carefully this matter of being a buddha or ancestor through all the hours of the day and in all our day-to-day activities. Functioning as a buddha or ancestor does not violate the sentient being, nor does he or she [as a buddha] take away from, deprive, or alienate that sentient being.[58] Nevertheless, the body

56. According to *Zengaku Daijiten*, Buddhist scholasticism taught that there is a gap or sequence from teaching to practice to realization, in that order. In Japanese, this is referred to as *kyō-gyō-shō* (教行証). In Zen, however, the three are intertwined and occur simultaneously. Another expression that shows the relationship between the three is *san soku ichi · ichi soku san* (三即一・一即三): the three are one, any one is simultaneously inclusive of all three.

57. The buddhas and ancestors have never debased or polluted the teaching, practice, or realization of the Buddhadharma by adding something to what was not there originally, nor has the teaching ever constituted an obstacle to the buddhas and ancestors.

58. That is, to function as a buddha in our day-to-day lives does not preclude in any way the loss of the individual. Yet, when functioning as a buddha, a consciousness of "I'm doing 'good,'" etc., does not arise, because "functioning as a buddha" implies an all-inclusive activity. The activity embraces the individual; hence, there is no conscious separation between self and other (person, or thing or event).

and mind of the functioning buddha have been cast off. The cause and effect of good and evil bring us to practice; cause and effect cannot be changed by will nor can cause and effect be contrived by human imagination.[59] There are times when cause and effect bring us to practice. Since the cause and the effect have been cast off, their fundamental feature becomes clearly evident. This is because they are the cause and effect of *refraining from*; they are absolute and transcend conscious effort—they are impermanent, and they are clearly evident and unhidden.

That the *various evils* are all contained within *refraining from* will manifest clearly in practicing diligently in this way. Aided by this manifestation of *refraining from*, we will be able to see the principle of refraining from various evils clearly and be able to sit immovably.

When continuously refraining from various evils in the living quick of time, these evils do not give rise as the cause of the next effect—there is only *refraining from*. Nor do these evils perish from some cause—there is only *refraining from*. When various evils are viewed impartially, then all the dharmas are viewed impartially. People are to be pitied who do not understand that *various evils* are born of a cause but that the cause itself is *refraining from*. As it is written in the *Lotus Sūtra*, "The seeds of Buddhahood sprout through causation."[60] Therefore, following causation, the seeds of buddhahood will be born.

III.

It is not that various evils do not exist, but rather that all there is, is *makusa* (莫作), *refraining from*. Nor is it a matter of evils existing; again, all there is, is *refraining from*. Neither are evils empty; there is only *refraining from*. Nor do they have a substantial form; all there is, is *refraining from*. Evils are not of themselves *refraining from*; for all there is, is *refraining from*.

59. Cause and effect are not something that can be imagined or created in one's head.

60. This passage is found in the chapter "Expedient Means" in the *Lotus Sūtra*, or *Saddharma-puṇḍarīka-sūtra*, in Burton Watson, trans., *The Lotus Sūtra* (New York: Columbia University Press, 1993), 41.

For instance,[61] it is not that the pine tree in the spring exists or does not exist—it is not a thing that is humanly created. Nor is it a matter of the chrysanthemums in the fall existing or not; it is simply that they are not a humanly derived creation. All the buddhas as well are neither existent nor nonexistent—there is but *refraining from.*

The existence or nonexistence of such things as the temple pillars or stone lanterns, the monks' fly chaser or the staff, is not in question; there is only *refraining from.* It is not a matter of jiko, our whole self, either existing or not existing; there is only *refraining from.*[62]

Making every effort to examine wholeheartedly in this way is itself a manifesting of the kōan; it is the kōan totally manifested.[63] See everything from the perspective of universal truth, i.e., the kōan; see everything from what is presently and actually being manifest, i.e., *genjō.*[64]

61. In Kishizawa Ian Rōshi's *Shōbōgenzō Zenkō* (*Lectures on the Shōbōgenzō*), he writes, "From this point, Dōgen Zenji will, in a sense, spread out his wares through various examples. Looking at 'For instance,' what he will be illustrating here are examples of how all the *dharmas* are fundamentally, 'refraining.'" Kishizawa Ian 岸沢惟安, *Shōbōgenzō Zenkō* 正法眼蔵全講 [Lectures on the *Shōbōgenzō*], vol. 4 (Tokyo: Daihōrinkaku, 1972), 176.

62. The notes in Mizuno Yaoko's four-volume *Shōbōgenzō* have helped elucidate several obscure passages. Mizuno defines the sense of "refraining" in this passage as "absolute truth having no connection to human actions." Mizuno Yaoko, *Shōbōgenzō*, 2:236.

In his commentary on this chapter, Kishizawa Ian Rōshi says that, "Refraining here is the same as *shohō jissō*—all things are what (or as) they are. There is no such thing or entity as 'evil.' *Shoaku* is another way of referring to the myriad of dharmas. Therefore, representing all the dharmas there are, Dōgen picks up the pine tree, the chrysanthemum, all the buddhas, the supporting pillars, the stone lanterns, the fly chaser, the staff—the objects and structures of everyday life." Kishizawa Ian, *Shōbōgenzō Zenkō*, vol. 4 (1972), 178.

63. Here, Dōgen turns the phrase *genjō kōan* around to make *kōan genjō suru*. That is, he uses *genjō* as a verb (現成) meaning to manifest the absolute truth of life in the present.

64. Literally, Dōgen is identifying the subject with the object. Mizuno interprets this passage as "Considering from the perspective of the kōan, considering from the perspective of genjō—manifesting." Mizuno Yaoko, *Shōbōgenzō*, 2:236.

There is an equivalence being drawn between *genjō* and *kōan*, and between *shoaku* and *makusa*, as well as between *u* and *ji,* from *uji*. That is, in these three expressions,

Despite the fact that evil can in no way be created, how can we avoid feeling remorseful over some terrible thing we mistakenly feel we have done? Such feelings of remorse also derive from the power of practicing *refraining from*.

However, hearing that the various evils are the same as *refraining from* and cannot be created, and then deliberately contriving to commit an unwholesome act is like heading north hoping to arrive in the southern country of Otsu.

Refraining from various evils is not limited to Sōzan's "The well looks at the donkey." It is the well looking at the well and the donkey looking at the donkey, too. Moreover, it is also the person seeing the person and the mountain seeing the mountain. As this was in response to Toku-jōza by Master Sōzan who had asked the senior monk to explain further the meaning of the "body of the buddha" that changes in response to the needs of the sentient being, this is [the same as] shoaku makusa. [The original story from which this was taken, reads:] "The *dharmakāya*, or true body of Buddha, is, as it were, formless; still, it takes a form in response to each matter.[65] It is like the moon reflected in a drop of water." Since

---

"genjō kōan," "shoaku makusa," and "uji," there is no separation—between manifesting or revealing (genjō) and *ultimate reality* (the kōan), between the various evils (shoaku) and refraining (makusa), or between the living quick (*u*) and time (*ji*).

If we take the phrase *shoaku makusa* literally, it indeed says "refrain from various evils," but what we have done then, is to separate the action from the activity, the doer from the doing. A literal translation would go against the spirit of Mahāyāna Buddhist thought.

65. This refers to matter as in material things or people (sentient beings), but broadly speaking, the situation or circumstance as well. According to Mizuno, the reference to the donkey and the well appears in Sōzan's *Iro no Honsoku*, the kōan of the donkey and the well. The original story of the Buddha's true body appears in the *Konkōmyō-kyo* (金光明経). In Case 52 of the *Shōyōroku* 従容録, or *Book of Serenity*, compiled by Wanshi Shōgaku (Chi: Hongzhi Zhengjue 宏智正覺, 1091–1157) in the twelfth century, we find: "It is said that the Dharma body [which is synonymous with jiko] is like the empty sky. It manifests a myriad of forms—just like the moon is reflected on the surface of the water. How do you explain this principle of taking various forms?" Toku said, "It is like a donkey looking at his own reflection in the water in a well." Sōzan said, "You put it quite

"responding to each matter" is the same as *refraining from*,[66] it appears as a form that must also be *refraining from*.[67] That the cosmic body of Buddha is formless is like striking out with the left hand; it is striking out with the right one—there are no hindrances. It is like the moon in the water; the water is obstructed by the moon.[68] All the examples I have given of *refraining from* are unquestionable illustrations of the manifesting of the quick of life.

The existence or nonexistence of such things as the temple pillars or stone lanterns, the monks' fly chaser or the staff is not in question; there is only *refraining from*. It is not a matter of jiko—whole self—either existing or not existing; there is only *refraining from*.

IV.

In the expression "Carry out all sorts of good," "all sorts of good" refers to the second of the three inherent qualities of evil, good, and unmarked. Although all sorts of good are contained within the quality of goodness, it is not as though some sort of good is simply on hand, waiting for a practitioner to enact it. When some good is being fully carried out, all good is inevitably present. Though good acts have no inherently fixed form, they gather all good quicker than iron is drawn to a magnet. Their strength exceeds even that of the most destructive hurricane-like *vairam-*

---

well, but you are only able to express 80 percent of it." Toku said, "How would you put it, Master?" Sōzan replied, "It is like a well looking at the donkey reflected in the water."

66. Mizuno's footnote reads, "This 'refraining' has nothing to do with a person's conscious restraint." Mizuno Yaoko, *Shōbōgenzō*, 2:237.

67. The form that is taken is not one that a human being can consciously take. Rather, it is the true form. In this case, *makusa* takes on the same sense as *shohō jissō*—everything is what it is, as it appears.

68. In the text, *hisui chūgetsu* 被水中月, Dōgen literally says the moon covers or is covered by the water, although Mizuno Yaoko interprets this to mean that the moon *obstructs* the water. The traditional reading is the moon *reflected* in the water. Bringing the previous sentence into play, the moon *appears* in the water, but it has no solid *form*.

bhaka winds that blow.[69] Notwithstanding all the phenomena occurring naturally in this world or the destructive or horrible deeds of all the nations and peoples dwelling therein, this gathering of good deeds can never be impeded.[70]

Still, that which is perceived as "good" is the same or different depending on the society and social context. [As it is written in the *Lotus Sūtra*,] "Just as the buddhas of the past, present, and future preached," they did so to the people of the time and ways in which they lived. There are a myriad of buddhas, whose appearances all vary—some have lived for an immeasurable length of time, others only for a short time; some buddhas are colossal, others are infinitesimally small. Still, "all of them taught the Dharma teaching of nondifferentiation."[71] There are those whose simple faith guides their capacity to move others and who base their practice on such faith, and there are those whose capability to move others is based on their comprehension and understanding of good derived from the depths of their practice of the teaching of good.[72] The functioning of each is very different. They almost appear to be teaching totally different Dharmas. A concrete example of this difference would be how a literal

69. *Vairambhaka*, Skt: (Jpn: *biranbu* 毘藍風). Hisao Inagaki writes: "a very strong wind that blows at a time of cosmic change [the beginning and end of the universe]" in *A Dictionary of Japanese Buddhist Terms*, Nagata Bunshodo, 1985, 12.

70. Alternately, "Neither the power of the entire cosmic creation nor the karmic deeds of all the nations can stand in the way or obstruct good deeds."

71. Dōgen has taken the phrase "Dharma teaching of nondifferentiation," as well as the one above, and incorporated it into his text.

72. *Shingyō no ki, hōgyō no ki* (信行の機, 法行の機). First of all, *ki* (機), in this case, is short for *kikon* (機根), that is, one who has the capacity or ability to actually carry out the practice of the Buddha Way. *Shingyō no ki* refers to those who have a simple belief or who literally believe the teaching and who practice. *Hōgyō no ki* refers to those who practice with a keen intellect and comprehend the teaching deeply. There is a Pure Land and Shin Buddhist expression that may help elucidate further: *ki-hō ittai* (機法一体). In this case, *ki* refers to sentient beings, while *hō* (法) refers to Amida Buddha. *Ittai* (一体) means that A and B are, literally speaking, "one body" or identical. So, a sentient being and Amida Buddha are *not two*.

upholding of the precepts by a śrāvaka becomes a breach of them by a bodhisattva.[73]

Goodness does not arise out of causes and conditions, nor does it disappear due to causes and conditions. Although all good takes the form of a dharma, no dharma is intrinsically good.[74] If, from the beginning, the causes and conditions, appearance and disappearance, and all sorts of good are sound, then they will be sound throughout as well. Although all good takes the form of some act being carried out, such carrying out is devoid of any ego; neither is there a "self" that is carrying out such actions.[75] This carrying out does not take place outside of oneself, nor can *carrying out good* be known by another. This is because knowledge and view of self and other lie in the purview of a dualistic conscious knowing that by nature separates self from other, "my" view from "another's" view. In each and every living action, there is the sun; there is the moon—that is *carrying out.*

When *carrying out* is fully implemented, although the kōan[76] is totally

73. The Japanese in this entire paragraph is not easy to piece together and I suspect that if he had had the time (and had known what difficulty later practitioners would have with it), Dōgen would have clarified or simplified it. I have chosen to translate this passage along the lines it has been interpreted by Kishizawa Ian and Kōshō Uchiyama, as well as Ishii Kyōji's modern Japanese translation. Readers should read other translations to see what other translators have done with it.

74. In this case, *dharmas* refer to entities and phenomena, including situations and circumstances.

75. Kishizawa Ian Rōshi interprets this passage this way: "Since all good takes the form of some act being carried out, etc., 'all good' and 'carrying out' are the same thing. That is, in carrying out an action there is no awareness of it being good or evil. We cannot see or evaluate our actions as good or evil while we are doing them." Kishizawa Ian, *Shōbōgenzō Zenkō*, vol. 4 (1972).

76. Here, the meaning of *kōan* is "ultimate reality." Originally, a kōan was a public document or pronouncement carrying great weight or authority that required investigation. From there, the word came to be used in Zen to mean an expression of absolute truth. There is an expression *kōfu no antoku* (公府の案溶く), which refers to taking up those enigmas or questions about life apart from human sentiment or bias.

present, there is no beginning to the kōan, nor has it been continuously residing somewhere.[77] Moreover, this *carrying out* is the fundamental practice. Although this is the total *carrying out of good*, there is absolutely no way to measure such good. Even though the present *carrying out* is the implementation of vivid actions, there is absolutely no way to calculate their effect. [Alternatively: Though this *carrying out* is done with a most vivid and alert eye,[78] we cannot measure the accomplishment.] The true Dharma does not manifest in order to be measured. The measure of clear and vivid actions is not the same as calculating human measurement.

Various kinds of good deeds cannot be verified in terms of existing or not existing, nor can they be characterized as taking some form or of having no form, and so forth—there is only *carrying out*. In whatever place or time good manifests, there will be *carrying out*. In this *carrying out*, all good will manifest. Though this manifestation of *carrying out* is absolute,[79] it neither comes into being nor falls into decay, nor is it subject to the conditions of cause and effect. *Carrying out* in living, in residing, in dying and so forth, is also like this.[80] When a single act of good is actually being carried out, the true ground of reality and the entire

77. We have to continue to practice living in a present where nothing is fixed. Kishizawa Rōshi comments, "As Dōgen stated earlier 'good is not standing around waiting to be performed by some practitioner.'" Kishizawa Ian, *Shōbōgenzō Zenkō*, vol. 4 (1972), 195–96. That is, good has no separate eternal existence of its own.

78. "Vivid and alert eye": in Japanese, *katsuganzei* (活眼晴). Ishii Kyōji says that katsuganzei is the vivid functioning of buddha nature. Ishii Kyōji, trans., *Shōbōgenzō* (Tokyo: Kawade Shōbō Shinsha, 1998), 2:382. The *Zengaku Daijiten* defines the term as "vivid eye" and "the vision to discriminate skillfully among all things." Komazawa University Publications Committee 禅学大辞典編纂所, ed., *Zengaku Daijiten* 禅学大辞典 (Tokyo: Daishukan Shoten,東京：大修館書店, 1985), 163.

79. Here, Dōgen is not using the word *kōan* as it is popularly understood in the Rinzai tradition: some sort of insoluble puzzle to be worked on during zazen. The word here simply means "absolute" or "nondualistic." It is being used in the same sense as it is in *genjō kōan* or the *kōan*, meaning "absolute manifestation of the present."

80. Alternately: "Likewise, although this manifestation of *carrying out* is absolute, it is not subject to being born, residing for some time, and then later, no longer manifesting."

body of all the dharmas is being carried out.[81] The cause and effect of this singular good act is the same as manifesting the kōan. It is a mistake to think that cause comes first followed by effect; cause is complete in itself; effect is complete in itself. The cause is incomparable; the dharma [as an action] is incomparable. The effect is incomparable; the dharma [as an action or phenomenon] is incomparable. Depending on the cause, we can surmise the effect. Still, we cannot say that cause comes first and then comes the effect, because the cause is complete as it is and the effect is complete in itself.

V.

Clarifying this mind of [one's] total self:[82] *refraining* is self, *refraining* is clarifying, *self* is present as this, *self* is mind, *refraining* is this, *refraining* is mind, *carrying out* manifests mind, *carrying out* manifests clarifying, *carrying out* is this, *carrying out* expresses self. That is why it is said to be the teaching of all the buddhas. It is like the various buddhas and

81. The "true ground of reality" is *shinjitchi* (真実地), while the "whole body of all the dharmas" is *jinbō zenshin* (尽法全身). The *Zengaku Daijiten* defines *shinjitchi* as "the realm of deep realization" (satori). Dōgen Zenji's most vivid reference to *zenshin* appears in *Shōbōgenzō* "Ikka no Myōju" (一顆明珠, "One Bright Pearl"). "... *Zenshin* [the entire body (of the Universe)] is the true Dharma eye, it is the body of truth, it is [contained in] this single expression, it is pure light, it is exactly what it is." An alternate translation of this last line is "... zenshin (全身)—the whole body of the Universe is zenshin (全心)—all life."

82. In *clarifying this mind of total self*, Dōgen uses the four characters in the third line of the gāthā: *ji* (自) or "total self," *jō* (浄) "clarify" or sometimes "purify," *go* (其) "this," and *i* (意) "mind." He is trying to show that each element, though standing by itself, is still connected to each of the others. In the original Chinese, there are only these four characters. And whether the verb *jō* is being used transitively or intransitively cannot be determined. Some translators choose to use the word intransitively and translate the first character *ji* as "naturally," rather than its other meaning of "self," so the passage becomes something like "naturally purifies the mind." However, since the Pāli word *sacitta* means "one's own mind," I feel that translating the four characters as "personally clarify" or "personally clarifying your own mind" makes more sense and is closer to the original Pāli.

numerous heavenly beings;[83] although there are both similarities and dissimilarities between them, those heavenly beings are not the same as the various buddhas. Or, it can be compared to the buddhas and *cakra-vartin*; there are similarities, but not all benevolent secular rulers are the same as the various buddhas. You need to carefully and thoroughly examine these principles.

Although there are those who never examine the meaning of "all the buddhas," though seemingly making extraordinary effort, their useless suffering is just that of ordinary beings; it has nothing to do with practicing the Buddha Way. *Refraining* and *carrying out* are like the horse arriving before the donkey has left.[84]

VI.

Haku Kyoi[85] of the Tang dynasty was a lay disciple of Bukkō Nyoman,[86] in the lineage of Baso Dōitsu.[87] When he was a high government official in Hangzhou Province, he called on Dōrin Chōka.[88] During their

83. In Japanese, the "numerous heavenly beings" is a translation of *jizaiten* (自在天). Originally, the heavenly beings in Buddhism were adapted from the Brahmanic deities with Shiva being the head creative deity.

84. In this Chinese Zen expression *rojimiko bajitōrai nari* (驢事未了馬事到来なり), the "donkey" is a metaphor for an ordinary, perhaps confused, unenlightened being, while the "horse" carries the image of dignity and someone who is highly enlightened. Or we could say the former represents delusion and the latter represents realization, or *satori*. The sense behind the expression is that ordinarily one might be apt to think that a person who starts out in Buddhist practice is deluded, but over time, becomes enlightened, and all the delusion disappears. However, the point Dōgen is making is that these two states coexist in the same ordinary being.

85. Haku Kyoi (白居易; Chi: Bai Zhuyi; 772–846) was known famously as Haku Rakuten (白楽天).

86. Bukkō Nyoman (佛光如満; Chi: Ruman Fuguang; dates unknown).

87. Master Daijaku of Kōzei (江西大寂) was better known by the name Baso Dōitsu (馬祖道一; Chi: Mazu Daoyi; 709–88).

88. Dōrin Chōka (道林鳥力; Chi: Daolin Niaoke; 741–824). Chōka means "bird nest." It is said that he lived several years on a branch of a large pine tree, hence the unusual name.

talk, Kyoi asked, "What is the gist of Buddhadharma?" Dōrin replied, "Refrain from committing various evils and carry out all sorts of good actions." Kyoi responded, "If that were the case, even a three-year-old child could say that." Dōrin replied, "Although a three-year-old child may be able to express it, not even an eighty-year-old can actually carry it out." Hearing the reply, Kyoi, thanked him gratefully, bowed, and left.

In fact, though Kyoi was a descendent of General Haku,[89] he was also a poet, unparalleled over several generations. It is said that he was reborn twenty-four times, each time becoming an increasingly adept poet. He was sometimes referred to as the Mañjuśrī of literati or the Maitreya of poets. There was no one who had not heard of his poetic artistry. The influence of his verse spread everywhere. However, when it came to the Buddha Way, he was just a beginner and was not yet mature. In regard to *refraining from various evils* or *carrying out acts of good*, he couldn't have understood what was behind such an expression, even in a dream. Kyoi probably speculated that Dōrin earnestly encouraged people to *refrain from various evils* and *carry out acts of good* at the conscious level. He was totally unaware and had never heard of the universal truth for all ages, of the Buddha Way from ancient times up to our own time, in regard to *refraining from evil* and *carrying out good*. He most likely said such a thing because he did not have the virtue of having yet learned Buddhadharma, nor had he ever stepped into a place where the Dharma was actually practiced. Make no mistake, even if we are cautioned to intentionally avoid various evils and, with every intention, encouraged to carry out good deeds, the actuality takes place in absolute refraining.

VII.

In every respect, Buddhadharma heard for the first time from a wise teacher or heard many years later as a result of authentic practice will be

---

89. General Haku (白; Chi: Bai) was a well-known general who served during the Period of the Warring States in China (third century BCE).

the same. This is called "right from the beginning, right at the end,"[90] or "subtle cause, subtle effect."[91] It is also referred to as "buddha cause, buddha effect."[92] Since the cause and effect of practicing the Buddha Way, however, are not like the concepts of *ijuku*[93] or *tōru*,[94] if the cause is not based on true reality, then an effect of corresponding quality cannot be expected. Being well grounded in the Buddhadharma, Dōrin was able to express the truth in this way.

Even if all spheres were to be totally engulfed by evil[95] or all dharmas entirely swallowed up, *refraining* remains the liberating factor.[96] Since all types of good are always good, the nature, form, substance, and impact of *carrying out* [such deeds] will always be equally good.

Kyoi showed no trace of having understood this, hence he said: "*Even a three-year-old child could say that.*" He said such a thing because he personally lacked a deeper understanding of expressing Buddhadharma.

90. In Japanese, *zushin bishin* (頭正尾正). Literally, the expression means "if the head is right, the tail will be right." *Head* and *tail* are metaphors for *beginning* and *end*, respectively.

91. In Japanese, *myōin myōka* (妙因妙果). *Myō* (妙) in Japanese can mean "subtle," or "marvelous," and by extension, "immeasurable," that is, "beyond the ability of the human mind to grasp."

92. In Japanese, *butsuin bukka* (仏因仏果). A cause based on true reality is a translation of *butsuin*, or "buddha cause," while an effect based on the same quality is a translation of *bukka*, or "buddha effect."

93. *Ijuku* (異熟) refers to an argument whereby the moral character or quality of the effect of a good or evil action differs from the cause.

94. *Tōru* (等流) refers to an argument whereby the moral character or quality of the cause of a good or evil action is the same in character or quality as the effect.

95. Here, surely Dōgen had to be thinking about all the intrigues going on between the various religious groups, as well as the fighting and battles that took place during his lifetime between the political powers during the Kamakura period. Perhaps the discourse between the various powers, both religious and secular, was shrill and confrontational—not so unlike our own age, all over the world.

96. That is, even if evil pervaded and held hostage all the aspects of our daily lives—politics, economics, civil rights, etc.—since evil is not an inherent nature of any of these things, we are still liberated simply by *refraining*. A Japanese translator renders this passage as "refraining from evil is not lost."

Poor Kyoi, what are you saying? Since you had never heard of the reality of the Buddha's teachings,[97] how could you know anything about a three-year-old child? How could you know that a newborn child could speak the truth? If you truly knew what a three-year-old knows, you would know all the buddhas in the three worlds—past, present, and future. Without an understanding of all the buddhas in the three worlds, how could you possibly understand a three-year-old?

Never think that you understand someone or something simply because you have encountered them firsthand, nor think that you do not understand someone or something just because you have never met them. Penetrating the minutest particle, you will penetrate all worlds without exception.[98] When you thoroughly comprehend just one dharma, you understand all dharmas. And if you do not understand all the dharmas, you cannot be expected to comprehend even one dharma. When you have thoroughly learned and penetrated one dharma, you will be able to see into all the dharmas and, equally, one single dharma. If you know well even the tiniest particle, you will understand all the worlds without exception. Therefore, it is foolish to think that a three-year-old child cannot speak the truth or to assume that what a three-year-old child says is childish and simple. Consequently, for followers of the Buddha, the most crucial matter is clarifying the direct and indirect causes of life/death.

The ancient buddhas have said that, at birth, all are born as lions. Here, a lion refers to the power of a *tathāgata* to turn the wheel of Dharma; it *is* the actual turning of the wheel. Further, another ancient one has said, "Everything that arises in our life/death is the true form of the most fundamental Self." Therefore, clarifying the true form of our most

97. The Japanese phrase is *buppō no kafū* (仏法の家風). Normally, the word *kafū* refers to the traditions or customs of a particular house; in this case, it is the Buddha's "house" that is being referred to. Further, this is a reference not just to the traditions or customs of the Buddha but to the reality of Buddhadharma.

98. "... the minutest particle": in Japanese, *ichijin* (一塵). There is an expression *ichi soku banpō, banpō soku ichi* (一即万法、万法即一). That is, a single dharma is not different from all the myriad dharmas; the myriad dharmas are not different from a single dharma.

fundamental Self with the resonance of a lion cub's roar is the most crucial matter. So it is not a simple thing to be taken lightly. To clarify the actions that underlie a three-year-old child is to clarify the actions of all the buddhas, because they are not necessarily different. Since it had never even crossed his mind that a three-year-old child could voice Buddhadharma, Kyoi foolishly said what he did. Dōrin's Dharma-voice was louder and clearer than a roll of thunder. Even if a three-year-old child could not say the same thing, it is said that a three-year-old child fully expresses Dharma. Kyoi never heard the child roar like a lion cub and totally misheard Dōrin's turning of the wheel. How can we not continually feel the compassion of Master Dōrin's "Even though a three-year-old child may express the Dharma, not even an eighty-year-old can carry it out." We must winnow through and practice very carefully that such a mind is an expression of the truth said by a three-year-old. And we must equally winnow through and practice the truth of an eighty-year-old being unable to carry it out. Trusting the Dharma-words of a three-year-old does not mean that everything such a child might say is Dharma-words. Though an old man may not be able to carry out those words, *how* is one unable to carry them out? In this way, based on practice, we must winnow through just what Buddhadharma is; understand it and express it as fully and clearly as we can.

> Presented to the Assembly at Kōshō Hōrinji Monastery, in Uji of Yamashiro Province, on July 16, 1240.
> Transcribed by disciple Ejō in his quarters, on February 26, 1243.

4. Commentary on "Shoaku Makusa"

KŌSHŌ UCHIYAMA

Translated by DAITSŪ TOM WRIGHT

Zazen is viewing both good and evil with the same eye.

There are lots of people in the world who want to be do-gooders. We can often see these people going to a temple or church. And, being totally caught up by (if, indeed, not possessed by) morals and ethics, they love to hear preachings on doing only good and not being bad. At the same time, of course, many Buddhist priests and teachers of ethics and morals accommodate these people's whims by preaching about just the things these do-gooders want to hear.

Such sermonizing, however, has no connection with the truth of human life. The society that most people tend to see is one devoid of almost anything inspiring or good, where violence and evil seem to permeate everywhere. Consequently, sermonizers talk away about things unrelated to the reality around us. And those who come to listen walk away with the temporary relief of thirst one might feel from drinking a cold soda pop on a hot day—there is never any intention of connecting what is being said to one's actual living situation. Also, among some of these do-gooders, there are those who, after hearing about doing good and not doing bad, go around parroting the teacher's words to others. They boast about how they enjoy the benefits from the "good" they do.

When we first hear the expression "Refrain from evil and carry out various acts of good," we might be inclined to think that it is preaching to us to be morally good and not commit bad or unwholesome actions.

However, it should go without saying that Dōgen Zenji would never have taught such a thing. That sort of moral nuance, which would make these do-gooders so happy, just never comes up in the text. If anything, what we find is food for reflection regarding the very foundation of the ethical formulation of carrying out wholesome acts and not doing ill. So the contents of our discussion become all the more complex.

As there are always many twists and turns in every fascicle of *Shōbō-genzō*, making any discussion far from simple, we need to read the text fully aware that a superficial or literal reading will never do.

I.

A *gāthā* of the ancient buddhas says:

Refraining from committing various evils
Carrying out all sorts of good actions
Personally clarifying this mind
This is the essential teaching of all the buddhas.

We find this teaching to be held in common by the first seven buddhas and, subsequently, by our ancestors as well. These teachings were transmitted from the earlier buddhas to their successors and were received directly by the latter from their predecessors. This holds true not only for the first seven buddhas; this is the teaching common to all buddhas. We must ardently practice and carefully examine these universal truths.

In one of the sūtras we read every day, we chant, "Bibashibutsu Daiosho, Shikibutsu Daiosho, Bishafubutsu Daiosho, Kurusonbutsu Daiosho, Kunagonmunibutsu Daiosho, Kashobutsu Daiosho," and then "Shakya-munibutsu Daiosho." Śākyamuni Buddha comes seventh. In other words, Śākyamuni Buddha didn't invent the Buddhist teaching; it was transmitted from previous buddhas long before him.

The gāthā, or poem, above is a precept held in common by these first seven buddhas. This is what has been transmitted. If the literal meaning were all that was being brought up here, it would be a simple matter. However, looking at this from a Buddhist perspective, we have an enormous problem facing us.

What is most fundamental to the teaching as Buddhadharma is contained in expressions such as *innenshō mujishō* (因縁生無自性), "the provisional arising of all dharmas has no independent cause," or *goonkaiku* (五蘊皆空), "the five elements compromising human existence are empty." "The provisional arising of anything has no independent cause" means that there is no concrete thing that we can point to that is fixed. "The five elements compromising human existence are empty"—there is nothing we can grab onto or take hold of. Or in the *Heart Sūtra*: *fushō fumetsu* (不生不滅), "no birth, no death"; *fuku fujō* (不垢不浄), "not sullied, not pure"; and *fuzō fugen* (不増不減), "no increase, no decrease." Nothing is added, nothing is taken away. All of these expressions are fundamental to Buddhadharma. Despite this, we read here about the existence of good and evil. How can this be?

When I was a young schoolboy, there was a class on morality. We were taught to do good things and to never do bad or unwholesome things. Now I am sure that both those teaching the class as well as us students all thought that in this world there are good things and bad things that actually exist. But to the extent that this problem of good and evil is dealt with in Buddhism, it must be done so on the basis of the concept of emptiness. It is there that one must clarify the significance within oneself by oneself. That is why Dōgen says, "We must ardently practice and carefully examine these universal truths."

> The actual Dharma teaching and Way of practice of the seven buddhas necessarily include the transmission and reception of that reality and of that practice. Further, it is the internal and direct transmission of how things are, and it is held in common by all the buddhas. It is without exception the totality of the teaching of the various buddhas. Moreover, this is the teaching, the practice, and the actualization of the entire myriad of buddhas.

The *Dharma* and *Way* in this passage refer to Buddhadharma, or *Buppō* (仏法) and *butsudō* (仏道). What does Buddhadharma mean here? I have yet to read any book on the Buddhist teachings that states exactly what this key concept is supposed to mean. To define it in my own words, I coined the expression "the actual reality of life." In contrast to Buddhadharma is *sehō* (世法), literally, "secular dharma," but in this case, it means the ways and values of different societies in the world. Sehō, as opposed to Buppō, implies viewing life once removed from reality. It is a view of life that constantly seeks to balance A with B, self with other.

In other words, a secular or worldly view of life doesn't look at reality, but rather views everything in narrow terms, for instance, that of market value. For example, money receives its value only when it is compared to something else. The actual reality of what we call money is that it is nothing more than a piece of paper. Yet, in extreme cases, people are even willing to kill in order to get a hold of a few sheets of this paper. One's position or job is another example of weighing one thing against another. It may sound impressive if we introduce ourselves as the chairperson of this or the president of that company, but in actual reality we may be simply no more than some senile old fool.

Buddhadharma has nothing to do with these sorts of conventional social values. Buddhadharma is always a matter of discerning the true condition of things. And butsudō, or "Buddha Way," means to live according to that true reality, not according to the lowest social denominators of behavior.[99]

Our text says that the Dharma and Path of the seven buddhas necessarily includes the "transmission and reception of that reality and of that practice." However, in this case, *transmission and reception* do not simply infer the passing on of some technique or skill from teacher to disciple. Transmission in Buddhism is not the same as receiving authorization or permission from one's teacher to teach flower arrangement

---

99. That is, the social fabrications of how we are supposed to live and by what values.

or the tea ceremony. The buddha Vipassī transmitted Buddhadharma to Vipassī and the buddha Vipassī received the transmission from Vipassī. Śākyamuni Buddha transmitted Buddhadharma to and received it from himself. This is the meaning of the line that follows: "It is the internal and direct transmission of how things are, and it is held in common by all the buddhas." It is not a matter of some mysterious thing being transmitted from Vipassī to Sikhī and then from him to Vessabhū. Each of them, individually and completely, internally "refrains from evil, does all sorts of good and clarifies personally his (or her) own mind" as the structure of jiko within themselves.

As soon as we hear the word *buddha* as in the expression "the entire myriad of buddhas," we are apt to dismiss it as having nothing to do with ourselves. We assume the discussion is about someone else. But that is not correct. The myriad of buddhas refers to all of us—actually, to all human beings.

In other words, as the internal structure of jiko, or our universal identity,[100] the Buddha Śākyamuni practiced "refraining from evil, doing all sorts of good," clarifying personally the significance of this as the essence of the teaching of the various buddhas. And then, Mahākāśyapa, by himself, did the same and not as some sort of authorization he received from Śākyamuni Buddha. That is why it is not just the first seven buddhas, but all human beings practicing the Buddha Way who, as "the teaching, the practice, and the actualization," practice refraining from evil, do all sorts of good, and clarify personally their mind as the essence of the teaching of the various buddhas. The expression "the teaching, the practice, and the actualization" means our everyday lives. *How* we live a lifestyle refraining from evil, doing all sorts of good, and personally clarifying the mind as the essence of the teaching becomes transmitted within us, permeating

---

100. The Japanese word *jiko*, when used in the Buddhist sense, is not an easy one to translate. Besides "universal identity," the term could also be translated as "whole self" or "all-encompassing self" or "all-inclusive self."

our day-to-day lives. This is the internal transmission common to all buddhas, the very basis of this whole fascicle.

> The "various evils" here refer to one of the three qualities of things/ actions—those three characteristics being good, evil, and unmarked. The nature of the various evils precedes conscious effort.

In Buddhism, all things [or actions] are categorized as being good, evil, or unmarked. Scholastically speaking, they are roughly defined in the following way. Good is that which is most appropriate or most suitable or in conformity with Buddhadharma. Evil is that which goes against what is most fitting or is not in agreement with Buddhadharma. Another definition is that good is that which becomes a power for bringing benefit to both oneself and others. Evil, on the other hand, is that quality that turns its back on reason or truth, becoming a force that invites suffering into the present and future. And that quality which does neither is what is termed "unmarked." These are the traditional Buddhist definitions of good, evil, and unmarked.

> And this holds true for good and unmarked things/actions as well. Though they are not sullied by human judgment and are truly how they appear, the qualities of all actions are revealed through the myriad dharmas.

The fundamental quality or inherent nature, in Japanese *shō* (性), in Buddhism refers to a fixed entity or thing. So that evil has no fixed quality simply means that although we speak of evil, there is no such *thing* as evil itself. The same is true for good and unmarked. Neither exists as an independent or fixed thing.

The character *ro* (漏) means "to leak or seep through something." While we are alive as human beings, our greed, passions, feelings, and sufferings seem to leak or ooze out of us. In today's idiom, we might use the word *secrete*. So, in the text, that evil and markless are not sullied means that they are not some secreted byproduct. In other words, "unmarked" or "not sullied" means the same as "all things are as they are."

> In different societies, that which is considered evil or unwholesome some-
> times appears to be the same, sometimes it does not. In former and later
> times, sometimes evil appears to be identical, sometimes it does not.

Before World War II, if a man and woman were to embrace in public in Japan, they would have been arrested for corrupting public morals and decency. But after the war, such sights have become socially acceptable. Hence, Dōgen writes, "In former and later times, sometimes evil appears to be identical, sometimes it does not." Or, before the war, when French films were popular, you would often see scenes of men and women embracing. At the time, I'm sure many Japanese had that image of the French, but there is in fact an established etiquette for hugging one another in French culture. For example, a man wouldn't just go touching a woman's breast as he greeted her. That would just be considered vulgar. Whereas the Japanese after the war would boldly touch whatever they could get away with. They thought they were, in a manner of speaking, imitating the French, but if French people ever saw such things, they surely would have thought Japanese men were all just a bunch of perverts. Hence, Dōgen writes, "In different societies, that which is considered evil or unwholesome sometimes appears to be the same, sometimes it does not."

> Evils in the heavenly realm may or may not be the same as evils in the
> human realm.

The lucidity of Dōgen Zenji's mind is unmistakable. In *Shōbōgenzō* "Senjō" ("Purifying"), he writes, "By nature, it is not necessarily so that water is pure. Nor is it by nature necessarily impure."[101] There is no

---

101. From *Shōbōgenzō* "Senjō" (洗淨, "Purifying"). Although "to purify" is a close

certainty that water is inherently pure. Nor is it certain that it isn't. However, Dōgen goes on to say, "Following and trusting in Buddhadharma
wholeheartedly is purifying." In other words, for Buddhadharma to
function as Buddhadharma, it has to be practiced, and that is how he is
using the word *purifying* here.

> Much less, looking at the Way of the buddhas and the ways of the con-
> ventional world, there are enormous differences regarding what is good,
> evil, and unmarked.

For example, it is common in our society today to believe that if we
educate and refine ourselves, building up our moral character and dis-
ciplining ourselves, we are improving ourselves and becoming better
than others around us. This is all thought of as doing good. In practicing
the Buddhadharma, however, this is not the case. Setting aside such
preoccupations with self-improvement, following the Buddhadharma
begins by throwing away our selfish, egotistical desires. We cannot say
in Buddhism that being more famous or cultivated than other people
is a good thing. Descriptions of the Buddhadharma are just not that
simplistic. There is an expression in Buddhism that goes, "The attitude
of a śrāvaka upholding the precepts is breaking them by a bodhisattva."
If a monk with a *śrāvaka* attitude says, "I keep all the precepts," there
you have his or her ego popping up. Since such statements are nothing
more than an expression of ego, from the Mahāyāna viewpoint, the precepts have already been broken. Of course, the same danger is present
in zazen, too.[102]

---

translation of *senjō*, Dōgen uses the term on a deeper level to mean "clarify." That is, by
practicing Buddhadharma sincerely, we will gradually and naturally clarify what it means
to become more of who we truly are.

102. Readers should note carefully here that neither Dōgen nor Uchiyama use the
term *hīnayāna*, meaning "small vehicle," to refer to a particular Buddhist sect or school.
They are talking about an individual person's attitude, not their religious affiliation. For

Zazen is the Dharma teaching of all the buddhas. There is also [a kind of] zazen found in the non-Buddhist schools. Although it looks the same, such schools make the mistake of coloring it or clinging to mistaken views. Therefore, it is not the same as the zazen of all the buddhas and bodhisattvas.

A tradition of [something like] zazen also exists among that line of the Buddha's disciples who practiced it to attain liberation for themselves only. This tradition also can be found among practitioners who liberated themselves without the assistance of a teacher. Though it looks the same, these people practice it in order to regulate their minds or to seek only to attain nirvana. Therefore, theirs, too, is not the same as the zazen of the buddhas and bodhisattvas.

In other words, the problem with the zazen practiced as something other than a bodhisattva practice is that it is imbued with an agenda. It is practiced from a narrow point of view. For example, the so-called śrāvakas practice zazen to become purified, attain harmony, and eventually enter nirvana. There is a goal to reach. Practicing zazen with that attitude is simply not the same as practicing it as Buddhadharma. Here is where worldly common sense of what is good or admirable totally differs from what is seen as good or worthy in the Buddhist sense.

> Good and evil occur in time, although time is neither good nor evil. Good and evil take the form of dharmas, although the dharmas are not of themselves good or evil.

That which is considered good and evil changes according to the time or occasion. Before and during the war, support for the war effort was considered good, but after losing the war, all those who had supported that effort were now branded criminals and were punished for their crimes.

Dōgen and Uchiyama, trying to "save" oneself first, or trying to "improve" oneself in order to get ahead of others, is an example of such an attitude.

The other day I saw a very humorous short limerick-like verse.

In the silver seat
Our future oldsters
Feigning sleep

Picture a couple of young people on a train, sitting in the seat reserved for the elderly or disabled. As soon as some elderly person gets on the train and looks around for an empty seat, the young people pretend to be asleep. Yes, it's true that these young people are the elderly of the future, but certainly not yet. Good or evil is determined by time.

Time, or *toki* (時) in Japanese, is related to the word meaning *speed*: *toshi* (速). Even though we might assume that the Hankyu commuter train runs fast, when we get down near Osaka, we can see the high-speed train shoot by us like a bullet. So we completely reverse our idea of how fast we thought the Hankyu was running. Time appears as a relative speed. Likewise, our ordinary value judgment of good and evil is also relative. Still, relativity itself is neither good nor evil. This is the sense of the passage "Time is neither good nor evil."

Human beings, too, show their good features or bad ones as a combination of factors, but there is no such fixed entity as a good person or an evil one.

I myself virtually killed my first two wives. When I reflect on my actions of those days, I badgered them to death by showing them only bad or negative qualities. I've never stopped thinking that my behavior was inexcusable. If only they were still alive today, perhaps I might have made them just a little happier by acting more positively than I did. Still, the sort of behavior I did reveal also occurred in time.

"Dharmas" in the previous passage refers to the way something is. Dōgen says that whatever way something appears, that way is not in itself good or evil. Recently, I had a chance to take a glimpse into the world of an elderly home. For some reason, wherever you go, there always seems to be someone who wants to be the boss, along with some poor fellow who tends to be shy or weak and, hence, always has to take the bullying. So I wrote my own verse:

One old man, soon to die
Treats with cruelty
Another old man, soon to die

Neither the perpetrator nor the victim is going to be around for more than a year or so, perhaps three or four at best. One way or another, they are both going to kick the bucket, regardless of whether they are cruel or kind. In that sense, "the dharmas are not of themselves good or evil." Nevertheless, at the same time, "As a rule, the principle of cause and effect is clear and impersonal; without a doubt, those who commit evil deeds will fall, and those who carry out good deeds will rise."[103] A brutal, violent, or senseless deed will stay with the person his or her whole life. This is for sure. It is, in this sense that, "Good and evil take the form of dharmas."

> Since all dharmas are held equally, all evils are held equally. In the same manner, because all dharmas are viewed equally, all sorts of good are also seen impartially.

Whenever this word "dharma" appears, I have again and again rendered it in more colloquial idioms to mean the genuine or true reality of life. As this true reality of life, all things and situations exist precisely because we personally experience life. I see, I hear, I think, etc.; these things come about because of my personal life experiences. Therefore, viewing everything from personal experience, they are all equal, that is, of equal gravity.

103. This is from Dōgen's *Shōbōgenzō* "Shinjin Inga" or "Deep Faith in Cause and Effect."

People who sit zazen can readily understand this. When we do zazen, everything is seen as having equal gravity. All things take form on the foundation of our own personal life experience. This is why zazen is also called *tōji* (等持): "all things are regarded equally or impartially."

Ordinarily, we live in a world we ourselves have created in which we think "this is good" and "that is bad," or "I loathe that, but I like this," etc. But before zazen everything is laid out on a foundation of equality or impartiality. When we are actually sitting zazen, a whole myriad of thoughts and feelings bubble up. But since doing zazen is different from just sitting there thinking, we let go of whatever is on our mind and return to zazen. Suddenly, all the thoughts that had appeared so clearly until now simply vanish, and we are back looking at the wall.

We can never say that evil is something extrinsic or external to us. No matter what sort of good or evil a thing or action might be, when we view it from whatever form it might take on the foundation of the actual reality of life, we see it impartially. As I have been saying for these many years, living a life of zazen is never a matter of throwing out the bad and picking up only the good. Zazen is not a matter of grabbing onto some "satori" (悟り, sometimes 覚り) and throwing away all delusion. Rather, a life of zazen is seeing them both with an impartial eye. This is where, for the first time, tōji comes into play. Hence, the passage, "[Since] all dharmas are held equally, all evils are held equally. In the same manner, because all dharmas are viewed equally, all sorts of good are also seen impartially." There is just no set or determined thing as good or evil. Although we tentatively refer to good or evil, from the foundation of life in zazen, we let go of all preconceptions, etc.; here, good and evil can be held equally and seen impartially.

Looking at the Buddhist teachings is like getting
a panoramic view of the varied layers of the deep
mountains—it is profound, comprehensive, and subtle.

> Nevertheless, in cultivating the one supreme living and enlightened real-
> ity—*anuttarā samyak-saṃbodhi*—we hear the teaching, practice it, and
> bear the awakened fruit of that practice. This Way is profound beyond
> measure; it is all-inclusive, all-encompassing; it is subtle and it is deep.

First of all, let us take a look at the Sanskrit term *anuttarā samyak-saṃbodhi*, transliterated into Japanese as *anokutara-sanmyaku-sanbodai* (阿耨多羅三藐三菩提). Of course, the Chinese (and Japanese, too) had to define the term, because the Chinese characters first used to write it were considered phonetically. No one could guess the meaning just from looking at the characters. So, the term was translated again into understandable Chinese as *mujō-shōtō-shōgaku* (無上正等正覚). *Mujō* (無上), means literally "nothing above," that is, "supreme"; I have expressed this in my own words as "arriving at the ultimate place of settling." The next word, *shōtō* (正等), traditionally means "correct and equal." *Shō*, however, can also be understood as "stopping at one," since the character is formed from the two characters *one* (一) and *stop* (止). More colloquially, I have expressed this as "the one reality of life." *Tō* (等) has been defined as "not two"—not different, equal. It is often combined with the Chinese character *hyō* or *byō* as in *byōdō* (平等), which means "something in common," or "not different from one." So, although *byō* is commonly translated as "equal," its Buddhist sense is that there is nothing outside of the one life. Finally, *gaku* (覚) means "to enlighten" or "to awaken" to something.

Now, let us take a look at this expression from a more practical angle. If you consider the role that thought plays in our perception of material things or in our interpretations and understandings of events, they begin to fall apart. For example, just looking at this cup on my desk, some people might think it is very beautiful, while others would regard it as some cheap thing I picked up at a flea market. Everyone has a different idea. Nevertheless, the actual reality is that there is nothing besides this cup sitting here. *Mujō,* or "nothing above this": there is no actual reality that transcends or is outside of this cup. It is a reality that is singular; there is no reality outside of it. In that sense, all things are a single, actual reality. There is no looking at the actual reality of a thing and saying "this is good" or "that is bad." It is to that one actual reality that we awaken.

In the harsh world of what is commonly taken for reality, we lose sight of the true living actuality. People are brought up and educated to lose sight of it. For example, the world an infant sees at birth and the one we see as adults are essentially no different except that the small child questions what this or that is. A child's world has not yet solidified. Still, as a member of the human species, even a small child possesses the ability to abstract. When a mother breastfeeds the child several times a day, the child makes a connection between the mother's face and her breast. In this way, the mother teaches the child the words "mama" and "breast," and over time, the child learns to abstract the words "mama" or "kitty" or "doggie" or whatever apart from the individual realities the words refer to. Eventually, the child, in a sense, learns to grab onto things through the use of words.

Words are nothing more than symbols. However, the living reality is never a symbol. Strictly speaking, the living reality of a mother is that she is changing moment by moment. This is true of all things, but because of our ability to abstract, we are taught to grasp things as fixed entities and we ultimately lose sight of the living reality.

So, if we peel away the words we have learned, will we be left with the living reality? Unfortunately, it is not as simple as that. The fact is, as long as we exist as human beings, that very power or ability we use to abstract, forming words and language, is itself a living reality. We are often admonished not to cling to language, and sometimes we hear evasive comments like "Such a matter is difficult to explain in words."

But such attempts to avoid using language to the extent that it can be helpful in elucidating matters should be resisted. This is what is behind Dōgen Zenji's statement, "This Way is profound beyond measure; it is comprehensive, all encompassing, it is subtle and it is deep." Sawaki Rōshi frequently used the expression *yūsui* (幽邃) to describe the teachings, and for years I have made every effort to express in my own words what he conveyed with *yūsui*, meaning "secluded," "quiet," or "solitary." Recently, I have tried to render it in my own words, though my rendering of the concept happens to be more scientific than literary: my description of jiko (universal identity or universal self) as being made up of a self that is one/all (one over all) and, at the same time, all/all (all over all). In sum, as long as we are alive, we live as a single, whole entity.

Mathematically, we could symbolize this as 1. At the same time, this "1" can also be formulated as $1 = 1/1 = 2/2$ or even as all/all. This $1 = 1/1$ = all/all is critical. Saying "I live here in this way" is, at the same time, saying that "I am living as the world I personally experience," which in Buddhism is termed *jin issai jiko* (尽一切自己), "all comprehensive self." Further on in the text, Dōgen Zenji uses the expression *jinchi jinkai jinji, jippō* (尽地、尽界、尽時、尽法). *Jin* (尽), means "all" or "thorough" or "exhaustive"; this is his way of emphasizing the sense of inclusivity. Applying the principle to myself, it means that I am living my life as all things and worlds. And when I die, all things and all worlds die with me.

Most people don't ordinarily think like this. They hold on to some vague idea that one comes into being on this stage called society, that we live out our life on this stage as one member of the society, and that death is simply exiting the stage. This is an example of seeing only the one/all aspect of self. What this idea also reflects, however, is the false assumption that one can find peace of mind only when one is surrounded or supported by a group.

The other day, for instance, someone remarked to me, "I would be terribly afraid to live like you do—a way that has no connection to any other people." In other words, this man feels very uneasy if he is not doing the same things everyone else does. I think this sort of thinking is an example of living as one of a herd. It is the kind of mentality that becomes overwhelmed with a sense of bitter loneliness whenever anyone turns away or decides to move on without you.

The truth of the matter is that no one else can live my life for me. Self alone can live out self. Living a life of all/all, there is no room to feel lonely or sorry for oneself. If I happen to fall into some hellish circumstances, then that is where I have to live. There is no one who can live in my stead. This is an undeniable truth of life.

When it comes to zazen, we sit as a self of all/all. That is the sense of the expression *jijuyū zanmai* (自受用三昧): the samadhi of a self that accepts and gives life to all. When we identify with this attitude of all/all, any way I may fall is okay, because ultimately, regardless of how we categorize experience, as positive or negative, it is all my world.

At the very same time as I have talked about the all-inclusiveness of jiko, as long as we also live in the day-to-day world as individuals, we are living as all/all while simultaneously living as one/all. Precisely because we are fundamentally living as all/all, "anything is okay" is no longer okay. You can't substitute poop for miso in the soup no matter how similar they might appear. There is right and wrong. It is true that where jiko is complete and we live realizing that whatever way we might stumble it is all our life—that is where we find absolute peace of mind. But if we are about to take a fall, it is better to fall somewhere out of the path of that oncoming truck—because if we fall in front of it, well, we're dead.

Again, while on the one hand, we are living as all/all—the total universe— at the same time, we also have to live as one/all, as an individual being that is constantly in the process of having to choose whether to go left or right. Now, when we actually go about making those decisions, we use our thinking minds in the process. At times, we agonize at length, unable to make any decision. But, actually, just mulling things over in our minds is not a very good way of making decisions; our thinking minds are incapable of making irrefutably correct decisions.

So, how can we live our lives making the only decision possible and doing so from the most settled position there is? Such discussion must be made on the foundation of whatever the actuality of life is; this is okay, and that is okay. The living reality of life has a sort of magnetic pull, and being pulled by the natural power of our life force itself is crucial.

Each and every one of us living as one/all can stand up or sit down only when all/all is being pulled by the earth's gravity. Or, while being pulled by gravity, we jump up and down, or fly in an airplane, or whatever. If we were detached from this gravity, we would just float off. In this same way, as we live out our lives as individuals, as one/all, it is vital for us to be impelled by the living reality of life as all/all. As long as we are separate individuals, one/all, we live our lives constantly making choices, but each choice always needs to be facing in the direction of that all-inclusive self or jiko. In Buddhism, choosing in this way is called *chōjō* (澄浄), which means "to clarify" or "to purify." Also, in Buddhism, the definition of faith is the same—to clarify or purify. So, ultimately, living by faith simply means to be pulled along by the living reality of the life force. Making choices in this way, that is, choosing to be led by our actual life force, is the meaning of the third line in the opening gāthā: "personally clarifying the significance of this mind."

Where the whole universe exists as nothing brought forth and nothing torn down, nothing purified and nothing defiled, nothing added and nothing taken away, nothing coming in and nothing going out, there is most definitely a direction in making those value judgments when choosing this or that. This is the context for "refraining from evil, carrying out good."

In Pure Land teachings, Amida Buddha is the all/all, while I am the one/all. And this I, as one/all, is being set free by Amida Buddha, who is all/all. Or, to put it another way, Amida Buddha and I are not two separate entities. As long as I live, Amida Buddha is the direction I approach. This is faith in action. Another way to express this would be through the prayer *Namu Amida Butsu* (南無阿弥陀仏)—I take refuge in Amida

Buddha. Therefore, it follows that where there is faith, there is naturally going to be a sense of "refraining from evil, carrying out good." Of course, there are good and bad choices that can be made. But, in this case, our discussion will turn in a different direction than good and evil as determined by the biases of culture or society or the state. This is why Dōgen writes, "This Way is profound beyond measure; it is all-inclusive, all-encompassing; it is subtle, and it is deep."

Refraining from evil is a universal principle that transcends human speculation.

We can hear and understand about this unsurpassable enlightenment from experienced teachers or learn about it from reading the sūtras; one of the first things we hear from those who have practiced for a long time is the teaching on refraining from various evils. If we are not told about refraining from various evils, then our instruction is not the same as that of the buddhas' true teaching; it is nothing other than some malevolent casuistry. Make no mistake; learning "various evils refrained from" is the true teaching of the buddhas. "Refraining from various evils" is not to be identified with that which people ordinarily conjure up in their minds. Hearing the teaching of "awakening to the living reality" is the same as hearing one on refraining from various evils.

This teaching is profound beyond measure, all encompassing, and subtly complex, or, as Sawaki Rōshi referred to it, *yūsui*: profoundly deep and calm, not easily accessible, yet thoroughly detailed. Just what is profound, all encompassing, and subtle? By hearing it from experienced teachers or from reading the scriptures, through expressing it and listening again and again, in time, it will become clearer. And, gradually, we will come to understand, for the first time, *refraining from committing various evils* as Buddhadharma.

Just because fundamentally all things were neither born nor will they perish, are neither filthy or pure, are neither increasing or decreasing, and are all empty—this does not give us license to commit whatever foul deeds we might have in our minds. When we hear "refraining from various evils," we also need to take it in with the understanding of not committing bad actions.

[However,] the meaning of "refraining from various evils" is not what people ordinarily imagine it to be. As I said earlier, refraining from evil is something that occurs as a natural phenomenon, an absolute principle; it is something that transcends human intention. It has nothing to do with human design.

Earlier, I defined *samyak-saṃbodhi*, or just *bodhi*, as awakening to the ultimate reality of life. Put another way, it is a satori of an ultimately settled living reality. Or, we might call it the *way* of awakening to such a reality. Dōgen Zenji expresses it as "explication of awakening to the living reality," that is, *bodai no setsu* (菩堤の説). Hearing this explication as a teaching is referred to as "hearing or listening to the teaching," or *monkyō* (聞教). And it is this teaching that is heard that sounds the same as "refraining from various evils."

> They sound the same, because both are the words of awakening to the one living reality. In fact, they are totally awakening words. For that reason, the words themselves are fully living [awakening] words. For the words to be heard as the teaching of the one living reality, and to be moved by them, we vow to hold dear refraining from various evils and to practice it.

"Refraining from various evils" is a definitive expression, a clear path. Generally speaking, when we think of a path, it usually indicates an area that was once very wild or untraveled and then one person comes along and tramples through it. Then the next person who comes along somehow, and for no particular reason, tramples through the same area. Then comes another and yet another, until the wild area finally becomes a path or way.

In a similar way, expressions we use eventually become a saying. First, one person says something and another person hears it. That person repeats it to yet another person and the saying becomes a natural expression. Likewise, in Buddhism, one monk says something and others following him repeat the saying. Of course, whether a saying should actually become a path or not is a separate issue.

At this point in the text, *refraining from various evils* is at the level of being a saying or an expression; it is not yet a path. But next we have Dōgen saying, "In fact, they are totally awakening words." That is, they are an expression that is awakened to the truth of life. "For that reason, the words themselves are fully living [awakening] words." The expression itself is the truth of life.

> Where various evils can no longer be created, there the virtue of practice manifests directly. This living actualization does so in all lands and all worlds, as all times and all dharmas. This vivid actualization of the entire universe is the parameter of various evils refrained from.

This is one of Dōgen Zenji's unique workings with language in terms of freshness and lucidity. Every day I walk along the banks of the Uji River and, afterward, sometimes compose something like poetry.

The Expansive Sky

Pain, sadness, anger
I leave them as they are
While looking up into the sky
Into the vast and magnanimous sky

Beneath the spacious sky, some people are working
Some are hiding from the bill collector
Others are taking their final breath

Surrounding these human goings-on
Are the verdant, forested mountains and streams
Or parched deserts or vast oceans

And in their various places live
The multitude of plants and animals carrying on
Their diverse and respective activities

The spacious sky looks down on all of this
That vast and magnanimous sky—
Becoming nothing but a speck, one particle,
I rise up and enter into this emptiness.

I see my daily walks, looking up at the sky, as my *dōjō* (道場), or place of practice. The truth of the matter is I am easily given to fits of anger. I'm frequently looking around for a way to pick a fight. Taking in a deep breath, I look up into the sky and the will to continue fighting dissipates. It is in this way that the virtue of practice manifests directly. But, needless to say, if you look up into the sky right in the middle of some big quarrel and think, "What kind of fool would look up in the sky and quit a juicy fight like this?" Well, then the virtue of practice will not manifest directly.

Perhaps you might be disposed to think that since a person has been practicing a long time, surely they must be in possession of the virtue or power of practice. Unfortunately, there is no such thing as a totally complete practitioner. There just are no manufactured, "satorized" human beings. You know, that satori thing is very fast; it runs away very quickly. The satori you may have bagged in the morning is already beginning to smell bad by noontime. You have no choice but to get rid of this morning's satori that same morning. It is not like something you would put in the refrigerator thinking you will snack on it later on in the day. It only comes raw, uncooked!

The only thing that is important is calling forth and nurturing the aspiration to give life to one's practice again and again and again. Concretely speaking, this simply means returning to one's practice in each moment. Satori is *satorizing*: realizing that practice is itself satori—and then settling on that.

We are often apt to think that when a man and a woman find themselves alone together something *must* happen. Just a little opening, even just a crack, and there arises this frame of mind, a mood, that causes one to give way to one's desires. Actually, though, nothing at all *has to happen* merely because two people are in the same room alone. It's just not necessary to feel so obligated to do something. At those times, if you just take the time to look up in the sky, the feeling can easily dissipate.[104]

"Virtue of practice" is a subtle thing. It manifests directly, [covering] "all lands and all worlds, as all times and all dharmas"—the whole universe. When all is said and done, what else can we do but aspire to manifest this virtue of practice again and again and again. Of course, there come times when we are unable to aspire again and again. Those are simply the times when we don't aspire, and they, too, are all right. But then, again, in the very next instant, we aspire once more and then again and yet again. Thinking that I can't aspire, that I am just no good, is holding fixedly onto that very idea that renders us helpless or no good. Letting go of the idea that I cannot do it or that I am no good is itself our practice.

104. An alternate translation for the above two paragraphs: "What is critical here is to return to the virtue of practice a million times. What this simply means is to continue our practice in every one of our day-to-day activities. People often ask what satori is. Actually, realizing that *satori* means "returning or continuing to practice" is itself satori, and then settling there.

"For example, we might entertain the idea that when a man and a woman are alone together, something must happen between them. Looking for that unguarded moment, we entertain the illusion of doing 'it' with him or her. Just being in the same room together doesn't automatically mean two people have to do something. When you start getting that feeling, just look up in the sky and the whole illusion crumbles."

The past is gone, it's finished.

The future is simply direction.

What is critical is to face that direction and act.

Refraining from is not merely talking about not doing bad things.

Of all the things in the world, there is no such fixed thing as some stone inside a plum that exists as good or evil. There was a great Sōtō Zen reformer in the Edo period called Menzan Zuihō.[105] In his work *Jijuyū Zanmai*, Menzan writes, "Evil is like bubbles on the surface of water or like the shadow of things. In the light that cannot be reached by discriminatory thought, there is nothing to feel an aversion for." Even though we speak of something being evil, it is not a matter of figuring out in your head what is evil and what is not. Then, he writes, "Evil should not be loathed nor, needless to say, should it be desired. This is called refraining from evil. Good, too, is like a phantom or an illusion. Likewise, it cannot be reached by human reason or thinking. There is nothing to hold on to. Neither liking goodness nor hating it—this is called doing all sorts of good."

By simply telling people to do good things and not do bad things, we are putting the squeeze on them for when they do something bad and, at the same time, taking pride in how good we ourselves are. By doing so, our good goes sour and becomes evil. We should always bear in mind that good and evil are similar to fantasies and to bubbles on the surface of stagnant water. Moving into the depth of life that is not fixed is, in itself, *refraining from various evils* and *carrying out all sorts of good*.

There is something truly special about the Mahāyāna teachings. When moving this deeply into the issue of good and evil, one's whole world changes. Here, as Dōgen writes, the "virtue of practice manifests directly." In the second chapter, on "Expedient Means," of the *Lotus Sūtra*, there

---

105. Menzan Zuihō (面山瑞芳, 1683–1769), was born in what is now Kumamoto Prefecture. Menzan wrote many commentaries on various chapters of the *Shōbōgenzō*.

is a passage that goes, "Call out the name of the Buddha just once and all sentient beings will attain buddhahood." That is, one's whole world completely changes, and all people complete the Buddha Way. They all complete the Buddha Way through their life attitude, moment by moment.

So in Dōgen's text, even though we read "refraining from committing various evils / carrying out all sorts of good," doing so is not a matter of thinking that something good and something evil exist and then going around liking the good and hating the bad. All there is, is to carry out not fixing or grabbing onto anything. In doing so, one's whole world changes. In the beginning of the *Sūtra on the Bodhisattva Avalokiteśvara* (Jpn: *Kannongyō*), it is written, "Even if there might be immeasurable numbers of sentient beings, to take on their sufferings, if one hears the name of the Bodhisattva Avalokiteśvara and genuinely cries out just once with all one's spirit, in that very moment, Avalokiteśvara will penetrate that cry and all beings will be released from their suffering." That is, just calling out "Namu Kanzeon[106] Bosatsu (南無観世音菩薩)," the bodhisattva will hear your cry and come forth to free all beings from their pain and suffering. Right in that moment, everything will change. That is what Mahāyāna Buddhism is about.

It is the same with our zazen. There is a passage in Dōgen's *Hōkyō-ki* (寶慶記) or *Record of the Hōkyō Period*,[107] that goes, "*Sanzen* is casting off body and mind." Later, in the *Hōkyō-ki*, Dōgen states, "Casting off body and mind is to do zazen." That is it. There is nothing else to do. Some people who hear the expression "casting off body and mind" conjure up some super special satori experience, arguing one thing and another, but no arguments will ever hit the mark.

106. Kanzeon is the Japanese for Avalokiteśvara.

107. Uchiyama went on to say "The *Hōkyō-ki* I just quoted from is a compilation of notes Dōgen Zenji wrote down based on comments made by his teacher, Nyojō Zenji. I firmly believe that they form the fundamental underpinnings (source) of Dōgen's thought."

Summarizing the above, *sanzen* (参禅) is defined as dropping off body and mind, and dropping off body and mind is the same as just doing zazen. This is the sort of zazen we need to do. Attempting to have some satori experience by doing zazen is not the zazen of dropping off body and mind. Sitting, aiming only at letting go of everything, the moment of letting go—this is casting off body and mind.

Likewise, *refraining from various evils* does not mean trying one's best not to do bad things. Rather, we must let go of the very intention of not doing bad things, of not committing evil: that is when "various forms of evil can no longer be created."

Or, taking the example I used earlier about a young man and woman alone in a room together, thinking "something" has got to happen, it is precisely because they feel some twisted sense of *responsibility* to do something that twisted events take place. You just have to let go of such a sense of obligation. Even after you have begun an argument, take one good look into the depth of the sky, and the argument has been let go. Throughout our lives, all sorts of things are inevitably bound to arise, but with that feeling of looking up into the sky, we can let go of everything. And, in doing so, the virtue of practice manifests directly. And this virtue functions "in all lands and all worlds, as all times and all dharmas." From the perspective of the magnanimous sky, our petty human workings look like dung beetles crawling in a cesspool. Getting dragged around by every little thing that comes along, in effect, we ourselves become like dung beetles. What a waste of our life.

Verbal expressions on Buddhadharma, such as "carrying out good" and "refraining from evil," are not simply intended to hold people in check by telling them not to do bad things. Expressions of Buddhadharma are sublime or majestic precisely because they aim at that place where "various sorts of evil cannot be created." It is in this area that Buddhism differs fundamentally from simplistic morality sects.

But if one reads this passage of aiming at being "where various forms of evil can no longer be created" and goes around bragging that he or she can no longer do any evil, this is nothing but arrogance. It is the same as saying that one is a saint. In truth, all human beings are simply ordinary people; there are no such things as saints. At least, I have never met one. But you know, there are any number of people thinking that somewhere in this world there must be a saint among us, someone worth worshipping. There are a lot of people running around all over the place looking for a saint. And, of course, where there is a demand, there will always be a supply. There are many people just aching to be worshipped. You have to understand, however, that both types are pretty unsophisticated. One human being venerating another human being is just not something that should go on. Ultimately, all human beings are without exception, just ordinary human beings with desires and passions. What is critical here is that it is *this* ordinary human being right here, now, who just aims at being where "various forms of evil can no longer be created."

The passage "then the virtue of practice manifests directly" follows right after this. Some people of a very strong-willed nature are sure to nurture the illusion that the power built up by their practice will enable them to do just about anything. But that is not at all what is written here. Dōgen Zenji is talking about the attitude we bring to our practice; the issue is one of our life's stability. That is why he continues: "This living actualization does so in all lands and all worlds, as all times and all dharmas. This vivid actualization of the entire universe is the boundary of refraining from various evils." This "living actualization" is an eternal stability encompassing the whole universe within our life. It is there that we settle and simply allow the virtue of practice to manifest directly in our lives here and now.

So, the first thing we have to do is clarify the foundation on which our life is built. And that foundation shouldn't be one that borders on the criminal, rather it should be a foundation whereby "various forms of evil can no longer be created." It is on this foundation that we sit firmly and arouse that bodhisattva spirit within us, the foundation on which "the virtue of practice manifests directly." Such a foundation for our life is, to put it yet another way, personally awakening to the reality of the life of one's jiko. At the same time, "This living actualization does so in all lands and all worlds, as all times and all dharmas." If we take the broad view, looking from the perspective of the reality of the eternal life that encompasses the whole universe, then the little goings-on on the surface of the earth amount to nothing. This "amounts to nothing" is the meaning of *refraining*.

Looking at a pile of money from the perspective of eternal life, we realize the pile of money means nothing. Precisely because a person wants to make a name for him or herself, they fall apart as soon as their position gets pulled out from under them. If you hadn't been set on becoming famous, then getting jerked around wouldn't have meant a thing. Why, if you just let go of it, even sexual passion doesn't amount to that much. I don't know whether to be happy about it or break down in tears, but it is true: as you approach my age, the fire of sexual passion begins to wane. But, when you are still young, attachment to sexual passion can be a real problem.

In Buddhism, when you become a disciple of the Buddha, you receive the ten precepts, called the *jūjū kinkai* (十重禁戒), and you must promise to keep them. The surface meaning of the first precept, the precept of not killing (*fusesshō-kai*, 不殺生戒) is not to take the life of any living thing, especially that of a human being. However, what you have to remember is that this precept is based on the boundaries of Dōgen's "This living actualization does so in all lands and all worlds, as all times and all dharmas."

To put it another way, the basis of this precept is the eternal life of the whole universe. Therefore, you cannot kill anything even if you would wish to do so. Since there is no independent and permanent self, as the *Heart Sūtra* puts it, "nothing is born, nothing dies; nothing is soiled, nothing is pure; nothing increases, nothing decreases." If we think there is something to be killed, and then go ahead and try to kill it, our mistake is doubled. In addition, since the eternal life of the universe is also the basis for the precept admonishing us not to steal, this precept is not something that an individual maintains, since there is no such thing we can point to as being our possession. When I conjure up the idea that there is something that I as an individual can possess, and then I act by taking something that belongs to someone else in order to make it mine, I only compound my original mistake. It is the same regarding the precept that admonishes against improper sexual conduct. Since all our actions are [fundamentally] actions of eternal life that encompass the universe, whenever we attempt to bring these actions into actions that "I" want to do, we make a double error.

This eternal reality of life encompassing the universe that I have been describing is not an all-encompassing life force we go about living out from this moment on. In fact, we are always living eternal life that includes the whole universe, whether we think so or not, whether we believe it to be so or not—this is a universal truth. Our existence here in this way is certainly not due to a deliberate effort to make our hearts beat. Even when we totally give up and fall into the deepest of sleep, our heart still keeps on beating and we continue to breathe normally. This is because the eternal life of the whole universe is functioning properly. In other words, we are alive in this way as incontrovertible truth; it doesn't matter whether we think so or not, or whether we accept it or reject it. Abiding by or in this absolute truth is the most important thing we can do.

In the Pure Land school of Buddhism, it is taught that Amida Buddha calls to us. And those who live their lives in response to that call are said to have *shinjin* (信心), or "believing mind." Amida Buddha is said to be immeasurable and unlimited. To put it slightly differently, Amida Buddha is the same as "all lands and all worlds, as all time[s] and all dharmas." The immeasurable and unlimited nature of Amida Buddha is what manifests. In other words, letting go of the thought that always grasps "I" as an individual entity is the same as the "refraining" in our text. Then, living reality manifests as it truly is. That which forms as thought is a mental fabrication. We let go of this mental fabrication. And in doing so, the fabrication falls apart. Letting go of mental fabrication is also casting off body and mind. There is a place where all that is not fabricated is as nothing at all. And it is just practicing this "nothing at all," or *mushō* (無生), without any substantial or permanent body, that is all-important.

We never practice zazen in order to experience "satori"— we are complete before we begin to practice!

> II.
> When a rare person actualizes this very time—even when living in, or only coming from or going to, a place where evil might be expected to abound; or where encountering occasions when carrying out evil deeds would seem only natural; or when keeping company with those who seem to act in evil ways—no evil is ever committed.

I have rendered the sense behind the opening phrase "When a rare person actualizes this very time" in my own words: "the actually living person in the actual living moment." When this comes about, then "no evil is ever committed."

I never cease to be amazed when people go to the barber and have their beard shaved; they seem so relaxed as the barber brings his razor over and sets it against their throat. All that has to happen is for the barber to suddenly harbor a confused/muddled view of life and—*Bam!*—you have yourself an incident. This would be even worse than if the mind of a banker in charge of all those bills blurs the line between what is legal and illegal. Our society is filled with such examples; the local pistol-toting policemen walking around, some driver behind the wheel of a two-ton car—each and every one of them first needs to act with that mind of "just such a person actualizing just such a time."

There is a poem by Sen Rikyu, the famous tea master, that goes,

For the dipper that travels between
The hells of hot and cold
There is no pain
Since it is without a mind

The water ladle gets dipped into cold water and hot water, but since it does not possess any feelings of its own, it knows no hell. Take away a person's sentiments or emotions, and he or she knows no heat or cold.

Inevitably, though we might try our best to avoid such people, it is very likely we've had occasion to mix with people who think very little of doing things that are obviously not good. However, just because one is in bad company doesn't inevitably mean that one has to do bad things; by setting aside our personal emotions, we can avoid unprincipled actions.

Now, by this, I'm not suggesting that one become some sort of vegetable. Rather, you give full attention to using your head. What is essential is to enable our heads to function as the eternal life that fills the universe. In this way, "no evil is ever committed."

> Since it is the functioning and power of *refraining from* that is being entirely revealed, we cannot say definitively that various evils are necessarily evil; not even a weapon can be said to be intrinsically evil!

Refraining from, in this case, is the same as opening the hand of our thought-grasping mind and is also the same as returning to the reality of life; there is just nothing to be concerned about.

When I first became a priest, there was a nasty fellow whose position placed him above me as a senior brother. He was constantly carping at me and giving me a hard time. I realized one day that whenever I would allow myself to get emotionally involved with his meanness, I would inevitably wind up getting hurt and upset. But if I would just let go whenever I encountered his nastiness, I would be completely impervious to anything he did.

"We cannot say definitively" means that there is just nothing fixed that is evil. There is nothing inevitable about possessing a gun; that is, just because someone possesses one, doesn't mean he or she has to go out and shoot someone with it.[108] "Not even a weapon can be said to be intrinsically evil."

> It is a matter of picking up and putting down.
>   When we thoroughly live out truly living time, it becomes clear and utterly natural that evil does not break the person and that the person can't destroy evil.

There are various ways that the things we handle in our daily lives can be wielded. Hence, "When a person actualizes this very time"—when we encounter something as the true reality of life—evil does not break the person [nor can] the person destroy evil—nothing can be hurt by the encounter. When we see a thing as it truly is, it loses its associations with good and evil. Even a gun is nothing more than a hunk of metal. Neither is a car necessarily a tool for killing someone. If you don't consume it, you won't die by merely looking at something that is poisonous. Whatever the object is, if you use it poorly, you could snuff out human life with it—it all depends on how the object is used.

> By the time we gather our wits and physically begin to practice, the lion's share [of that practice] has already been accomplished. This is the quick of *refraining from*.

---

108. One cannot really argue with Dōgen or Uchiyama's example here, however, I am sure that the context of the comment refers to the world of a Japan where ordinary citizens (except for hunters) cannot legally own guns.

This passage may appear somewhat puzzling on first reading, but if we examine it in light of our practice of zazen, it just seems natural. Let us say we get it into our heads that we want to do zazen. To do this, of course, we have to physically practice it. By deciding to practice and taking up the posture, "the lion's share has already been accomplished"; prior to making any effort, the greater portion of the practice has already been completed.

"This is the quick of *refraining from*" means that after the practice is finished, there is nothing left over. Here is the essence of the practice of zazen and of Buddhism. As long as we are caught by an attitude of "I do zazen," we are still not doing zazen in its true spirit. Truly doing zazen means practicing in the spirit of zazen being the same whether we do it or not; we need to practice a zazen without form. When we do zazen with an attitude of aiming at some sort of satori experience, then after we have sat there is something left over—satori. We can hardly call such a zazen "the quick of *refraining from*."

The zazen taught by Dōgen Zenji is already completed prior to practicing it. It is one after which nothing remains. This is the sort of zazen that fills the universe.

> We practice, bringing into play the totality of body and mind. And we who practice physically and mentally do so substantively—with the full power of the four elements and the five constituents that comprise our body and mind. This fuller body does not contaminate our true self, our *jiko*. It is always in this very present that our whole body naturally practices.

No matter who we are, when we do zazen, we do it both physically and mentally.

The "four elements and the five constituents" refer to the earth (solidity), water (moisture), fire (warmth), and wind (movement), and to form, perception, conception, volition, and consciousness, respectively. In short, these elements could be encapsulated as our body and mind.

The strength to practice with the four elements and five constituents lies in our sitting erect with our bones and muscles. As soon as we do this, we are sitting zazen. It is nothing special. In the same way our hand becomes a fist when we close it into a ball or becomes our *gassho* when we bring both open hands together, when we sit erect, fold our legs, and place our hands in our lap, this becomes the form for zazen.

Historically, "not contaminating" (*zenna sezu*, 染汚せず) has been defined in various ways. One definition is "to neither pick up nor put down" (*fushusha*, 不取捨). Another sense of this expression is "this is good, so I will pick it up, and that is bad, therefore, I will put it down." Another definition is "to not contrive, plan, or devise" (*fushukō*, 不趣向); that is, to not busy oneself thinking about what to do next while in the middle of doing something else. If you are going to sit zazen, then just sit zazen. When we sit physically and with full attention, zazen becomes actualized; we don't wonder about what to do next or what direction we should go in, and we make no attempt to "pick up" satori or "throw away" illusion. We just do zazen. When we start entertaining the idea of getting something beneficial for ourselves, like satori, when we sit, then we end up contaminating zazen.

As I have always been saying, Dōgen's Zen is nothing other than doing zazen with our bones and muscles. That is it.

The power of the whole body and mind that we are practicing right now brings the body and mind of previous times into the practice.

The strength, or power, to practice right now includes all prior or preceding physical and mental activity. For example, even our muddled thoughts, such as "Should I sit zazen today or shall I go out drinking?" can and do exist within our practice.

Since becoming a disciple of Sawaki Rōshi, I have spent some thirty-five years living a life of zazen. During that time, I have sat sesshin every month. There were even periods when we had sesshin two or even three times a month. Each of those sesshin, of course, was a three- to five-day period of continuous sitting. The night before the beginning of the sesshin, an indescribable feeling would come up whenever I thought about having to sit for the next five days. But, then, the next day would come, and once sitting began, since I would be submerged in doing zazen, the whole thing just seemed natural. And since I simply entrusted everything to zazen, time would seem to pass all by itself. This is because "The power of the whole body and mind that we are practicing right now brings the body and mind of previous times into the practice." The anxiety I typically felt the previous night would be swallowed up in the practice. In this way, the five days just flowed by.

> And, just as our practice enables the mountains and rivers, the earth, the sun and moon and stars all to practice, they, in turn, bring us to practice.

Buddhadharma means that I live inclusive of the entire world I experience. People often think that they are born into an already existing world and that they live as members of that world. However, such a thought is not Buddhist. Rather, the life force of my true self is at the same time the eternal life force of the entire universe. It is the entire universe that enables me to practice. To do zazen implies that, simultaneously, the world of zazen opens up.

Occasionally, you find people who, when they start drinking, like to talk about Zen. Of course, no amount of talk about zazen is zazen; it is just the canapé accompanying the sake. If you are going to drink, just drink. If you are going to sit zazen, just sit zazen. When you do that, the world of zazen is also revealed. When you just sit zazen, for example, the atmosphere in the zendō becomes very sober. That atmosphere pulls us around and sets us to doing zazen. When you go out drinking, the mountains and rivers, the earth, the sun and moon and stars also become drunk and, before you know it, the drunken mountains and rivers and moon and stars only get you more drunk. If you sit zazen, the realm of zazen opens up. If you go out drinking, the realm of drinking opens up. You create your own world.

This is not merely a one-time realization; it is the vibrant attitude in all times. Because it is the living vision of each and every moment of time, it induces all the buddhas and ancestors to practice, it induces them to listen to the teaching, and it induces them to carry out the fruit of their learning.

Normally, we conceive of time as flowing from the past, into the present, and toward the future. In reality, however, the past and future are only depictions in our mind, which is always in the present. There is no such existing entity as past or future: hence, "the living vision of each and every moment of time."

"All the buddhas and ancestors" actually refers to the very person who is practicing; it should not be taken to mean some vague person in general. If I am practicing, then I myself am all the buddhas and ancestors. I don't mean to arrogantly assert here that I am the Buddha. Rather, to the extent that I am sitting zazen, zazen is buddha. Because that is the zazen I am practicing, zazen is the embodiment of the buddhas and ancestors. Moreover, not just the zazen being practiced, but all the activities in my day-to-day life must embody or manifest the most fundamental life force, that is, the teaching, the practice, and the "fruit" or realization (*kyō-gyō-shō*, 教行証). As I have mentioned so many times before, in regard to the zazen we do, we do not do it with the intention of picking up some satori experience. If we just sit zazen, we don't contaminate it.

The buddhas and ancestors have never vitiated the teaching, practice, or realization; hence, these things have not been an encumbrance to the buddhas and ancestors.

The teaching, practice, and realization wholly comprise the buddhas and, as such, are uncontaminated. Therefore, they pose no obstacle to buddhas and ancestors.

When we are sitting zazen, various thoughts pop into our heads. Naturally, what things arise vary with the individual. As for me, beautiful ladies often appear very clearly in my mind. But if we just let go of whatever appears, all that remains before us is the wall. What is essential in practicing zazen is this: as soon as we let go of what was so clear in our minds just a moment ago, it disappears, and we are left with just the wall.

Originally, the Buddha was called *Nyokonyorai* (如去如来), which was later abbreviated to simply Nyorai, or in Sanskrit, *Tathāgata*. This means "suchness," or "like coming, like going." That is, a buddha is "one who appears to come and go." When doing zazen, various ideas seem to float into our minds; they seem to come in (*nyorai*), and when we let go— poof!—they seem to disappear (*nyoko*, 如去). When we do zazen, we let go again and again and again—we let go one billion times! When I say zazen is buddha, I do so with the idea of nyokonyorai in mind. Quite often, when people think of a buddha, they imagine some unusual state, someone having a great realization. That is what some people imagine. However, when we sit, we let go of such imaginings. That is the zazen of Dōgen Zenji.

> Consequently, in being brought to practice, no buddha or ancestor has ever tried to circumvent the facts of the past or to take flight into the future. Acting as an ordinary sentient being or as a buddha poses no obstacle to what is widely thought of as a "buddha" or "ancestor." Still, we need to consider constantly and carefully this matter of being a buddha or ancestor through all the hours of the day and in all our day-to-day activities.

It would appear that in the time of Śākyamuni Buddha sexual desire was the most troublesome issue. There was one monk who actually thought of cutting off the root of what he thought was causing him such anguish in order to become impotent, but he was severely scolded by the Buddha. Rather than severing desire, there is meaning in practicing while giving full recognition to one's sexual appetite. Forcing oneself to be impotent is an attempt to escape from the past. Likewise, contemplating suicide as preferable to carrying the burden of one's present life is an attempt to take flight into the future. These are not the actions of the buddhas and ancestors. Being a true practitioner means to practice with whatever body we have been given.

"What is widely thought of as a 'buddha' or 'ancestor'" refers to the stereotypical image we often have of the Buddha or of Bodhidharma. Being a buddha is not a matter of our becoming an "ancestor" only when doing zazen; such ideas of Buddha as separate are in the way and have to be thrown aside. Whether we speak of sentient beings or of buddhas, fundamentally, they are not two different entities. As part of the eternal reality of life that fills the entire universe, all beings and buddhas are the same. The critical matter for us lies in how we manifest that reality right now. When we practice manifesting the teaching, the practice, and the realization, *that* is buddha. When we don't practice manifesting the teaching, *that* is the sentient being. We have to consider carefully just how to manifest as a buddha in our daily actions.

> Functioning as a buddha or ancestor does not violate the sentient being, nor does he or she [as a buddha] take away from, deprive, or alienate that [sentient] being. Nevertheless, the body and mind of the functioning buddha have been cast off.

Distinguishing here between "buddha" and "sentient being" and applying that distinction to our day-to-day life, we could say that safely driving our life is the buddha, while driving it recklessly or inattentively—or falling asleep behind the wheel—is the sentient being. Still, even though we may drive safely, this safe driving in no way alienates or deprives the reckless or sleepy driver of anything. We have the choice as to what sort of driving we want to do. Neither safe driving nor reckless driving is a matter of slogans. Waking up to the reality of our life, letting go of concepts and fancy words, we need to drive our own life in accordance with the reality of who we are, of our whole self.

Cause and effect are identical; doing zazen,
we actualize Buddha.

> The cause and effect of good and evil bring us to practice; cause and
> effect cannot be changed at will nor can cause and effect be contrived
> by the imagination.

Needless to say, hoping to have some kind of satori experience that will
transform any egregious act you might commit into a "good" deed is just
not going to pass muster. In reality, cause and effect remain what they
are. How can one be so narrow-minded as to expect to be seen driving
safely, while in fact, driving recklessly? Likewise, you must never expect
practice to create or force change in cause and effect. Just because you
didn't get arrested for taking a bribe or made a safe getaway after running
someone over with your car, that doesn't mean everything is all right or
that you are permanently off the hook. Sawaki Rōshi often used to say
that if you imitate the notorious robber Ishikawa Goemon, even if you
only steal a little, you are still a genuine thief.

People think they are safe in taking bribes as long as they don't get
caught. Or, even if they do get caught and prosecuted, they think they
are still innocent until the verdict is passed down. Or, even if the verdict
goes against them, they still have the right to appeal. Why, they don't
see themselves as criminals until the Supreme Court hands down a final
decision! The fact of the matter is this: the instant we take the bribe, we
become an authentic criminal.

In the same sense, imitating the Buddha, we sit zazen. "Oh, I'm no
Buddha, I merely imitated him," you say. But that's no good. If you actually sit zazen, that is being a buddha. If we carry out good acts, then that
is doing good. If we commit evil ones, then that is doing evil. Cause is
not different from effect.

> There are times when cause and effect bring us to practice. Since the cause
> and effect have been cast off, their fundamental feature becomes clearly

evident. This is because they are the cause and effect of *refraining from*; they are absolute and transcend conscious effort—they are impermanent, and they are clearly evident and unhidden.

When we drive safely, that is being safety itself. When we drive in a dangerous manner, that is, in effect, being danger itself. Precisely because cause and effect are not different, this cause-and-effect brings us to actually driving: that is, to actually practicing.

"Their fundamental feature" is not creating or contriving anything; *makusa*, "not creating" or "refraining from," means to let go of all notions and concepts. Here, that causes and effects are "absolute and transcend conscious effort" means that "good" and "evil" as concepts have no fixed cause; "impermanent" means, of course, that everything is changing in every moment. It is foolish to entertain the idea that everything is now "safe" because you have had a realization while sitting zazen. The actual reality of life is impermanent in every moment. That is why, moment by moment, we consider what needs to be done. Moment by moment, we sit zazen.

"They are clearly evident" means that actual reality cannot be clouded over, while "unhidden" refers to actual reality itself. Actual reality is free of cause and effect; actual reality is simply what it is. "Since the cause and effect have been cast off" refers to the opening of the hand of thought, because casting off corresponds to acting in accord with the actual reality.

> That the *various evils* are all contained within *refraining from* will manifest clearly in practicing diligently in this way. Aided by this manifestation of *refraining from*, we will be able to see refraining from various evils clearly and be able to sit immovably.

If we practice in this way, moment by moment, we see that, generally speaking, there is no fixed entity that can be called "evil." "Aided by this manifestation of *refraining from*" means that we are pulled by the actual reality of life. So, the power of sitting immovably enables us to see evil as an illusion—this is what becomes perfectly clear.

For example, we can't actually drive a car with only some general notion of how to steer or when to apply the brakes. Trying to drive based only on some rough idea of how to drive is clearly treacherous. Only when we let go of such concepts and just act in each moment with full awareness can we call our actions safe driving.

> When continuously refraining from various evils in the living quick of time, these evils do not give rise as the cause of the next effect—there is only *refraining from*. Nor do these evils perish from some cause—there is only *refraining from*.

The expression *shōtō immo no toki* (正当什麼時), that is, when "refraining from is truly actualized," means when the reality of life is fully acting as the reality of life. "When continuously refraining from various evils" refers to a cause from the past that continues into the present and follows into the future. Such a theoretical cause-and-effect does not, in reality, exist. When we open the hand of thought, there is no such fixed thing. The reality of life of not creating[109] becomes manifest as the reality of life.

"These evils do not give rise as the cause of the next effect." It is not that we are no longer pulled by cause-and-effect, but rather that cause-and-effect itself is *refraining*. Likewise, "Nor do these evils perish from some cause—there is only *refraining from*." It is not a matter of cause or effect disappearing somewhere when evil has perished. With no consideration about the arising or perishing of cause-and-effect, there is only *refraining*.

For example, when a young man finds a young woman he likes, infatuation takes over, and he just assumes that she is simply the most beautiful woman in the world. From there the action begins. Now, I'm not saying

---

109. "The reality of life of not creating" here means not creating or imagining something in our head.

the two of them shouldn't get together. I'm just saying that he has to open his eyes. He has to realize there is no justification for assuming she alone is the most beautiful woman in the world. If he doesn't, he's apt to act foolishly and get caught in the web of arising and perishing of cause and effect. Practicing Buddhism means to become emancipated from this web of transmigration.[110] True emancipation is the practice of opening the hand of thought.

We often hear people talk about luck or seeing some so-called "good" omen. Or the opposite: how misfortunate or ominous something is. We need to let go of luck or omens, of notions of misfortune or how ominous something is. This is emancipation. It is from there that we have to act.

> When various evils are viewed impartially, then all the dharmas are viewed impartially.

The Buddhist term *tō*, that is, "equal" or "impartial," has a special nuance of its own. In our daily lives, we experience both good things and bad. Sometimes we eat, sometimes we do hard work, sometimes we sit zazen. From the perspective or foundation of the personal life experience of our most universal yet totally personal identity, all experiences have equal value. As Buddhadharma, that is the sense of tō: impartial. It is also in that sense that zazen is referred to as *tōji*: "to hold all things or view all things impartially." There is a temple in Kyoto with the name Tōji-in, literally, the "temple of holding impartially." Anyway, sitting zazen means to do just that: hold impartially, or view with an unbiased eye. When sitting zazen, all sorts of notions, fantasies, and impossible or unrealistic ideas arise, but whether they arise or fall away, the moment we think that we must not entertain them, we are no longer holding things impartially.

---

110. Uchiyama's use of the term *transmigration* is quite different from what most people would expect. He doesn't use it to refer to reincarnation, but to mean acting from one deluded thought to the next, in this lifetime.

Whether memories or fantasies pop up or dissipate, all we need to do is continue to let go of what arises.

It is precisely when we act to get rid of the fantasies and attempt to put ourselves into "better" circumstances or situations that zazen cannot just be what it is. Comfortable circumstances are nothing more than a matter of temperature and humidity. When we have to sit on a hot muggy day, our head just seems to boil over and all sorts of fantasies rise to the surface. Nevertheless, it is quite enough just to sit still and hold the zazen posture. Around dusk perhaps a high-pressure area moves in and a cool breeze begins to blow—and without doing a thing, we find ourselves in a very comfortable circumstance. Why, we might just feel so good that we start thinking, "Oh, everything's perfect. Maybe this is satori . . .?" But we have to let go of even that sort of thought. Doing zazen means to take the posture and open the hand that clings to thought. Doing just that is doing perfectly commendable zazen. Whether fantasies arise one after another or whether you sit there with a perfectly clean slate, let go of either one. Seeing both, illusions or realizations, with the same eye is what is critical here.

Unfortunately, there are an increasing number of explanations of Buddhism that have no connection to Buddhism, too many accounts that simply aren't grounded in the religion. Two illustrations of what I am referring to are embodied in such naive expressions as "an ordinary being who has changed and enters sainthood" (*tenbon nyushō*, 転凡入聖) or "illusion falls away and one enters nirvana" (*tenmei kaigo*, 転迷開悟). Such nonsense. On the other hand, although the way of expression is quite different from Zen, talks I have heard by Pure Land priests accord very well with the Buddha's teaching. They don't talk about such fantasies as illusion "falling away" and turning into satori. Rather, our body, just as it is—everything, in fact—is all contained in Amida Buddha. Now that is the Buddha's teaching.

> People are to be pitied who do not understand that *various evils* are born of a cause but that the cause itself is *refraining from*.

Because various evils are observed from the outside, cause-and-effect arises. However, when you are right now in the middle of an act, no cause-and-effect arises. What is significant here is this *you*—the very one who is presently acting. To the extent that you are alive fully as you, from the standpoint of this universal identity, cause and effect are *refraining*. When we are alive fully as we are, it is impossible to see ourselves. That we exist only as observers—this, Dōgen says, is pitiable.

> As it is written in the *Lotus Sūtra*, "The seeds of Buddhahood sprout through causation." Therefore, following causation, the seeds of Buddhahood will be born.

The seed called "buddha" arises from causation. However, causation is fundamentally *refraining* that is not fixed. The actual reality of life itself is nothing special. Look up at the ceiling of the room you are reading this in. It has a face of undetermined *refraining*. Everything in the universe is that way. The seed called "buddha" arises as a consequence of some cause. However, the cause arises out of an indeterminate *refraining*—that is, out of nothing special.

The ground of self is self alone.—*Dhammapada*
To rely on the other is to be always unsettled.—*The Suttanipāta*

III.
> It is not that various evils do not exist, but rather that all there is, is *makusa, refraining from*. Nor is it a matter of evils existing, again, all there is, is *refraining from*. Neither are evils empty; there is only *refraining from*. Nor do they have a substantial form; all there is, is *refraining from*. Evils are not of themselves *refraining from*; for all there is, is *refraining from*.

Not only do these lines have a high degree of sonority, they also demonstrate Dōgen Zenji's kindhearted thoroughness. He begins with how evils neither exist nor don't exist and then takes the discussion to the point where "evils are not of themselves *refraining from*; for all there is, is *refraining from.*" A discussion on the existence or nonexistence of something has to do with the view or perspective of an observer, but the discussion here is from the viewpoint of jiko—all-encompassing self, and, from that viewpoint, self is the actual reality of life. Here the actual reality is just how alive one is. In that moment, we let go of the fabrications or images or ideas that form in our heads. Here, it is not a matter of negating or disowning our assessment of various evils; what is crucial is to just *refrain from*: that is, let go.

> For instance, it is not that the pine tree in the spring exists or does not exist—it is not a thing that is humanly created. Nor is it a matter of the chrysanthemums in the fall existing or not, it is simply that they are not a humanly derived creation.

When we hear the words "refrain from various evils," we are apt to interpret them as some sort of admonition or warning not to do bad things. However, that is not what Dōgen means here. Makusa—*refraining from*—is nature as she is; this is what Dōgen is alluding to by the spring pine tree and the autumn chrysanthemums. Sawaki Rōshi used to rephrase this passage as "no playing or trifling with." Imagine sticking your hand inside a fishbowl with a couple of goldfish in it and stirring your hand around. The poor fish swim around for their lives in desperation, not knowing what is going on. Even now I can see in my mind Sawaki Rōshi gesturing with his hand in an imaginary fishbowl. And isn't swimming around for their lives in desperation exactly what an awful lot of people in the world are doing? *Shohō jissō* (諸方実相)—all things are just what they are; it is not a matter of whether or not they exist. Everything in nature is just what it is; we really shouldn't be playing around and tampering with everything.

> All the buddhas as well, are neither existent nor nonexistent—there is but *refraining from.*

When people think of *buddha*, they inevitably assume there must be some great, blessed person existing outside of themselves, but that is just not true. You shouldn't go around looking for buddhas outside yourself. Our true identity as jiko—whole self—sees all the buddhas within practice. What we practice is just letting go without producing anything—this is the deeper sense of *refraining*.

> The existence or nonexistence of such things as the temple pillars or stone lanterns, the monks' fly chaser or staff is not in question, there is only *refraining from*. It is not a matter of *jiko*, our whole self, either existing or not existing; there is only *refraining from*.

These are the same items Dōgen brings up in the "Uji" fascicle: those large round pillars supporting the main hall of the temple, the lanterns on either side of the Buddha statue. The *hossu* (拂子) was a sort of fly chaser used to chase away the flies and mosquitoes in India, while the precautionary staff (*chūjō,* 拄杖) was used by itinerant monks when they went into the forests to warn animals that a human being was coming through. So here Dōgen has listed a number of things used in everyday life.

When most people see this word *jiko*, they will generally only see it as "self" in opposition to "other." However, the actual reality of jiko in its all-inclusive dimension isn't structured in such a way. This all-inclusive self lets go of the way our individual minds frame thoughts; jiko is the ultimate limit of life.

> Making every effort to examine wholeheartedly in this way is itself a manifesting of the kōan; it is the kōan totally manifested. See everything from the perspective of universal truth, i.e., the kōan; see everything from what is presently and actually being manifest, i.e., *genjō*.

When we begin to see things in this way, an absolute reality, that is, the kōan, is manifested—which is, at the same time, a total manifestation (in Japanese, *genjō*).

In the *Diamond Sūtra*,[111] there is a passage that says, "All things in this world are ephemeral. They are like dreams or phantasms. Everything is short-lived and fragile, like bubbles on water or like shadows, like dewdrops, like a bolt of lightning. See clearly all creations [dharmas] in this way." That is, all things are impermanent, which, of course, also means that all things are just as they are—shohō jissō. Therefore, you should look and see all things as they truly are.

Regarding this passage, further on, there is another passage in the *Diamond Sūtra* that reads, "Give rise to a spirit wherein there is no place to reside." The emphasis here is to act or function *as* impermanence, to function *as* shohō jissō.

The line "See clearly all creations [dharmas] in this way" tells us to just sit zazen without moving, observing clearly and with open eyes. So, in contrast to this passage of no-movement, we have the other passage telling us to act or function as impermanence. Together, the passages suggest acting or functioning while residing in impermanence. The second one says to create a place with no residing. This is not so easy. It's not enough to personally experience all things being as they are: rather, we need to act or function in accord with all things being as they are.

Dōgen's text continues, "See everything from the perspective of universal truth, i.e., the kōan; see everything from what is presently and actually being manifest, i.e., *genjō*." View all things that are being presently manifest before your eyes and enable them to function. It is possible to see things from both a particular and overall contextual perspective.

---

111. *Kongō Hanyaharamita-kyō* (金剛般若波羅蜜多経), known commonly as the *Diamond Sūtra*, is one of the Perfection of Wisdom sūtras in the Mahāyāna tradition. Kumārajīva (鳩摩羅什, 344–413 CE) is thought to have translated it from Sanskrit into Chinese early in the fifth century. Buddhist scholar and practitioner Dr. Kansho Honda has informally commented on these passages as, "It is essential to live a life with an attitude of no fixations."

Despite the fact that evil can in no way be created, how can we avoid feeling remorseful over some terrible thing we mistakenly feel we have done? Such feelings of remorse also derive from the power of practicing *refraining from.*

However, hearing that the various evils are the same as *refraining from* and cannot be created, and then deliberately contriving to commit an unwholesome act are like heading north hoping to arrive in the southern district of Otsu (Ch., Yue).

It is a big mistake to think that since everything is *refraining*, it is okay to do something bad. It is like walking north in order to arrive in the south.

Refraining from various evils is not limited to Sōzan's "The well looks at the donkey." It is the well looking at the well and the donkey looking at the donkey, too. Moreover, it is also the person seeing the person and the mountain seeing the mountain. As this was the response of Toku-jōza to Master Sōzan who had asked the senior monk to explain further the meaning of the "body of the buddha" that changes in response to the needs of the sentient being; this is [the same as] shoaku makusa. [The original story from which this was taken, reads:] "The *dharmakāya*, or true body of Buddha, is, as it were, formless; still, it takes a form in response to each matter. It is like the moon reflected in a drop of water."

Now, a donkey looking into a well is indeed devoid of any human sentiments. However, it is an animal (a sentient being) looking, so Toku-jōza's reply doesn't go far enough. Therefore, Sōzan replies that the dharmakāya is like a well (an inanimate thing) looking at a donkey. Still, for Dōgen Zenji, neither is a complete answer, so he adds, "It is the well looking at the well, and the donkey looking at the donkey, too." Going this far, Dōgen has arrived at *refraining*. It is a mistake to set up *shoaku*—"various evils" in opposition to makusa—*refraining*. You shouldn't see them as two separate entities. The dimension here is always one of self that is only self.

As I mentioned in my introduction to Dōgen's *Instructions to the Cook* (*Tenzo Kyōkun*, 典座教訓), "Mind extends throughout all phenomena, and all phenomena are inseparable from mind."[112] That is, all things exist as my own personal life experience. At the same time, I live out all things while I am personally experiencing my life. These two—I and all phenomena—are entirely and completely one. This is self that is only self; it is complete self. All I do is enact that self. When doing so, there are not two separate entities. There is no balancing between "this" and "that" going on. This is crucial. This is also the aim or direction of our practice. No matter how many years we do zazen, our work is to never balance oneself against some "other." Zazen is also *jijuyū zanmai*, the samadhi of receiving all things and enabling all things to function freely and fully, and *jiko giri no jiko* (自己ぎりの自己)—"all-encompassing self" or "self that is only self."[113] The way Sawaki Rōshi used to put it is "self selfs the self."[114] Śākyamuni described it by saying, "The ground of self is self alone," in the *Dhammapada*. Finally, in the *Suttanipāta*, appears the passage, "To rely on the other is to be always unsettled." This has to be one of the most important teachings of Buddhadharma. The basis of self is only oneself. There is nothing more absolutely true than this. Relying on something outside of yourself, placing all your hope in someone or something else—for example, in money or wealth, or in position or status—is nothing more than depending on what goes on in the stock market, on things that are constantly fluctuating!

112. The Japanese expression here is *isshin issaihō issaihō isshin* (一心一切法、一切法一心). That is, all phenomena or dharmas are a reflection of mind that is both discerning as well as universal. Kōshō Uchiyama, *Jinsei Ryōri no Hon—Tenzo Kyōkun ni Manabu* 人生料理の本—典座教訓に学ぶ, Sōtō Shumucho, 1970.

113. *Jiko giri no jiko* might be more literally but awkwardly translated as "self that extends to the extreme limit of self." *Giri* comes from the expression *girigiri* which implies the sense of something utmost or of an ultimate limit. Hence, in this case, the reference is to a self that is all-inclusive or all-comprehensive.

114. *Jiko ga jiko wo jiko suru* (自己が自己を自己する). Here "self" is used as subject, verb, and object. Literally, the term is as indecipherable in Japanese as in English.

An acquaintance of mine dropped by recently. He said his son, whom he had tried to raise so carefully and on whom he had placed all his hopes, had gone rotten. His son had gone so far as to get involved in some criminal activity and was being investigated by the police. The man just broke down completely and lamented how it would have been better never to have had a child.

Parents might have a kid, dote on him, and pin all their hopes and dreams on him, but that is a major mistake. Likewise, I hear that some people run around looking for a priest whom they blindly believe to be some sort of saint and place all their trust in the person. What nonsense. After all, priests are just human beings. Who would be so naive as to believe in the existence of such a "holy person"? Let me say this: The greater and "holier" you see the person behaving, the more you can be certain that there is something hidden—the reality is never the way it appears.

In the end, the fundamental teaching of Buddhadharma is "That which self can rely on is self alone" and "To depend on another is to remain unsettled."

In the *Long Āgama Sūtras* (*Jōagon-kyō*, 長阿含経), it is also written, "Take refuge in self, take refuge in Dharma [the teaching], take refuge in nothing other." This teaching has the same sense as my expression, "whatever the situation, self is self alone." The ground of self is the practice of one/all clarifying and settling into the Self of all/all. When we read, "the person seeing the person, the mountain seeing the mountain," the emphasis is on the wholeness or totality of the person or mountain in itself prior to any comparison to anything outside.

That the body of Buddha "takes a form in response to each matter" is in the same sense as *refraining* in the text. It is not some relative refraining that employs comparative values. Rather, it is a *refraining* whose very structure dwells immanently within jiko—whole self. Traditionally, this is called the "seed of buddha" or more simply, the very life force of the self. Now, this all-inclusive self can work or function in any myriad of ways. That is the true reality of the life force. However, if you are always thinking about how your reputation will be affected or how something will appear to others—in other words, thinking only in terms of weighing what to do against how it will be taken—you will never be able to fully function in life. When I coined the expression *deau tokoro waga seimei* (出会うところ我が生命) or "everything we encounter is our life," what I meant was that we should throw all of our energy into that which is directly in front of us.

> Since "responding to each matter" is the same as *refraining from,* it appears as a form that must also be *refraining from.*

Even when working, if we let go of any notions or sentiments that might arise in regard to it while we do it, we are able to do the work completely. After becoming ordained, I worked as the *tenzo,* or cook, in the monastery throughout the war and the years following. Looking back on those days, it was a time I was always hungry. But luckily, if you were assigned to the kitchen, there were chances to nibble a little here and there. So it was one job I always took on gladly. But, of course, if you have that sort of attitude, something is sure to go wrong. So, around 1948, I really gave the matter some thought: Could there be anything more miserable than to have taken all the trouble to become ordained only to spend my time stealing food? So I resolved then and there not to go around sneaking food anymore. And from that time on, I was able to immerse myself in the work of the tenzo and to do it completely without screwing up.

As those familiar with Zen monasteries in Japan already know, the cook is in charge of preparing the meals alone, while everyone else sits zazen. So when zazen finishes, the cook has to be able to put all the food on the table right then with no delays, especially in the dead of winter when everyone has been sitting for several hours in the cold. When they're finally done and they come down for dinner, even putting just hot rice and miso soup on the table, along with some nice pickled dish, is no laughing matter. If you take time out to sneak a bite to eat, even if it is only for a few seconds, you might be able to finish the soup, but the rice may not be ready, or some similar issue will arise. You wait a few minutes for the rice to finish, but the soup cools down, the tofu gets tough, and the miso loses its flavor. These are the sorts of things that occur when your mind is on something else. If you genuinely aspire to put the best meal together with the ingredients you have and you earnestly make every effort to do so, then the meal will surely come together.

From that time on, I was able to appreciate Dōgen Zenji's *Instructions to the Cook* and to throw all my energy into the work of the tenzo. Dōgen writes, "Both day and night allow all things to come into and reside within your mind. Allow your mind [self] and all things [the work] to function together as a whole." What I understood from this passage is that truly working means that you and the work have to function as a single unit. This is true, of course, not only for the tenzo, but for mendicant begging as well; you need to become totally one with it. Actually, I think this applies to any type of work in our society. Politicians, too, are—or should be—performing as a sort of tenzo; they and their work should be just like the moon reflected in the water. They should be able to make policies that reflect letting go of the "hand" of special or vested interests.

"That the cosmic body of Buddha is formless is like striking out with the left hand; it is striking out with the right one—there are no hindrances." Swinging out with the left or right hand is like swinging in the air; this is the same as *kokū* (虚空): literally, "the empty sky," but in Buddhism, "empty without any obstacles." Regardless of what befalls us, there is no hitting *or* missing the mark.

"It is like the moon in the water; the water is obstructed by the moon": [you and your work come together and you perform it being fully absorbed in it, while at the same time, who you truly are becomes reflected in the work.

All the examples I have given of *refraining from* are unquestionable illustrations of the manifesting of the quick of life.

> The existence or nonexistence of such things as the temple pillars or stone lanterns, the monks' fly chaser or the staff is not in question; there is only refraining from. It is not a matter of jiko—whole self—either existing or not existing; there is only refraining from.

It is exactly this sort of letting go that in itself is genjō—"presently manifesting." *Genjō* implies that the present becomes more of the present. To put it another way: everything, just as it is, becomes that much more of what it is.

Gain is illusion, loss is realization. Carry out good with fullest sincerity.

> IV.
>
> In the expression, "Carry out all sorts of good," "all sorts of good" refers to the second of the three inherent qualities of evil, good, and unmarked. Although all sorts of good are contained within the quality of goodness, it is not as though something good is simply on hand, waiting for a practitioner to enact it.

The "three qualities" here are the same as those mentioned earlier in the text: the qualities of good, evil, and unmarked or neutral. That is, as an individual (one/all), I live from day to day, constantly making decisions and distinguishing whether something is good for me or bad for me or neither one nor the other. However, the truth of the matter is that there is no such solid entity [with an intrinsic value] that is simply waiting around for me to put it to use or discard it.

I first became a monk when I was thirty years old. Until that time, I was just a pasty intellectual. So when I became fed up with all the intellectualizing, I became a monk under Sawaki Rōshi's guidance and moved into the monastery at Daichūji in Tochigi Prefecture. The atmosphere there was very different from that which we see in ordinary society; if there was anything you were able to give someone a hand with, then you did it without questioning. The very first thing Rōshi said to me on my arrival there was "If there is some work to be done, you've got to roll up your sleeves and do it." For someone like me who had been living the life of a pale-faced intellectual, rolling up those sleeves was a monumental task. What's more, I had this habit of being argumentative. When I first heard Rōshi say that if we could be of help to someone, we should get right to it, my first reaction was "Wait a second, hold on there." I decided to ask him about it. My argument was that, in general, if I do some work for the sake of some other person, I only wind up doing what that person should really be doing for himself. So then I become the cause of someone else's laziness. Consequently, aren't I simply contributing to other people's vices and immorality?

Rōshi came back, "You can find that same argument in Tolstoy. One day he left his house for the day intending to give money to the poor. But, when he arrived down in the slum district, he began thinking, 'If I give money to that guy, he's just going to drink it all away. And, if I give it to the guy over there, he'll most likely just become lazy and do nothing.' In the end, he wound up back home without having given a penny to anyone. Almost all you intellectuals are exactly like that. That kind of thinking, however, never occurred to me. If there is something helpful you can do that will make someone happy, right here in front of you, then just do it!"

I heard these words directly from Rōshi shortly after I became his disciple. Right then, my whole attitude changed, and I strived to serve others. When I look back on it now, I'm sure that Sawaki Rōshi's well-known words during the final years of his life, "Gain is illusion, loss is satori," derived from his own attitude of those earlier days. What is important here is not only being willing, but actively pursuing what is disadvantageous for one's "own" position. Think, "Oh, I lose," and then just let go. That is satori. Wherever you hesitate to let go, even in the slightest, it's no mistake to say that that hesitation is the extent of your delusion (*mayoi*, 迷い).

In other words, good is to be found only in the carrying out or functioning.

> When some good is being fully carried out, all good is inevitably present. Though good acts have no inherently fixed form, they gather all good quicker than iron is drawn to a magnet. Their strength exceeds even that of the most destructive hurricane-like *vairambhaka* winds that blow. Notwithstanding all the phenomena occurring naturally in this world or the destructive or horrible deeds of all the nations and peoples dwelling therein, this gathering of good deeds can never be impeded.

When you enact a single good deed, all good comes together. Dōgen says metaphorically that all good gathers around faster than iron filings adhering to a magnet, and that good acts are stronger than the *vairambhaka* winds that are said to blow at the very beginning and the very end of the world. Expanding on this metaphor, Dōgen says that the speed and strength of this gathering together of all good are so great that not even all the destructive power of man's worst connivings and structures can prevent it.

The other day a female college student called on me. After just sitting there for some time, eventually tears began to roll down her cheeks. When I asked her what had brought her to see me, she said she had come because she had just read my book on *Instructions to the Cook*. Then, she became more relaxed and related her problem.

"I want to become an English teacher, but for that, I have to go abroad to study. And to do that, I have to get a scholarship, because I don't have enough money. But to get a scholarship, I have to study unbelievably hard. At school," she continued, "I have plenty of classmates, but I don't talk to any of them. I only have one friend, and recently, since I've been studying so hard, I've even lost her. Now I feel so lonely, I don't know what to do."

The first thing I told her was that it was unwholesome to have just one friend and hardly associate with any of her other classmates. Every human being is born into this world naked and alone and leaves it the same way, so everyone experiences that loneliness. Still, as long as we are alive, we wear some sort of clothing for a while. It is only natural that we meet many people and make many friends. But don't misunderstand this to mean that we should go about looking just for specific friends who appreciate and feed our narrow egotism. Rather, it is on our part that we need to develop a sense of serving and helping others, whoever they might be. She said she read my book, but the whole thing clearly emphasizes the fact that everything we encounter is our life. Not only people, but also all the things and events that come into our life are precisely that—the encounters of our life. You need to see all these things as your "children" and then strive to take proper care of them.

A child is one who thinks of having his or her parents do everything for them. But once you have become a college student, it should be a matter of course that when your mother has work to do, you start thinking about how you can help her out. When you start doing that, she will begin to show you a brighter face, too. In that way, when you go to school, you need to begin seeing your classmates as a part of yourself and to give them a hand whenever you can, too. If there isn't anything in particular you can do, then at least help out by showing a smiling face. You shouldn't poison the people around you by always showing a sour face.

After my having said those things to her, the young woman seemed to have understood and left. Then, just the other day, I received a letter from her in which she wrote that my advice had indeed helped her to brighten up. That, for me, was a relief.

As I get older, it's gotten more and more difficult to sit zazen. So in my last years, I've been chanting *Namu Amida Butsu* instead. This is a recent poem I wrote with that title.

Namu Amida Butsu

Amida is *immeasurable life*
This is the life of whichever way I fall—
This is my life
Namu is to return to life
Return, that is, to my Life
Whether I think so or not
Whether I believe it or not
Pulled by the magnetic power of
The undeniable reality of my life
In speech, in body, and in mind[115]
Always now, here, at this time, in this place
Am I enabled to function as Namu Amida Buddha
This is the meaning of buddha
A buddha is a true adult.

I'm afraid, as usual, that this is my poor imitation of a poem. However, the sense of it is this:

In Japanese, the sense of *amida* is translated as *muryō* (無量), which means "immeasurable," but in a way that has nothing to do with a large quantity or size. On the altar in Shin Buddhist temples, we can often find written *Namu Muryō Ju Nyorai* ("Take refuge in the immeasurable Tathāgata") and *Namu Mugekō Nyorai* ("Take refuge in the Tathāgata of unimpeded light"). Whichever way we fall, *muryō* is our all-inclusive self that is our life.

Namu, usually translated as "take refuge," means to return to life—that is, return to my life that is all-inclusive. My personal life experience includes all things. Or, to turn the phrase around, I am alive by personally experiencing all things as my life. The kind of life I am living is one in

115. That is, through words, actions, and awareness.

which I am alive regardless of whatever might befall me, whether I think something is so or not, whether I believe it is so or not. Likewise, regardless of our beliefs or ideas, we are always being pulled by the magnetism of undeniable reality. It's just that we simply aren't aware of it.

In the very same way that we are pulled by the force of the earth's gravity, whether we realize it or not, we are also being pulled by the force of absolute reality. This is not something that comes about only because of some condition, like passing an exam (or gaining satori); it's a matter of having that frame of mind of always functioning to return to one's life—this is the deeper sense of *Namu Amida Butsu*. This is the meaning of *hotoke*[116]—which is another reading of *Butsu*. All buddhas are true adults; this is the definition of buddha. *Hotoke* or *Buddha* is the true meaning of being an adult.

Namu Amida Butsu is not simply a mantra one recites with the mouth. You have to recite it with your body. And further, you need to recite it through your day-to-day activities. Whether you pass or fail, you have to live out *Namu Amida Butsu*. We sit in the palm of Amida Buddha. He is saving us from his position in the Pure Land. That is where he resides. So, since it is Amida's *Namu Amida Butsu*, returning to the life of Amida, functioning as *Namu Amida Butsu*, means we need to chant his name with our mouth, our body, and our whole heart.

Now, my explanation here may vary slightly from the "official" version. However, for me, I dare to say that *Namu Amida Butsu* is Dōgen's *shushō ichinyo* (修証一如), his "identity of practice and enlightenment," and his *shōjōnoshu* (証上の修), his "practice that transcends enlightenment." My poem may be a bit short on poetic structure, but I would like you to try and appreciate it from this alternate view. Concretely and practically, carrying out good as Buddhadharma is to work and function with such an attitude.

116. In Japanese, the character for *buddha* is also read *hotoke*. One explanation of the origin of the word is that it refers to one who has been liberated from the sufferings of all deep-seated cravings, called *bonnō* (煩悩).

To put it another way: everything we encounter is, in a sense, an off-spring of our life as a self not balanced or opposed by any other, a self that is all-encompassing. It is with this attitude that we take care of the various matters and events that come up in our lives. This attitude applies, of course, to all the people we encounter in our lives as well. Actually, there is nothing that we encounter that is not a part of the content of our life. The practical functioning of this all-encompassing life is the sense of "when good is being fully carried out."

When we are sitting zazen, zazen comprises the life of jiko—our whole life. Moreover, in our day-to-day life, this is the meaning of *shikan* in the term *shikan taza* (只管打坐), or "just sitting."[117] "When good is being fully carried out," Amida of Immeasurability comes to welcome us. Amida gathers good "quicker than iron is drawn to a magnet and is stronger than the Vairambhaka winds."

There is a similar passage in Dōgen's *Instructions to the Cook* that reads, "Do not overlook one drop in the ocean of virtue [by entrusting the work to others]. Cultivate a spirit which strives to increase the source of goodness upon the mountain of goodness."[118] When we carry out this one grain, or one drop, there all the buddhas of the three worlds (past, present, future) will appear. And further on in the text, "Handle even a single leaf of a green in such a way that it manifests the body of the Buddha."[119] It is this attitude of enabling the sixteen-foot-tall Buddha to appear even when working with a single leaf. And then, "This, in turn, allows the Buddha to manifest through the leaf."[120] Welcome the Buddha even when cooking a single leaf—this is the way to handle veg-

---

117. Here Uchiyama Rōshi is suggesting that the Chinese term *shōtō immo no toki* (正当什麼時), meaning "when something is being fully carried out," is the same as the expression he used, *shikan*. In Nakamura Gen's *Bukkyōgo Daijiten*, we find the term *shikan* (只管 or 祗管) defined as *hitasura* or *ichizu ni* meaning "earnestly," "solely," "or with all one's heart"; *immo* (恁麼) is defined as "a thing or situation as it actually is."

118. Uchiyama, *How to Cook Your Life*, 4.

119. *How to Cook Your Life*, 7.

120. *How to Cook Your Life*, 8.

etables. Working with that sort of attitude is what the spirit of the tenzo is about.

I worked as a monastery cook for twenty years and, in doing so, that was my aim. There is no passing or failing here. Working just this much or just that much to "pass" is merely a matter of technique. Instead, what we're aiming for is *just doing* the tenzo's work. I'm not talking about skill or technique; I'm talking about a deep maturing in attitude.

When I first started out as a tenzo, naturally, I was called on to cook the rice, but no matter how hard I worked at it, all I could manage was "rainbow" rice: at the bottom, it was pitch black, next to that came a layer of ordinary burned rice, somewhere in the middle the rice was only half-cooked, and floating on top was a soupy-looking gruel. Everyone was so impressed I was able to cook up so many layers of rice in the same pot!

Moving into the Depth of All/All As One's Universal Identity.

> Still, that which is perceived as "good" is the same or different depending on the society and social context. [As it is written in the *Lotus Sūtra*,] "Just as the buddhas of the past, present, and future preached," they did so to the people of the time and ways in which they lived. There are a myriad of buddhas, whose appearances all vary—some have lived for an immeasurable length of time, others only for a short time; some buddhas are colossal, others are infinitesimally small. Still, "all of them taught the Dharma teaching of nondifferentiation."

Before commenting on the overall sense of these passages, I need to talk briefly about a few of the terms that come up.

The entire quote from the *Lotus Sūtra* is "Just as the buddhas of the past, present, and future preached, I will also do the same and preach the Dharma teaching of nondifferentiation."[121] The Dharma teaching

---

121. Burton Watson, in his excellent translation of the *Lotus Sūtra*, translates,

of nondifferentiation appears in the *Lotus Sūtra*. First of all, what the teaching means is that the preaching, the lifespans, the dimensions, the countries, and the cultures of all the buddhas are all different. For instance, Śākyamuni Buddha lived for eighty years, while Amida Buddha lives for an immeasurable length of time. Also, Śākyamuni is said to have stood over fifteen feet tall, but there have been even much larger buddhas. Then there are lands or countries that are corrupt or barbaric, as well as lands like the Pure Land. It's not that the buddhas are different. Rather, various buddhas appear in response to the needs and characteristics of the people. This is referred to as *ōbutsu no gishiki* (応仏之儀式), the principle of the correspondence of the buddhas. In short, a buddha preaches the reality of life, or life that is fully life, never the law of discrimination.

> There are those whose simple faith guides their capacity to move others and who base their practice on such faith, and there are those whose capability to move others is based on their comprehension and understanding of good derived from the depths of their practice of the teaching of good. The functioning of each is very different. They almost appear to be teaching totally different Dharmas. A concrete example of this difference would be how a literal upholding of the precepts by a śrāvaka becomes a breach of them by a *bodhisattva*.

The word Dōgen uses here, *ki* (機), refers to the capacity or capability to move others; that is, corresponding to the teaching determines the extent to which one can move or affect others. A person with a simple faith is one who believes in someone's teaching and then practices it without any

---

"Following the same fashion that the Buddhas of the three existences employ in preaching the Law, I now will do likewise, preaching a Law that is without distinctions." (Watson, *The Lotus Sutra*), 45. The Buddhist understanding of the concept of "nondifferentiation," in Japanese, *mufunbetsu* (無分別), should not be confused with its modern-day meaning "to do something without thought." The understanding of nondifferentiation is that it takes place within the practitioner prior to any discriminative or differential thoughts. That is, nondifferentiation and differentiation are not opposites.

doubt or hesitation, while other people practice and function in their lives having derived comprehension and understanding through their own deep contemplation.

The so-called śrāvaka is one who simply lets go of greed, anger, and ignorance, while a bodhisattva is a Mahāyāna practitioner who truly aspires to live out his or her own life to the fullest. Although the precept may be the same, the understanding of it for the śrāvakas is different from that of the Mahāyāna practitioner. Let's say, for example, that we see a woman who is about to drown in a river and is calling out for help. Now if the śrāvaka who comes along even touches the woman, he has broken the precept forbidding a monk from touching a woman. For the Mahāyāna practitioner, however, he breaks the precept if he doesn't try to rescue the woman who is calling for help.

Now let us look at how the passage comes together and what the overall meaning of it is. The fact that what is recognized as "good" differs from society to society is like the principle of the teaching of nondifferentiation; even that is going to be expressed differently according to the time or circumstances or society. Hence, "some [buddhas] have lived for an immeasurable length of time, others only for a short time; some buddhas are colossal, others are infinitesimally small [. . . .] They almost appear to be teaching totally different Dharmas." That is, simple believers and those who have understood through exhaustive study and practice may interpret that same Dharma differently. That has to do with the dullness or sharpness of the practitioner even though the Dharma of nondifferentiation itself is the same. In that way, what is recognized as "good" depends on the society, even though they are speaking of the same Dharma of nondifferentiation. This is just like the seeming difference of Dharma between the śrāvaka and bodhisattva interpretations of what upholding the precepts means.

Goodness does not arise out of causes and conditions, nor does it disappear due to causes and conditions. Although all good takes the form of a dharma, no dharma is intrinsically good. If, from the beginning, the causes and conditions, appearance and disappearance, and all sorts of good are sound, then they will be sound throughout as well.

Just as in the previous section where it was written that evils do not arise or fall due to causes or conditions, here in this passage, good is not subject to causes and conditions either. Ordinarily, people are apt to think that something good exists as an entity outside of their own life experience and that good things or bad things come into existence or pass away due to causes and conditions.[122] However, here Dōgen is emphatically stating that such is not the case. This is really his most salient point.

Ultimately, thinking there is some good or evil existing outside of oneself and believing that one will choose not to do the bad thing in favor of the good thing is only a matter of comparison, an attempt at maintaining a balance. Then you're just talking about some generally or socially accepted moral code or ethics. That is not what the Buddhadharma is about. The Buddhadharma always has to do with what Dōgen called *jijuyū zanmai*—the samadhi of freely receiving and functioning. Another way to put it would be that Buddhadharma is about an all-inclusive self.[123] What, then, does it mean to say that good and evil are contained within this self?

We are born individually as one entity among all the entities, that is, as one/all. And as we grow, we assume that we ourselves comprise a single individual thing within all the things of all the various worlds. So, if we begin to doubt that anyone understands us, it becomes natural to feel alone. From an individual standpoint, as one person among many others,

122. Uchiyama Rōshi often told the story of Sawaki Rōshi who, one day, received a distressing letter from a devout follower. The writer of the letter was grieving because despite all her years of doing zazen, she developed cancer and wondered why. Sawaki Rōshi's reply was that no matter how many years you practice zazen, that has nothing to do with whether or not you'll get cancer or suffer any other kind of misfortune.

123. For "all-inclusive self," Uchiyama mingled Dōgen and Sawaki's words, using the expression *jin issai*, or "all-inclusive," and *jiko giri no jiko*, or "self that is entirely self."

we think about *this* being good and *that* being evil. In other words, we understand refraining from evil and committing good deeds within our horizontal relationship of giving and taking.

However, while I exist as one among all, at the same time, my intrinsic nature is one of all/all. To restate this idea a little differently, while self is, by birth, one/all, it is also, simultaneously, all/all. When we realize that, we give up acting as an ego constantly comparing and competing against other egos. That is actually refraining from evil. And, since intrinsically, we are all/all, we carry out actions as all/all. This is carrying out good deeds.

The problem is one of depth. To act as all/all and refrain as a narrow one/all, our all-inclusive self—jiko—must just deepen into itself. That is, it is a *vertical* relationship. This is the meaning of refraining from evil and doing good as Buddhadharma. This is also what is referred to as the identity of practice and enlightenment—*shushō ichinyo*. Through this practice, *our* self as all/all becomes manifest. To be manifest, here, means that the present becomes fully the present.[124]

To give a concrete example, let us say we are doing zazen. Since we are always intrinsically all-encompassing self, regardless of what befalls us, we need to aim at *falling* in the direction of sitting like a coiled dragon rather than nodding off half-asleep, of sitting like a tiger in the mountain rather than sitting there thinking and daydreaming. That is, we want to aim at holding the most alive zazen posture that we can.

Further, whether we think so or not, whether we believe it or not, whether we acknowledge it or not, everyone in the world is living out this intrinsic, fundamental self; it is our actual life. This is what we have to wake up to. When the topic of practice comes up, we get all confused and we start to think, "From now on, I'm going to practice very hard and become all-encompassing self." But, we are already actually living out

---

124. The present becomes fully the present is Uchiyama Rōshi's rendering of *genjō*, the two Chinese characters of *genjō kōan*.

all-encompassing self. We are right now breathing in the air that fills the universe, drinking the water that fills the universe, eating the food that fills the universe. Even our heart beating and blood circulating—these all come from the life of the universe. So, being pulled by the gravity that fills the universe, we carry out actions that fill the universe. This is "refraining from evil and carrying out good deeds."

Too often, however, we fail to act in a universe-full sense and, instead, act and behave according to our narrow sentiments and ideas; that is, we are controlled by secretions of our minds. We act out of the ego of one/ all self, which we call "I." Letting go of our egotism is the meaning of *refraining*. And, exactly when we let go, I who fill the universe encounter life that fills the universe.

What Dōgen is trying to say is that all situations and things and all the people we encounter—anything and everything—are all the "children" of the life of our universal self.

In *Instructions to the Cook*, Dōgen writes: "Both day and night, allow all things to come into and reside within your mind. Allow your mind (Self) and all things to function together as a whole."[125] There are some people with a liking for Zen who might pick this up and think that Dōgen is talking about some sort of mysticism, where the subject and object miraculously come together, but they would be way off the mark. Dōgen is not talking about anything mystical here. What he is saying is that we have to physically throw ourselves into our work and just do it. For example, in a passage where he writes that, as we wash out the pot, pot and ourselves merge into one, some people nurture the idea of somehow attaining to some such stage—but he's not writing about any sort of mystical state of mind. When we actually work as a tenzo, we clean the pot right down to the bottom, carrying out the work of washing as if it were our very own head.

From my early thirties until I reached fifty-five, all I did was work

125. Kōshō Uchiyama, *How to Cook Your Life*, 6.

that most people would say was very servile. It was only natural for me to entertain doubts about the value of my work. By that time in my life, all my school friends had risen to become department heads or even presidents of various companies, and here I was cooking rice in some little known and impoverished temple. It was no wonder I had a lot of misgivings about what I was doing. Still, I followed Dōgen Zenji's teaching and just let go of my doubts. Just letting go, I worked as hard as I could. Now, after all these years, you might think I would go out and try my luck in the world as a famous chef or something, but you'd be mistaken. Every encounter we have is our life, and just doing everything with that in mind was my fundamental attitude. It was precisely because of that teaching on allowing the mind and all things to function together as a whole in *Instructions to the Cook* that I was able to continue throwing myself into my work. For me, having this attitude toward one's own practice is very important.

Now, in what we have read so far, this same idea is expressed in "When various evils can no longer be created, then the virtue of practice manifests directly. This living actualization does so in all lands and all worlds, as all times and all dharmas. This vivid actualization of the entire universe is the boundary of refraining from various evils."

In other words, when we *just do* without thinking in terms of comparing or competing with others, then the virtue of practice manifests directly. All-encompassing or universal (whole) self manifests directly.

Refraining (*makusa*) is letting go of one's own egotistical self by not competing or comparing oneself with other people. Further, concretely in our daily lives, *refraining from various evils* and *carrying out all sorts of good* mean letting go of our egotistical self again and again. That is refraining. Carrying out good is not something that lies outside of us.

For example, I think having an opportunity to speak here is, for me, a good thing, and being able to address you has its causes. Abbot Hosokawa at Sōsenji temple, urging me to explain *Shōbōgenzō* and offering his place as a venue, is a primary cause. And there are various reasons and causes that brought you here. In other words, there are causes for all these things to have happened, so what does Dōgen mean when he says that goodness does not arise out of causes and conditions?

When I speak, I don't move my lips and think of these causes. I could list this or that cause, but as I speak, all of the faces of the people listening are being reflected on the retinas of my eyes. As I look at them, as an "I" inclusive of all of them—or to put it another way, as a self or jiko that is entirely and inclusively me—when I speak of Buddhadharma, I'm speaking totally as an all-inclusive self while trying to inspire them and convince them of such a self, so much so that I can see a whole new look in their eyes. Ultimately, I, inclusive of everyone, am here totally, just speaking, since everything I encounter is my life. So my words are filled with vigor.

In a nutshell, my speaking has a beginning and an end, and it also has causes that brought it about. However, the self that I am truly, all-inclusive jiko, is not something that can be seen objectively. All there is, is the doing of it. And, in the actual doing of it, there are no particular fixed entities as birth and decay, causes and effects, or good and evil. Just speaking—that is my practice here. As for this practice of just doing or just speaking, if this practice is correct, then the result will be correct. That is the sense of the term *zushin bishin*: "right from the beginning, right at the end."

The Buddhadharma Has Been Rephrased as "My Eyes Are Horizontal, My Nose Is Vertical"

Although all good takes the form of some act being carried out, such carrying out is devoid of any ego; neither is there a "self" that is carrying out such actions. This carrying out does not take place outside of oneself, nor can *carrying out good* be known by another. This is because knowledge and view of self and other lie in the purview of a dualistic conscious knowing that by nature separates self and other, "my" view from "another's" view. In each and every living action, there is the sun; there is the moon—that is *carrying out.*

Carrying out has nothing to do with comparing one's actions with someone else's actions. It's not an individual matter. In Dōgen's *Bendōwa* (辨 道話 or "Wholehearted Practice of the Way") we can find the following similar passage: "You should know thoroughly that you practice the Buddhadharma precisely when you let go of the dualistic view of self and other." While doing zazen, you begin to think, "Oh, I'm getting into some nice space here . . ." That's no good. For the most part, there is nothing as useless as self-observation during zazen. Self-observation is just an illusion; it has nothing to do with zazen. Zazen is nothing other than the samadhi of the freely functioning self, self that is only self. Moreover, *self,* here, means "self that precedes the dualistic and separating dichotomy of self and other." So, as long as you cling to the idea of somehow or another "getting" satori, you're still operating in the realm of duality and comparison. Sitting zazen like that is not doing true zazen.[126]

The attitude of a practitioner of Dōgen's zazen is one that just sits, seeing both realization and illusion with an equal eye. At that time, there is no particular consciousness of oneself.[127] Nor, is there any particular evaluating awareness of the quality of one's zazen. That is the sense of the passage "[Although all good takes the form of some act being carried out,] such *carrying out* is devoid of any ego; neither is there a 'self' that is *carrying out* such actions."

Sawaki Rōshi often used to say, "You have to just sit believing that zazen is the posture of the Buddha." Here, "Buddha" refers to self that

126. Uchiyama uses the quest for satori as an example of comparing one's present "unenlightened" self with one's future "enlightened" self. But, actually, any kind of zazen that is done with the attitude of trying to gain greater self-awareness or self-observation is not the "just sitting" zazen of Dōgen.

127. That is, there is no particular consciousness of oneself *as a separate or individual entity.*

is all-inclusive, that is, jiko. Therefore, it is at the same time the samadhi of the freely functioning self. To the extent you sit and take up the zazen posture both physically and mentally, there is no sense of balancing or comparing oneself to anything "outside." This *carrying out* does not take place outside of oneself, nor can *carrying out good* be known by another. That there is some fixed entity of "self" or "other" is nothing but a view. In our heads, we think, this is me and that is someone else—we take a viewpoint. According to Dōgen, "This is because knowledge and view of self and other lie in the purview of a dualistic conscious knowing that by nature separates self and other, of 'my' view and 'another's' view."

During zazen we let go of those viewpoints; all we do is just sit with all our energy. That is the sense of "a person's living actions," or *katsuganzei*, when Dōgen says "in each and every living action, there is the sun; there is the moon—that is *carrying out*."

Just as the sun shines during the day and the moon shines at night, everything in its own way vigorously lives out the reality of its life. Each and every thing just acts as a life that is all-inclusive.

> When carrying out is fully implemented, although the *kōan* is totally present, there is no beginning to the kōan, nor has it been continually residing somewhere. Moreover, this *carrying out* is the fundamental prac-tice. Although this is the total *carrying out of good*, there is absolutely no way to measure such good.

"When carrying out is fully implemented" simply means when we are *just doing something*. The key word here, *fully*, or *shōtō* (正當) is not being used in contrast to *not* fully. With not one exception, all of us are, in fact, living out the reality of the life of all/all, whether we think so or not, believe it or not, accept it or not. As an absolute undeniable fact, we are living all inclusively with no connection to whatever scenery takes place our heads. Therefore, there is no such thing as *partially* or *not* fully. Thus, by carrying out actions aiming at all/all, all/all manifests here, right now.

You can think of *kōan* in this passage as meaning "absolute fact" or "truth." This absolute fact is not a thing that can be hidden, nor does it disappear. Neither does it manifest and then die. So it is not something that just began. That is why Dōgen writes, "there is no beginning to the kōan." Still, since we are also living as a conditioned physical body, as one/all, if we aren't careful we begin to act or behave under the control of our self-centered thoughts and emotions.

If ultimate reality were a thing that resided somewhere, even if it weren't enacted, it should still appear. This is the meaning of "nor has it been continuously residing somewhere"; the kōan must be carried out. If we ignore that "this carrying out is the fundamental practice," and just act out of our egotistical whims, we'll fail to act as an all-encompassing self. That is why it is necessary to leave home and practice.[128] Further, if this were just a matter of me as a conditioned individual refraining from doing evil things and improving myself by doing good things, it would be possible to measure and calculate just how much good I have done. However, as long as we are referring to the "total *carrying out of good*," it is never just facing some *other* and then acting. And, because these actions are the actions of moving more deeply into all-over-all (all-encompassing self), there is no way to take measure of such deeds.

Even though the present carrying out is the implementation of vivid actions, there is absolutely no way to calculate their effect. [Alternatively: Though this carrying out is done with a most vivid and alert eye, we cannot measure the accomplishment.] The true Dharma does not manifest in order to be measured. The measure of clear and vivid actions is not the same as calculating human measurement.

Various kinds of good deeds cannot be verified in terms of existing or not existing, nor can they be characterized as taking some form or of having no form, and so forth—there is only *carrying out*.

128. "Home leaving" is the literal meaning of the Chinese characters *shukke* (出家). The term *shukke suru* is the verb and means to "leave the house" of one's conditioned value judgments, etc., and become a monk.

This zazen we do is just a wonder, a mystery, a marvel. We have to aim, but there is no "hitting the mark"! If we are going to talk about facing a wall and hitting the mark, then we are better off going to a pachinko parlor. If one of those balls goes in the right hole—*bingo!* Doing zazen, however, we aim with all our strength to sit properly, but there is never any hitting the mark; there is no mark at all.

A passage from the "Genjō Kōan" fascicle of *Shōbōgenzō* reads, "Even though Dharma fills body and mind sufficiently, there is a feeling of something missing..."[129]; since there is no mark or target, there is a sense of something being not quite satisfactory. What is crucial here is doing and acting with all our strength even with that feeling of insufficiency or incompleteness. We get all confused because we are always trying to fully satisfy ourselves. If there were some way to know that while sitting zazen we had become fully realized, this would amount to a calculating and measureable satisfaction. But then, that's not zazen; that's just thinking going on in our heads, a kind of self-observation. True zazen is just sitting with that feeling of insufficiency.[130] We don't do zazen in order to calculate our realization; we just act, just manifest the present.

The vivid eye—our intrinsic or natural universal identity, that which is from the beginning, all/all—cannot be measured. Even if it were measurable, it couldn't be done with the conditioned eye that sees only as one/all. There is no other way than for your own eye to open naturally. There is no other person[131] who can understand this. The "just aiming"

129. "Genjō Kōan" (現成公案), "The Kōan of the Present Becoming the Present." Here, genjō kōan also implies "absolute truth (the kōan) continually manifesting (*genjō*)."
   Dōgen's words are turning on the expressions *jūsoku* (充足), meaning "completely filled" or "satisfactory," and *tarazu* (たらず) the negative form of "enough" or "sufficient."

130. Alternately: "in a state of not feeling satisfied."

131. "Other person": *yonin* (余人). In the text itself, the term Dōgen used is *yohō* (余法); in this case, *hō* (法) means the same as *nin* (人), or "person." The sense of this peculiar use of "other person" includes our own conditioned self. So, in this case, "other person" is not being set in contrast to oneself; rather, "other person" includes the self of our own individual perceptions, ideas, etc., as well as other people.

Wisdom

WISDOM PUBLICATIONS

Please fill out and return this card if you would like to receive our catalogue and special offers. The postage is already paid!

NAME

ADDRESS

CITY / STATE / ZIP / COUNTRY

EMAIL

Sign up for our newsletter and special offers at wisdompubs.org

Wisdom Publications is a non-profit charitable organization.

BUSINESS REPLY MAIL

FIRST-CLASS MAIL   PERMIT NO. 1100   SOMERVILLE, MA

POSTAGE WILL BE PAID BY ADDRESSEE

WISDOM PUBLICATIONS
199 ELM ST
SOMERVILLE MA 02144-9908

of our universal identity of all/all is entirely different from the discriminating, calculating self of one/all.

In *Shōbōgenzō Zuimonki* as well, there is a passage that goes "As long as we attempt to evaluate and calculate what Buddhadharma is with our thinking mind, there is no way to do it in ten thousand lifetimes... we attain the Way only with the body." It's no good trying to figure out what Buddhadharma is with our thinking mind. All there is is the doing. Sitting at one's desk and contemplating the merging into one realm of subject and object the way so many Zen buffs like to do is utter nonsense. A similar passage in *Instructions to the Cook* reads, "The Way-Seeking Mind of a tenzo is actualized by rolling up your sleeves."[132] In other words, precisely in the midst of getting down to work can we find the so-called oneness of subject and object.

Just as in the case of *refraining* in our text, *carrying out* is also found within the internal structure of all-inclusive self. We might say that just as that fundamental life force in me is "all-inclusive self" facing "all-encompassing depth," these actions get carried out. This is the true life force. Take any weed along the roadside; it grows of its own accord. That's the life force. Therefore, we, too, with the life force we have been given, act while facing in the direction of an all-encompassing depth. This is not something that can be objectively observed as either existing or not existing, as having a form or no form. There is only *carrying out*.

> In whatever place or time good manifests, there will be *carrying out*. In this *carrying out*, all good will manifest. Though this manifestation of *carrying out* is absolute, it neither comes into being nor falls into decay, nor is it subject to the conditions of cause and effect. *Carrying out* in living, in residing, in dying, and so forth, is also like this. When a single act of good is actually being carried out, the true ground of reality and the entire body of all the dharmas is being carried out.

132. Kōshō Uchiyama, *How to Cook Your Life*, 5.

Without raising the issue of time or place, we just act. That is where various good deeds manifest.

Concerning the use of "absolute," let us look at the first character, *kō* (公).[133] The commonly understood definition that can be found in most dictionaries calls this "equalizing that which is unequal (or unjust) is *kō*, 'public.'"[134] However, if the conversation is going to express Buddha-dharma, then it has to be all-embracing. When the world is divided between equal or unequal, just or unjust, then the discussion is of emotional, divisive issues of society in general; it has nothing to do with Buddhadharma. For the discussion to turn to Buddhadharma, it has to begin prior to the division into equal or unequal, just or unjust.

In *Dōgen's Genjō Kōan* we find, "To uphold one's part or position is called *an*." In this case, "to uphold one's part or position" means for every individual to become more fully or naturally him- or herself. The commonly understood definition of *an* (案) is "to investigate or consider deeply."

In *Gokikigakishō* (御聞書抄), *kōan* is footnoted by Senne Zenji as the following: "*Kōan* (公按) as Buddhadharma means upholding the full functioning of unfairness/injustice within oneself. That is, injustice or inequality or unfairness as it is, is the total functioning of the kōan.[135]

133. In the text, Dōgen uses the word kōan (公案) for "absolute."

134. *Kō* can also be understood to mean "official" or "governmental." It also means "to reveal openly to anyone or to do something together with everyone else": hence "public." This definition is the cultural or relative definition of the term, not its religious definition, which Uchiyama Rōshi is explaining in his commentary.

135. Senne Zenji (詮慧禅師), a direct disciple of Dōgen Zenji, wrote a commentary entitled *Shōbōgenzōshō* (正法眼蔵抄), which is the earliest known commentary on *Shōbōgenzō*. Later, Senne's work came to be *Gokikigakishō* (御聞書抄), or more succinctly, *Goshō* (御抄).

In *Dōgen's Genjō Kōan*, Shōhaku Okumura quotes Uchiyama Rōshi, who in turn quotes Senne Zenji on equality and inequality: "In the worldly sense, *Goshō* defines *kōan* as 'equalize inequality' and 'keep one's position.' When we speak of *Buddha dharma* beyond comparison and dichotomy, where is the boundary between equality and inequality? Actually, there is no such distinction. Therefore, the true meaning of 'public' is the

This is the meaning behind the idea expressed in Dōgen's words "my eyes are horizontal, my nose is vertical": *gannō bichoku* (眼横鼻直).

Dōgen's expression about eyes and nose being horizontal and vertical respectively is simply an abbreviated way of saying that all things function in their own position. And, moreover, that in itself is equality or the balance of all things. Here, there is no line drawn between "level," "just," "balanced," etc., and their opposites, "askew," "unjust," or "unbalanced." Not level is at the same time level. It surely is no good for an eye to act like a nose. Each and every part, by functioning as it naturally functions, is protecting and maintaining its position. Here, there is true settlement without any comparison to anything else. I, just being myself, am what is crucial here. There has to be a sense of resolving to do what we intuitively feel is most vital and what we need to be doing, whether anyone recognizes us for it or not. It is when we carry out actions that are total—the kind of actions that connect with all things in the universe—that cause and effect or arising and decaying have no bearing.

"In living, in residing, in dying, and so forth" in a sense refers to one's starting point and subsequent actions. It is said that in the beginning one enters the Dharma; then, for a while, one resides, refining and deepening one's practice and, finally, goes beyond and leaves to teach others. But this living, residing, and dying are carried out without comparing oneself to others; the carrying out is all kōan.

Looking around these days, too many parents begin by choosing the "best" kindergarten in order to get their children into the "best" elementary school. And, a few years later, just to get the "best" job, young people compete to get into the "best" college or university. Then, those young people, thinking ahead about their retirement, look for the "best"

'not-two-ness' of equality and inequality. What is the 'position' when we say to keep one's position? Originally, there is no such fixed position. *An* is beyond such boundaries." Shōhaku Okumura, et al., *Dōgen's Genjō Kōan: Three Commentaries* (Berkeley, CA: Counterpoint, 2011), 151.

pension plan; and for that, they try to get into a top company. And finally, they retire—to get buried in the finest of cemeteries!

In other words, *this* living, residing, and dying is constantly being weighed against some fictional "other." So, why wouldn't it follow that people run around behaving like hungry ghosts[136] way past their prime without ever truly having become adults. A while ago, I was asked to speak at a gathering of a local parent-teacher association. Ultimately, the only concern of most of the people there seemed to be how their child would fare against all the "other" kids. They couldn't seem to shake off that mentality. With that kind of attitude prevailing in our society today, there is just no way to encounter Buddhadharma. Still, I think there were quite a few people there who did understand what I was saying, so I will keep on. If just hearing about a life without comparing means such an atmosphere can come about among families, and then in the society at large, that atmosphere will get passed on. Recently, I visited the new Antaiji monastery in Kutoyama in Hyogo Prefecture after quite some time. I could hardly believe how many of my own disciples were there. After all is said and done, just *carrying out* is what is truly important.

> When a single act of good is actually being carried out, the true ground of reality and the entire body of all the dharmas is being carried out. The cause and effect of this singular good act is the same as manifesting the kōan. It is a mistake to think that cause comes first followed by effect; cause is complete in itself; effect is complete in itself. The cause is incomparable; the dharma [as an action] is incomparable. The effect is incomparable; the dharma [as an action of phenomenon] is incomparable. Depending on the cause we can surmise the effect. Still, we cannot say that cause comes first and then comes the effect, because the cause is complete as it is and the effect is complete in itself.

136. In Japanese, the word is *gaki* (餓鬼), a Buddhist term often translated as "hungry ghost." The gaki is a demon-like person incapable of ever being satiated. The image often depicts a figure with a very narrow throat incapable of taking in enough and a bloated stomach.

In *Shōbōgenzō* "Genjō Kōan," Dōgen writes, "Penetrating fully and completely a single dharma, the totality of that dharma functions freely. Encountering a single practice is to carry out that practice with all one's effort." When I was assigned to be the cook at the monastery, I threw all my attention and energy into doing just that. When I am speaking to those who have come to sit zazen, I put all my effort into that. This is because I speak as a self that has no other opposing it, it is a self that is all-encompassing and includes all the dharmas, all times, and all realms and lands. My world is changing from one place to the next. So, when I say "just doing" or "just carrying out," I'm saying that I am acting out or carrying out all of my worlds simultaneously.

In this way, through the present *carrying out* as absolute and undeniable reality, the cause of good brings about a result of good; both cause and effect are present. However, this cause-and-effect is not a matter of chronology: a past cause bringing about a present effect, and that in turn becoming the cause for some future effect. All worlds are simultaneously being carried out; therefore, my actions are inclusive of the cause and the effect. So, practice embraces both cause and effect; it is an indwelling or internal cause and effect. Moreover, in Mahāyāna Buddhism, cause is *just what it is* and effect is *just what it is*—there is nothing outside of me as the true reality of life.[137]

Both cause and effect are just what they are, therefore Dōgen writes, "Cause is complete in itself; effect is complete in itself." In my own words, I have been expressing this idea by saying, "Being pulled by the incomparable gravity that fills the whole universe, there is only carrying out actions that embrace the entire universe."[138]

137. That is, there is no living entity that exists independently of ourselves. "Just what it is" is a translation of *shohō jissō*.

138. In other words, concretely speaking, Buddhist practice is nothing other than carrying out actions that are universal.

Let go of ideas of *jiko* and just act.

V.

Clarifying this mind of [one's] total self: *refraining* is self, *refraining* is clarifying, *self* is present as this, *self* is mind, *refraining* is this, *refraining* is mind, *carrying out* manifests mind, *carrying out* manifests clarifying, *carrying out* is this, *carrying out* expresses self. That is why it is said to be the teaching of all the buddhas.

In the *Dhammapada*, it is written that "The ground of self is self alone." Only a well-arranged, well-adjusted self can be relied on. There is no person to depend on other than oneself. It's just that, in this case, "oneself" isn't the same as the "I" that we go around holding onto as our self. Our true foundation, which we can rely on, is the well-arranged and well-adjusted jiko. So, what is the issue here with "well-arranged, well-adjusted?"

If I may state the conclusion first, "well-arranged, well-adjusted" is nothing other than the samadhi of freely receiving and functioning (*jijuyū zanmai*). Just carrying out that samadhi is the sense of "well-arranged, well-adjusted."

This is the same sense as "clarifying" (*jō*, 淨) in our text. In Japanese, to speak of *jō*, which can be understood as "refreshed," one might think of achieving some level of being refreshed and clear, but that would be a mistake. One's total self becoming more fully one's total self (jiko) lies in just facing the depth and clarity that is here. Just how *deep* we can go, or just how *clear* we can become, is not something that can be measured. It is a depth that is incalculable, a clarity that is immeasurable. "Clarifying" here is not a clarity or freshness that one can catch a glimpse of, thinking, "Oh, I just feel so clear and clean and ready to go." Nor is it a sense of "Oh, little by little, I'm beginning to feel clear all over." "Clarifying this mind of [one's] total self" is to just be and do right now. It is self of all/all aiming at just being and doing self that is all/all. It takes a certain amount of time to actually say the phrase "clarifying this mind of [one's] total self," but actually doing it has no length of time. There is no chronological hierarchy. And, in order to express just that, Dōgen Zenji wrote, so carefully and conscientiously, "*refraining* is self, *refraining* is clarifying, *self* is present as this, *self* is mind, *refraining* is this, *refraining* is mind, *carrying out* manifests mind, *carrying out* manifests clarifying, *carrying out* is this, *carrying out* expresses self." In refraining, there is self; in refraining there is clarifying.

Here, too, clarifying that is clear or clean or pure is not set in opposition to something sullied or polluted as in thoughts of greed, anger, or ignorance.[139] In the *Heart Sūtra*, it is written "no defilement, no purity, nothing added, nothing taken away"; transcending what is perceived as "pure" or "defiled" is what is truly pure or clear.[140] The "self" of "*self* is present as this" in the passage is not a "self" set in opposition to "other"; it is the all-inclusive, all-comprehensive self. Moreover, the "this" here is not a "this" that is pointing at anything. Also, the "mind" of "*self* is mind" is not referring to perceived consciousness. In just acting, or being, there is self, there is clarifying, there is this, and there is mind.

Now, this "just doing," "just being" I have mentioned—or this "just refraining," "just carrying out" without any comparison—is *musō* (無相), "without form." In our everyday world, we often think in terms of wife in contrast to husband, child as opposed to father, superior above subordinate, customer in opposition to salesman. It is a world of form, one balanced against another.

> It is like the various buddhas and numerous heavenly beings; although there are both similarities and dissimilarities between them, those heavenly beings are not the same as the various buddhas. Or, it can be compared to

---

139. *Ku* (垢). This character is sometimes used to translate the Sanskrit word *klesha*.

140. Anyone who just sits zazen experiences that thoughts have no substance and have nothing to do with just sitting.

the buddhas and *cakravartin*; there are similarities, but not all benevolent secular rulers are the same as the various buddhas. You need to carefully and thoroughly examine these principles.

The "heavenly beings" here is a reference to Shiva in the Hindu teachings. Normally, heavenly beings are depicted as having three eyes, eight arms, and three bodies. In that sense, they are similar to the three bodies that the various buddhas have.[141] However, the three bodies of the heavenly beings have a fixed appearance. That is, they have a form. On the other hand, the features or appearance of the three bodies of the buddha vary with the buddha. Therefore, they have no fixed form. In the *Diamond Sūtra* it is written, "If you see no form among the various forms, you have seen a *nyorai*, a perfect one," and "To separate from all forms, that is what is called 'various buddhas.'"

In our everyday world, we call this a blackboard, that a wall; for all things, we see a form or appearance. Yet all these forms have no fixed form. Take the pine tree in the garden, for example. An ant probably doesn't see a pine tree at all; it most likely thinks that it's just a very long pole to climb. And when the ant finally arrives near the top, it walks around and thinks there just might be something worth eating at the tip of that branch. Or, if we look down from some high altitude, no matter how large the pine tree might be, it probably looks like some mold on the surface of the earth.

It is said that a cakravartin, a kind of benevolent ruler, bears thirty-two marks. A buddha is also said to bear thirty-two marks; however, the

---

141. The three bodies (*trikāya*) of a buddha are (1) Dharma body (Jpn: *hosshin* 法身; Skt: *dharmakāya*) or "truth body," with no limits; (2) bliss body (Jpn: *hōjin* 報身; Skt: *sambhogakāya*) or an enlightened one who gladly receives from others and gladly teaches others (Amida Buddha and the Medicine Buddha are examples of this body); and (3) human body (Jpn: ōjin 応身; Skt: *nirmāṇakāya*) or body that manifests according to the situation and time.

difference is that the marks of the cakravartin are said to be visible,[142] whereas the buddha's forms have no form; they are *musō*. Here, the meaning of *musō*, in addition to "being formless," is that there is nothing in opposition. So, what is important is that a buddha acts not with form, but formlessly, with no visible form.

To the extent that we do anything, we take a form or posture. For example, we're sitting on a train, and an elderly person gets on. We stand up and give the person our seat. We have taken the posture of having given someone our seat. However, to be conscious of the other person's eyes looking at that seat, then becoming conscious of doing one's "good" deed for the day, and then saying, "Please, take *my* seat," is very different from *just doing*—that is, just getting up and saying, "Please, sit down." Just as there is a form in giving someone one's seat, the *way* of doing it should take no form; it has to be formless.

> Although there are those who never examine the meaning of "all the buddhas" though seemingly making extraordinary effort, their useless suffering is just that of ordinary beings; it has nothing to do with practicing the Buddha Way.

In the *Diamond Sūtra* we can find these words, "In truth, as Buddhadharma, a nyorai, a perfect one, does not gain supreme perfect enlightenment." "Supreme perfect enlightenment" is another way of saying satori; even the Buddha did not *gain* satori. There is yet another passage in the sūtra that reads, "I have never gained perfect supreme enlightenment or even a little of the Buddhadharma. This is what is called perfect supreme enlightenment."

In other words, a true buddha is without form. Those who are unaware of this and strive with all their effort to grasp onto some satori that takes a form, and then boast that "Oh, I've gotten satori!" have nothing to do with Buddhadharma.

142. *Usō* (有相).

Refraining and *carrying out* are like the horse arriving before the donkey has left.

The donkey symbolizes delusion (mayoi), while the horse symbolizes enlightenment (satori). It's a mistake to think that only after you have eliminated the various evils (i.e., all delusions), then, for the first time, will enlightenment arrive. *Refraining from various evils* or unwholesomeness and *carrying out good deeds* mean that when we let go of our egotism, a deed that is totally all/all is already manifesting itself. The satori of the true reality of life is just that. I'm afraid I'm repeating myself, but to blow away all delusion and aim at bagging satori—"Oh, I can see the light now!"—is no good at all. How we can let go of "myself" and just act here and now—that is all there is for us to do.

The heart of the matter: although a three-year-old child can express it, it's very difficult for even an eighty-year-old to carry it out.

VI.

Haku Kyoi of the Tang dynasty was a lay disciple of Bukkō Nyoman, in the lineage of Baso Dōitsu. When he was a high government official in Hangzhou Province, he called on Dōrin Chōka. During their talk, Kyoi asked, "What is the gist of Buddhadharma?" Dōrin replied, "Refrain from committing various evils and carry out all sorts of good actions." Kyoi responded, "If that were the case, even a three-year-old child could say that." Dōrin replied, "Although a three-year-old child may be able to express it, not even an eighty-year-old can actually carry it out." Hearing the reply, Kyoi, thanked him gratefully, bowed and left.

In fact, though Kyoi was a descendent of General Haku, he was a poet, unparalleled over several generations. It is said that he was reborn twenty-four times, each time becoming an increasingly adept poet. He was sometimes referred to as the Mañjuśrī of literati or the Maitreya of poets. There was no one who had not heard of his poetic artistry. The influence of his verse spread everywhere. However, when it came to the Buddha Way, he was just a beginner and was not yet mature. In regard to *refraining from various evils* or *carrying out acts of good*, he couldn't have understood what was behind such an expression, even in a dream. Kyoi probably speculated that Dōrin earnestly encouraged people to *refrain from various evils* and *carry out acts of goodness* at the conscious level. He was totally unaware and never heard of the universal truth for all ages, of the Buddha Way from ancient times up to our own time, in regard to *refraining from evil* and *carrying out good*. He most likely said such a thing because he did not have the virtue of having yet learned Buddhadharma, nor had he ever stepped into a place where the Dharma was actually practiced. Make no mistake, even if we are cautioned to intentionally avoid various evils and, with every intention, encouraged to carry out good deeds, the actuality takes place in absolute refraining.

Although Haku Kyoi came from a long bloodline of military men and was known as a truly great poet, when it came to the Buddha Way, he was just a beginner. He probably just thought that Dōrin was simply saying "be good and don't do bad things" as some sort of moral or ethical admonition. However, *refrain from various evils* and *carry out acts of good* as a teaching of Buddhadharma has nothing to do with ethics or morality or being "good" in the social sense. Buddhadharma has nothing to do with the absolute life of jiko facing outward and deliberately choosing to do so-called "good" or "evil." Rather, as an all-comprehensive jiko without any comparing of self and other, *refraining from various evils* and *carrying out acts of good* is the internal structure of the actuality of the life force.[143]

143. Without a doubt, this is one of the most important passages of Uchiyama Rōshi's argument about good and evil. It is almost out of habit that people relegate discussions of good and evil to the realm of ethics or morality. But this is exactly where Buddhist practitioners must delve more deeply into the teaching of Buddhadharma. Rōshi's statement is not meant to dismiss egregious misbehavior on the part of various teachers in

In the very beginning of this chapter, we read, "it is the internal and direct transmission." Here, it refers to all-comprehensive self. In other words, although the text indicates, "Refraining from committing various evils / carrying out all sorts of good / personally clarifying this mind / this is the essential teaching of all the buddhas" has been transmitted by the ancestors and received by the disciples, this doesn't mean that the gāthā has been transmitted and received. Vipassī Buddha himself, as the completed internal structure of all-encompassing self, transmitted and received *refraining from evil, carrying out good* within himself. Likewise, Śākyamuni Buddha himself, as the completed internal structure of all-encompassing self, transmitted and received *refraining from evil, carrying out good*. That is the meaning of "it is the internal and direct transmission" and is the basis of this whole fascicle. That is the sense of what is being talked about in this fascicle as *refraining from evil*, of *carrying out good*, of *personally clarifying the significance of this*, and of *this is the essential teaching of all the buddhas*. This is the true teaching and the actual Path of the seven buddhas, and necessarily includes that truth and that practice, to rephrase Dōgen.

Despite that, Kyoi dismissed Dōrin's teaching lightly by saying even a three-year-old child could say that. He said that because he was totally ignorant of the foundation of life in the teaching of Buddhadharma. Buddhadharma is fundamentally different from a society in which people run around constantly comparing themselves with others. The teaching of Buddhadharma is entirely one of a self that is all-comprehensive. So, if we are going to study and learn about Buddhadharma, then we need to understand its foundation.

---

many different so-called religious organizations—or on the part of anyone else who claims to have surpassed "good" and "bad." However, Uchiyama is trying to encourage those for whom acting morally is just common sense. And then, beyond that, as practitioners of Buddhadharma, we have to consider the meaning of good and evil on a deeper, internal level.

The Buddha Way is the gate of repose and quiet joy.

VII.

In every respect, Buddhadharma heard for the first time from a wise teacher or heard many years later as a result of authentic practice will be the same. This is called "right from the beginning, right at the end," or, "subtle cause, subtle effect." It is also referred to as "buddha cause, buddha effect."

Usually, it is in my nature to poke fun at or belittle the various things I see going on around me. And yet, somehow, the more I study and practice Buddhadharma, the more impressed I become regarding how wonderful it is. I find it incredible that this teaching of Buddhadharma pursues the ultimate truth of human life. Perhaps it is because there has been a continuation of the pursuit of the truth of human life in all its facets, beginning with Śākyamuni Buddha in India, and then carrying on with other magnificent people, spreading to China and Japan and elsewhere.

Further, from the first time one hears Buddhadharma to the latest time, the contents never change; the teachings are always the same. Take *refraining from evil* and *carrying out good* for example—nothing changes. That goes for the very ultimate point in human life, as well.

Whatever path we take, it is fundamentally all our own life. So when we speak of not taking something that doesn't belong to us, for instance, we keep in mind that there is in fact nothing to steal at all. Thinking that there exists something that we can steal, and then going and taking that thing, is a double mistake. To secrete the thought in one's head that there is something to steal defiles all-comprehensive self, wherein fundamentally there is nothing to steal. And then to actually go ahead and try to carry out such a deed is to defile a second time one's fundamental self, whose nature is pure and clear, without any blemish. In other words, in all senses of the expression "don't steal," self strives not to defile itself. Self, taking best care of self, is the sense of "personally clarifying the significance of this."

In the text, the Japanese for "right from the beginning, right at the end" is *zushin bishin*, which means literally that if the head is right, the tail will be right; if something is correct from the beginning, it will be correct at the end, too. Also, the sense of "subtle" in the expression "subtle cause, subtle effect" (*myōin myōka*) is that all interpretation or explanation is beyond human speculation or common sense.

All causes and effects that lie outside human speculation or common sense are, ultimately, shohō jissō: all dharmas are what or just as they are, the reality of life prior to or before any comparison with "other," the very life force of original self—that is the meaning of "subtle cause, subtle effect." Finally, "buddha cause, buddha effect" means that Buddha is the living out of cause and effect as all things just as they are.

Taking a closer look at shohō jissō or "all things are just as they are," or in my own words, the true reality of life, we find this passage in the *Diamond Sūtra* that reads, "The true form is without form." We project a form or appearance every time we draw a comparison with something "other"—"child" as opposed to the figure of "parent," "wife" as opposed to the figure of "husband," "superior" as opposed to the figure or appearance of "subordinate." These are all figures or forms or appearances. Having said that, whichever way we fall in our lives, there is no figure, no form, and no appearance to all-comprehensive self. There is no act that intentionally carries out an action based on balancing something in opposition. All there really is, is just doing. Where the "true form" or "true appearance" is without any form or appearance is what is behind "buddha cause, buddha effect."

Since the cause and effect of practicing the Buddha Way, however, are not like the concepts of *ijuku* or *tōru*, if the cause is not based on true reality, then an effect of corresponding quality cannot be expected. Being well grounded in the Buddhadharma, Dōrin was able to express the truth in this way.

Some people say that someone who likes to kill living things will eventually grow physically weaker and weaker. There is even an expression that goes "To one who kills eels and birds for a living will a child with bad eyes be born." I suppose there may be some aspect of truth to that; it may occur at some level where we simply cannot understand the complicated connections of cause and effect. Another example of *tōru*, the notion that the character of an effect is the same as the character of its cause, might be that of a person who eats lots of rich pork cutlet, sleeps well, and gets fat. Such a person could very well put on weight and get fat. However, cause and effect in practicing the Buddha Way are very different from cause and effect defined by ijuku or tōru.

By nature, we are all living out the reality of the life force. Therefore, if we act accordingly, that is, in accord with that life force, then the truth of that life force will manifest. That is cause and effect in practicing the Buddha Way. It's not like thinking, "I'm just an ordinary person, but if I practice very hard and somehow 'get' satori, I'll become a famous teacher." If you've already decided that you are just a dolt, then no matter what you do, you'll still be a dolt. Honestly and without exception, you, me, all of us are, by nature, living out the reality of the life force. So, what is most critical here is that we follow in accord with that living reality through our actions—just that. Just doing that—how can there be anything so easy! People keep thinking about what they can do to make more of a profit, or they ponder over how they can look important or distinguished to others, or they worry over how they can catch that girl's eye—it's no wonder everyone gets so tired! Not putting one's energies into such nonsense and taking care of what is right in front of our eyes—just doing that—is enough. Practicing the Buddha Way is just doing that, and that's why it is called the "gate of repose and quiet joy."

Dōrin Zenji understood that truth and that is why he spoke the Buddhadharma the way he did.

The most fundamental way to resolve the evils in society is by just cleaning up your own self.

> Even if all spheres were to be totally engulfed by evil or all dharmas entirely swallowed up, *refraining* remains the liberating factor.

Even if all across the world evil were to swallow up everything and spread everywhere—and today it certainly seems that wherever we look all we see is evil or corruption in government and politics, economic inequalities, education—"*refraining* remains the liberating factor." What does that mean?

"Hey, look over here! I'm Kōshō Uchiyama, and I'm going to get rid of the evil and corruption that's pervading everywhere." Sure sounds bold and resolute, but what does it amount to? Nothing. Looking outside yourself is nothing more than acting out your life as one/all—one person in opposition to the whole world.

Among my younger disciples, there are a few who feel that they can't just sit around doing nothing. This makes sense: a young person with no temple connections who actually aspires to become a priest usually comes here with a strong sense of justice. So, when something comes up about discrimination, they get all fired up and want to jump into the fray. One wants to do work to help people who are physically handicapped, so they leave the temple. Another one wants to leave to go live in one of the historically impoverished areas of Osaka, "if just to save even one person." I usually tell people like that to forget about it. But why do I say that?

More than anything else, the teaching of Buddhism is about cleaning up one's own life—that is the foundation of the Buddhadharma. For the most part, all societies are made up of groups of people who themselves are not settled and are ready to get into the mix at the drop of a hat; once you set out to correct something in society, you're very likely to just get dragged into the vortex and swallowed up by all the troubles.

The fundamental teaching of Buddhadharma is becoming a true adult.

To put it another way, we must straighten out our own lives first. I frankly believe the most fundamental way to resolve all the evils and sufferings going on around the world, or the social ills facing mankind, is nothing other than for there to be just one more human being straightening out his or her own life.

Sawaki Rōshi used to say that the reason or cause for which a system or organization forms itself is the same one that causes that system or organization to fall apart. It isn't a single system or organization doing any particular thing that is critical, but rather that each and every person just acts in the most honest and straightforward way. Rōshi used to put it this way: "It is just like the way a chicken picks up a grain of rice one at a time." Each person acting in that same upright way will pick up another "grain." I firmly believe that Rōshi's words resonate well, and it is my hope to abide by those words myself and to pass them on directly.

Even for those of you who come here every month to hear these talks, there is no "membership." Those who want to come, come. There is nothing that says you are required to be here. Usually, when people set up some sort of function or event, they'll establish a membership fee and pass out membership cards. That's not so difficult to do and you can usually get plenty of people to join. It's the same as paying an entrance fee in order to get in the movie theater. Since you've paid the fee, even if the movie isn't very interesting, you'll most likely stay until the end. But if the talk here isn't any good, folks will just get up and leave. A membership fee has the power to bind people. But binding people, what good is that? It's a big mistake.

During the days when I was the abbot at Antaiji, sometimes prominent or influential companies would send someone to ask if their employees could come for training, but I always turned them down. The reason I turned them down was that there would always be several people among them who would come not because they wanted to do zazen but because they were getting paid to come as part of their training. Such people would just have been a nuisance. To be clear, I never said that working people from companies were unwelcome; it's just that I wanted them to come as single "grains." I only wanted people to come to Antaiji who truly wanted to sit zazen.

During Dōgen Zenji's period as well, here and there, there were volcanic eruptions and continued poor harvests. It was also recorded that piles of dead bodies, victims of starvation, could be seen all along the dry bed of the Kamo River. Even during those times, Dōgen Zenji is said to have continued sitting zazen.

There's even a related story about the Buddha, Śākyamuni:

In India, the Śākya clan was said to have been a very good bloodline. However, the people of their very powerful neighboring country, the Shae, were said to have come from very humble origins.

It appears that King Hashinoku of the Shae clan came up with a plan of improving the clan's bloodline by somehow marrying a princess of the Śākya clan. However, King Śuddhodana of the Śākya clan did not want to have any daughter of his line marry into such a humble bloodline. But if he were to refuse, there was a very good chance that the entire Śākya clan could have been wiped out by their powerful neighbors. So, having little choice, he had the female offspring of a member of his family and a maidservant sent to the Shae clan. King Hashinoku, assuming that the woman who arrived was a princess of very good blood, welcomed her as his first wife. Eventually, the couple had a male child whom they named Ruri.

One day, when Prince Ruri was a little boy visiting his mother's home in Kapilavastu, the capital of the Śākya clan, an unfortunate incident came about. When certain members in the Śākya clan noticed the boy playing at the very top of the highest altar in the sacred hall of the clan, they scolded him severely and threw him out. Prince Ruri, thinking himself to be the prince of a great clan and, on top of that, deigning to visit his mother's birthplace, couldn't understand why he had been thrown out. So, Prince Ruri's attendant, a man named Kokubonshi, spilled the beans to the boy: "Your mother was nothing more than a maidservant in the Śākya clan." Now, for those people born into a royal or aristocratic family, they live off their pride, so if that pride somehow gets stepped on, all hell can break loose. On hearing what Kokubonshi had to say, Prince Ruri vowed to himself that when he got older he would take revenge on this insult and destroy the Śākya clan. And, from then on, he ardently practiced the martial arts, as well as military strategies and tactics. Eventually, Prince Ruri became an adult and, pushing his father out, anointed himself as king. Finally, the golden opportunity of overthrowing the Śākya clan arrived and, gathering up a huge army, Prince Ruri set out to attack Kapilavastu.

By that time, most of the best young soldiers in the clan had become disciples of the Buddha, leaving very few capable men to protect Kapilavastu. Facing the certainty that, if attacked, Kapilavastu would surely fall, attendants were sent to where Śākyamuni was staying, pleading with him for help. Listening to their pleas, he found a half-dead tree alongside the road that the advancing troops of the Shaes would have to pass. And there, he sat down in zazen, waiting for the enemy troops to pass by.

King Ruri, leading the Shae's forces, happened to glance down at the side of the road and noticed Śākyamuni sitting there. The king got off his horse, greeted Śākyamuni, and asked him, "Why are you sitting under this dying tree?" The Buddha replied, "Oh, King! Even though it may be dying, it is cool here in the shadow of one's home." King Ruri sensed what was behind Śākyamuni's words and reluctantly gave up his bid to attack the Śākya clan.

Then the vindictive attendant, Kokubonshi, again stirred the king to seek revenge. King Ruri set out once again with his forces to capture Kapilavastu. And for a second time, the king was moved by Śākyamuni and retreated with his troops. However, the third time was different. This time King Ruri just ignored Śākyamuni and went on to attack the capital. There, he proceeded to kill all the males in the Śākya clan and returned to his own kingdom with all the women. That evening, looking

off toward the scorched sky and the flames of the burning Kapilavastu,
Śākyamuni said, "Ah, this night my heart feels so heavy."

I read this story many years ago, but I've never forgotten it. Surely,
among the Buddha's disciples, there must have been some who felt that
they should take revenge against the Shae clan. That is just human nature.
However, Śākyamuni bore it all and refused to act. When Sawaki Rōshi
told this story, he commented that if the Buddha had allowed all that
hatred to boil up inside himself and then had taken up arms against King
Ruri, there would be no Buddhism today. It was precisely because he was
not one to get all in a heat like we do so often today, that he created a
cool shady place for us. Normally, our state of mind would be one unable
to hold down those raging feelings of revenge, hatred, or anger. But it
was precisely because Śākyamuni was able to sit still and let go of those
emotions that the true Buddhadharma began.

Looking at the state of affairs in the world today, nothing has changed
from the past; we see human beings continuing to wage war, this "-ism"
clashing with that "-ism," one religion denouncing another. We see frequent droughts, torrential floods, and volcanoes, with scores of people
dying as a result. At times, it even seems that nuclear war is imminent,
an event that could very well destroy the planet. And closer to home,
local politicians and bureaucrats seem to be stuffing their pockets with
bribes. Juvenile delinquents and cadres of loan sharks seem to lurk around
every corner, and we are relentlessly polluting our rivers and oceans. One
can't help but wonder what lies ahead for humankind. But it is just at
these times that if we get dragged about by our narrow ideas of justice
and equality, we become that very person who gets all caught up in the
heat of the times. For those who aim to truly practice Buddhadharma,
there is just no getting up off the seat whatever the circumstance. That is
where we find the depth of Buddhadharma. That is why we sit without
getting unsettled. We are putting ourselves in order. It is being an actual
model of such a way of living, for those who have left home as well as
for those living a lay life, that is so critical.

If I think carefully about just why I became a monk, I believe it was due to the influence of my grandmother who taught me origami when I was a child. She died in 1927 in Kyoto, on the same day as my grandfather on my mother's side died in Tokyo. As my parents were unable to travel to Kyoto when she was dying, my older brother and I were sent to represent the family. When we arrived, my grandmother was on the verge of death. As she had been having difficulty breathing, she had someone call for a priest to come read a sūtra for her. The relatives on that side of our family belonged to the Tendai sect, and as the priest leafed through the sūtra book, chanting for her, I could hear my grandmother say, "Ah, I feel so much better now."

Especially in her final years, my grandmother always seemed very settled to me. I've come to think that elderly people who are always complaining, unlike my grandmother, have little to give to their children or grandchildren. But anyone who in old age strives to straighten out their life by themselves, not just monks or priests, will surely have an influence—even on other children living in the neighborhood. That is why taking care of whatever has to be taken care of in one's life by oneself—that is, being a role model of a true adult—is so very important.

Every person needs to know that whatever illness or unfortunate situation they have fallen into, one has a mission to be a true model of straightening out one's life by oneself. And in order to do that, you have to dig deeper into yourself on a daily basis. This is the way of living out Buddhadharma.

> Since all types of good are always good, the nature, form, substance, and impact of *carrying out* [such deeds] will always be equally good.

As I have said many times, letting go again and again of one's egoism as one/all and carrying out the function of all/all—that is the attitude with which we truly express and manifest the life force of the whole self of jiko. This is the sense of *carrying out good deeds.*

Taking one's eyes off the value of survival and fixing them on a life that lives and dies.

> Kyoi showed no trace of having understood this, hence he said: "*Even a three-year-old child could say that.*" He said such a thing because he personally lacked a deeper understanding of expressing Buddhadharma.

The fact is that a three-year-old child *can* speak Buddhadharma.

So often, human beings who call themselves or think of themselves as adults are nothing more than quasi-adults or even pseudo-adults. They're only adults physically. These quasi-adults merely have a habit of conceptualizing and of following social rules—which society often views as part of "adulthood."

The head priest at one famous temple in Kyoto, for example, and his grown son both appear to be totally consumed with conceptualizing and social rules. I wonder if the basic problem is that each thinks of himself as the very epitome of "head priest." When they were newborn babies, neither father nor son would have nurtured the idea that he was the full embodiment of the sect's high priest. But as they grew into adulthood, little by little, they each began to believe in themselves as coming from a long bloodline of "head priests," that each was indeed the "head priest," even the inheritor of the position of "head priest." What a huge mistake. A three-year-old unsoiled by the conniving and strictures of social rules potentially can certainly speak Buddhadharma to a far greater extent than either of those guys.

However, that isn't what Haku Kyoi meant by his remark; he personally didn't possess a deep-enough understanding of Buddhadharma to speak of Buddhadharma prior to any social norms or rules. Rather he was merely speaking according to the common perception of three-year-olds.

> Poor Kyoi, what are you saying? Since you had never heard of the reality of the Buddha's teachings, how could you know anything about a three-

year-old child? How could you know that a newborn child could speak the truth? If you truly knew what a three-year-old knows, you would know all the buddhas in the three worlds—past, present, and future. Without an understanding of all the buddhas in the three worlds, how could you possibly understand a three-year-old?

Here we come to one of Dōgen Zenji's famous scathing remarks. In Japanese, the sense of this passage is "What the heck can I say, you doofus? You obviously haven't the slightest understanding of Buddhadharma. Since you had never heard a thing of the reality of Buddhadharma prior to words and letters, i.e., prior to language, how could you possibly know anything about the reality of a three-year-old child? If you are a person who knows the true appearance of the reality of the life of a three-year-old prior to language and all the agreed-upon conventions and rules of society, then you will know all the buddhas of past, present, and future. And, conversely, of course, if you truly lack understanding of the buddhas of the three temporal worlds, how could you possibly understand the reality of a three-year-old?"

Never think that you understand someone or something simply because you have encountered them firsthand, nor think that you do not understand someone or something just because you have never met them. Penetrating the minutest particle, you will penetrate all worlds without exception. When you thoroughly comprehend just one dharma, you understand all dharmas. And if you do not understand all the dharmas, you cannot be expected to comprehend even one dharma. When you have thoroughly learned and penetrated one dharma, you will be able to see into all the dharmas and, equally, one single dharma. If you know well even the tiniest particle, you will understand all the worlds without exception. Therefore, it is foolish to think that a three-year-old child cannot speak the truth or to assume that what a three-year-old child says is childish and simple.

There is an expression that describes when one encounters something but fails to see the reality of it: "seeing the appearance without understanding it." For example, you meet a woman and think, "Oh, she's beautiful." But what's beautiful? Her clothing? Her makeup? Either way, you haven't seen the reality of the person. When people go around saying, "Oh, that guy is great," they're usually looking at the person's position or title or degree. That's all.

If you really penetrate to the reality of just one thing, you will understand the reality of all things. One who fails to understand the ten thousand dharmas fails to understand even one. All dharmas work together with and communicate with all other dharmas. Therefore, if a person has a truly thorough knowledge of just one small thing, with no exceptions, he or she has a thorough knowledge of all worlds. The key is looking at the true reality of a thing.

Haku Kyoi didn't have a thorough understanding of the true reality of one small thing; in this case, he had no understanding of a three-year-old child. He thought that three-year-olds were incapable of expressing Buddhadharma, and so he spoke of them disparagingly. That is the very proof that he knew nothing.

> Consequently, for followers of the Buddha, the most crucial matter is clarifying the direct and indirect causes of life/death.

This is actually the opening line of the *Shushōgi*.[144] In my book *A Reader for a Course on Human Life* (*Jinseika Tokuhon*), I wrote about the life force that lives and dies, but many people told me that they couldn't figure it out. As for me, I couldn't figure out why they couldn't figure it out . . .

In ordinary society, if you mention the word "death," lots of people

---

144. *Shushōgi* (修証義), or *The Meaning of Practice and Verification*, is a compilation of excerpts from *Shōbōgenzō*. And this opening line was taken from the fascicle "Shoaku Makusa."

get the feeling that it's bad luck to talk about it, or they go run for the salt.[145] So, I suppose that's why they have difficulty talking about it and avoid looking into it. People today, particularly followers of Buddhism, even when they do bring it up, they seem to have this gloomy way of expressing it. But I don't bring up the subject of death because of some nihilistic or pessimistic view of life. Everything that is, is born, lives, and dies. That's why I bring it up.

People today think only about survival. They think that *just surviving* is a wonderful thing, but that talking about death is unlucky, that it's very inauspicious. Still, averting one's eyes from death, or refusing to talk about it, doesn't change the fact that all of us are inevitably going to die. For example, take those who work for a salary at a big company; they should do so with their eyes wide open, knowing fully that eventually they will have to retire. Could there be anything more foolish than being handed your notice of dismissal and saying, "Oh, I never gave a thought about ever retiring. What'll I do now?" I've seen many actual cases like this, and I've always been stumped as to why. The other day I was reading in the newspaper about a guy who wrote, "Despite the fact that I've worked all my life for the sake of the company, I assumed that when retirement came around, the executives and top management would surely keep me on for several more years, but when the day came and I was given notice on a single sheet of paper that I needn't come in anymore, I was totally shocked." This guy actually got off lightly with just being shocked. There are others who have written notes saying "The company is forever!" and then committed suicide. Everything in ordinary society eventually comes to an end.

The other day I had a guest who asked, "They say that mankind will eventually die. What do you think?" I was shocked that he was shocked when I replied, "Of course, everyone knows that." I mean, what is there

---

145. In Japan, it is customary to throw a bit of salt over the shoulders of someone who has just come home from attending a funeral. Salt is said to purify.

to be shocked about? It's only a matter of time before the earth and our solar system will die out. How could anyone be so foolish to think that even if our solar system does die off, mankind will surely survive? And yet people set aside a truth that is so obviously evident and run around full-steam, working to preserve the survival of their own ego. According to current scientific theories, mankind should be safe from solar extinction for another several million or billion years. But even the scientists who talk about that never seem to touch on the undeniable fact that human-kind will eventually fall. Even if humankind did survive for several billion more years, there can be no doubt that, at some point, human beings will die off. And for all anyone knows, the end of the earth may come much sooner than we imagine. There is just no proof or guarantee otherwise.

Of course, the same holds true for any human being. You might live to be one hundred years old or you could die tomorrow. But even if you were to live to a hundred, without any doubt, your day of death would come. That is why it is essential to absorb that fact and then reflect on how to live right now. For a long time, people have held the impression that a person's death is something sad or sorrowful. If you cling to the view that human beings can exist forever, then death might very well be seen as something sorrowful. However, if your understanding is that dying is a natural thing, then death is reasonable and obvious.

If you lose sight of the naturalness of your own death and fail to look carefully into who you truly are, then there is no way you will understand human life. Not seeing death as natural, and living only to survive, is nothing more than a skill for getting on in the world. What I want to emphasize is not developing some skill for "success," but rather how to walk one's own true life.

In so many homes today, a child is born and parents work to raise the child in a healthy way. Then they put them in a good school and, after school, special classes so they will eventually get into the best university, and so forth. Parents tend to hold these values as being the most impor-tant. Some parents almost religiously plead with their children to study hard—what nonsense. There's no need to force studying on a child who just isn't into it. Many of my disciples are quite promising; from the time they were in high school, they looked around at most of the colleges and universities and realized how ridiculous they all were. They figured that they would be better off becoming monks and came to Antaiji.

Thinking that your child is especially gifted just because he or she comes home with a good report card is the same as thinking that a goldenrod is the same as a redwood tree. A young redwood sapling will grow perhaps a very small amount a year. A goldenrod will sprout in the spring, and by summer it will have grown over two meters. But by fall, there's no trace left of the goldenrod at all! Parents today just seem so foolish, putting all their effort into raising goldenrods! The next generation will be a whole generation of goldenrods, and the redwood saplings will all get trampled underfoot. My whole intention here at Antaiji is to have an environment where I can raise redwoods that will someday become truly valuable trees.

Giant trees just won't grow if you don't give them lots of time to do so. I was just a novice monk until I was fifty-five years old. Even Sawaki Rōshi was fifty-six before he became a teacher at Komazawa University (駒澤大学) and became known by so many people. I believe that the world is going to need more people who are strong, who have resolved that to be a novice at least into one's fifties is just common sense. Of course, I'll be long gone by then. Do what you like! (I'm afraid if I get too indignant and lament over the times we're in, people will just think I'm a grumpy old man and ignore me.)

What it comes down to is a matter of people's sense of values. It is useless to think that muscling one's children into an elite educational path is what's most worthwhile. And to spend your life thinking that you'll be around for another several hundred million years simply because humankind might be is clearly the epitome of foolishness.[146]

146. The word Uchiyama Rōshi used to talk of the fool here is *chigu* (痴愚). Both

> The ancient buddhas have said that, at birth, all are born as lions. Here, a lion refers to the power of a *tathāgata* to turn the wheel of Dharma; it *is* the actual turning of the wheel.

From the moment I gave out my first cry as a newborn baby, I have been living out the true reality of life. That is why it is said Śākyamuni took seven steps in the four directions and declared, "In heaven or on earth, I alone am the most precious." What he meant by this is that a single universe of all/all had been born. There are some foolish people who say that this passage shows how arrogant Śākyamuni was, but such a complaint just shows that they themselves are only looking from the view of one/all.

To receive life into this world as myself occurs just one time in several hundred years. Well, actually, the truth is that I am the only human being to appear as "me" in all eternity. To appraise yourself as just being very inconsequential and to perceive yourself as merely one human being among all humanity (one/all) is no good. Because you have been born as a human being, you need to live that life with the sense of also being all/all, all-inclusive life.

> Further, another ancient one has said, "Everything that arises in our life/death is the true form of the most fundamental Self." Therefore, clarifying the true form of our most fundamental Self with the resonance of a lion cub's roar is the most crucial matter. So it is not a simple thing to be taken lightly.

No matter what befalls us, our highest priority, our highest value, needs to be living out the full and true reality of life.

Dōgen and Uchiyama use it when they are talking about themselves personally, or human beings in general, as not being adults.

To clarify the actions that underlie a three-year-old child is to clarify the actions of all the buddhas, because they are not necessarily different. Since it had never even crossed his mind that a three-year-old child could voice Buddhadharma, Kyoi foolishly said what he did.

In *Shiki*, Zakke Benkai poses "they are not necessarily different" as a question: "How would those actions be different?"[147] And in *Benchu*, Tenkei Denson has "It might be better to say 'since there are no differences.'"[148] After all, the actions of the very life force of a three-year-old, free of any habits or mannerisms, is not any different from that of all the buddhas in the three worlds. However, Haku Kyoi, without it even crossing his mind that there could be anything like speaking Buddhadharma prior to social customs and norms, blurts out, "Well, if that's the case, even a three-year-old can say that."

Dōrin's Dharma-voice was louder and clearer than a roll of thunder. Even if a three-year-old child could not say the same thing, it is said that a three-year-old child expresses Dharma. Kyoi never heard the child roar like a lion cub and totally misheard Dōrin's turning of the wheel. How can we not continually feel the compassion of Master Dōrin's "Even though a three-year-old child may express the Dharma, not even an eighty-year-old can carry it out." We must winnow through and practice very carefully that such a mind is an expression of the truth said by a three-year-old. And, we must equally winnow through and practice the truth of an eighty-year-old being unable to carry it out. Trusting the Dharma-words of a three-year-old does not mean that everything such a child might say is Dharma-words. Though an old man may not be able to carry out those

147. *Shōbōgenzō Shiki* (正法眼蔵私記) is a commentary on this passage by Zakke Benkai, also known as Zōkai Zenji (蔵海, 1730–88). He lived during the Tokugawa period in Kyushu (today's Oita Prefecture) and wrote *Shiki* toward the end of his life.

148. *Shōbōgenzō Benchū* (正法眼蔵辨注) was written about 1727–29 by Tenkei Denson (天桂传尊, 1648–1735), a Tokugawa scholar of Sōtō Zen.

words, *how* is one unable to carry them out? In this way, based on practice, we must winnow through just what Buddhadharma is; understand it and express it as fully and clearly as we can.

Right here, right now, a three year-year-old child is living the truth of life. The internal structure of the life of that child is living out the life of *refraining from various evils, carrying out all sorts of good*, and *personally clarifying* the significance of that. Therefore, even if the child can't put it into words, he or she is already expressing it. Now, as time goes on, that child learns language, becomes a social person, and begins to live within the strictures of social customs and values. I don't want to suggest that we shouldn't become a part of the social world. To whatever extent we live as a social being, we do need to know those social customs and agreements, etc. We certainly can't live our whole life as a child.

However, as the child grows and begins to live as a social being, before becoming aware of it, he or she develops the habit of absorbing the various words and signs one has learned and memorized as generalizations or concepts, ultimately losing sight of the true reality of things. But as adolescents begin to enter adulthood, doubt, as well as ambition, begins to well up regarding just what the correct way to live one's life is. The young person makes every effort in his or her search for the right direction, but unfortunately, there is no teacher around to give the young person truly good advice. As time goes by, the man or woman gets tangled up in a tough world and, before one knows it, decides to live just feeding one's egoism as one/all—one among all human beings. And, in the end, even as an eighty-year-old, he or she becomes unable to carry out the words of the gāthā.

On the one hand, even though a small child is surely like a lion cub, that doesn't mean that it is good to be like a child forever. To the extent we live in a society, we need to understand the rules and strictures of that society as one among all (one/all). Having said that, even though an old person loses sight of original, fresh life as all/all, such a life doesn't just end when dismissed as something we are unable to carry out. As Dōgen says, "Though an old man may not be able to carry out those words, how is one unable to carry them out?" In other words, how far can we go in explaining the depth and complexity of being unable to practice Dōrin's words? Here, I strive with all I can, to explain the depth and intricacies of Buddhadharma. I strive to understand it, to express it, to winnow through the intricacies of it, to say all I can about it. That is the sense of "In this way, based on practice, we must winnow through just what Buddhadharma is; understand it and express it as fully and clearly as we can."

That is, you have to make it your own.

Part III. Living Time

5. Uji[149]
Living Time
有時

EIHEI DŌGEN ZENJI

Translated by DAITSŪ TOM WRIGHT

I.

An ancient buddha has said, "The living quick of time[150] stands on the peak of the highest mountain. The living quick of time moves on the

149. The Chinese characters (有時) have been understood and translated quite differently by different translators. Most translators have chosen to read the term as *aru toki*, that is, "one time," "once," "on one occasion" or "for the time being," "just for the time being," "there is a time when," "at some time," or "now and then." And that is the usual way to understand it. However, in the text as a whole, I believe that Dōgen's overall message is that such a reading is not the way to understand time as Buddhadharma. Hence, to emphasize time as the immediate present and not to see Dharmas so much as things but as processes, Dōgen coined a new expression to read *uji* or *yūji*. I'm afraid that English expressions like "for the time being" or "sometimes" or "once" may invite misinterpretation because they seem to imply "stasis" or "limiting," while Dōgen wants to emphasize the immediacy and aliveness of every moment, which naturally include all the temporary processes that surround us. Certainly, the original Chinese can be read "for the time being" or "on one occasion," but I feel that Dōgen's sense of *immediacy* is lost. So, I have chosen to translate the term as "living time" or "the living quick of time."

150. "*Uji* is the moment-by-moment living quick of time (有時)." Kōshō Uchiyama, *Shōbōgenzō: Uji and Shoaku Makusa wo Ajiwau* 正法眼蔵：有時・諸悪莫作を味わう *(Shōbōgenzō: Appreciating Uji and Shoaku Makusa)* (Tokyo: Hakujusha Publishers, 1984), 20–21.

floor of the deepest ocean.[151] It takes the form of the three-headed, eight-armed brutish beast.[152] It appears as the figure measuring sixteen feet tall when standing and eight feet tall when seated. It takes the form of the precautionary staff or a monk's fly chaser; it is a pillar or a lantern. It is the common third or fourth child,[153] it is the earth; it is the heavens."[154]

By *uji*, or "living time," I mean that each moment of time reveals all existences, all worlds.[155] All the various phenomena are themselves time. The sixteen-foot golden body is itself time. Because of that, the radiant light[156] also manifests as time. Learn and practice the twelve hours in this way. The three-headed, eight-armed brutish beast is time. Because of that, it is not different from the twelve hours.[157] Although no one

151. These opening phrases have been attributed to Yakusan Igen. This story also appears in Dōgen's *Shōbōgenzō Sambyakusoku* (*Commentary on Three Hundred Kōans*; 正法眼蔵三百則), Vol. 2.

152. The *ashura* (阿修羅; Skt: asura), or three-headed, eight-armed beast, was originally an antigod of Vedic mythology. The Sanskrit word literally means "deity against heaven." In Buddhism, the ashura represents those characteristics of wrath, conceit, and stupidity in human beings. The ashura can also be thought of as representing the burning competitive spirit to gain or possess something, perhaps not unlike the Olympic spirit of competing to be the winner, or perhaps a warrior monk of the Crusades. Louis Frederic, *Buddhism: Flammarion Iconographic Guides* (Paris: Flammarion Press, 1995).

153. *Chōsan rishi* (長三李四): literally, the third son of Mr. Chō or the fourth son of Mr. Li, but more broadly, any Tom, Dick, or Harry; an ordinary person, the common man.

154. The Japanese phrase *daichikokū* (大地虚空) literally means the earth or ground and the sky or heavens. By subtle implication here, it could also mean all phenomena or existence as well as that which is transcendental.

155. In an edition of *Shōbōgenzō* entitled *Dōgen: jō*, *u*, or "world," is understood to be restricted to phenomenal existences or appearances; however, Uchiyama interprets this more broadly to include not only things, but circumstances and situations as well. Considering the scope of Dōgen's writings, the broader interpretation would seem to be more appropriate. Terada Tōru and Mizuno Yaoko, eds. 寺田透・水野弥穂子, *Dōgen: jō* 道元(上), volume 12 of the Nihon Shisō Taikei series 日本史相大系 (Tokyo: Iwanami Shoten 岩波書店, 1976), 256.

156. In Japanese, *kōmyō* (光明) refers to the function of a thing, in this case, buddha's radiant light.

157. The connection between this and the previous sentence may seem a bit difficult to grasp. We could say that the "three-headed, eight-armed brutish beast" is a metaphor-

has been able to measure the length of time, still, we customarily call twelve hours a day.

Traces of the past and the direction of the future seem so clear; no one truly questions these things. However, this is no assurance that, because there is no true questioning, we understand what time actually is. Fundamentally, all the phenomena and experiences we question are themselves not fixed. This time of questioning cannot possibly coincide with that which is being questioned in the very next moment of time. For a while, questioning itself simply exists as time. Jiko is fully arrayed and manifests as the entire universe.[158] Investigate and winnow through all the individual things, all the various phenomena and circumstances of this universe as particular times. No thing interferes with any other thing, in the same way that no two times clash with one another. Therefore, all living things aspire at the same time and, simultaneously, all life is aspiring time. The same holds true for practice and attainment of the Way. This principle of universal identity as time means to recognize one's total identity as it manifests through the myriad of phenomena and circumstances.

II.

Because of this underlying principle [of all things being precisely what they are], the whole world[159] appears in its ten thousand forms and one

---

ical image for how we as ordinary people spend our day—the twelve hours—running around here and there. In other words, we are both the "radiant light" as well as the "three-headed, eight-armed brutish beast."

158. This passage could also be translated as "Self is personally experienced as the entire universe" or perhaps "I personally experience the whole universe as it manifests through all things." I have translated the Japanese word *jiko* variously as universal self, whole self, and sometimes as universal identity; I feel that any translation that includes "self" is inadequate, because the word carries its own baggage for Westerners, especially in the field of psychology.

159. In Japanese, the word is *jinchi* (尽地). Dōgen frequently uses the character *jin* (尽) as the first of two-character expressions: *jin issai* (尽一切), meaning "everything or all things"; *jinji* (尽時), "all time(s)"; *jinkai* (尽界), "all worlds"; etc.

hundred grasses.[160] Learn to appreciate each and every grass and each and every circumstance; strive to enable all these things to manifest in the deepest [and fullest] way. Viewing all things in this way is the first step of practice. When all things arrive in their most settled place, a blade of grass is just what it is; a situation or circumstance is just what it is. Sometimes there is understanding [of a situation], sometimes there isn't. At times we comprehend what a blade of grass is, at other times, we don't.[161]

Because there is only time present, uji is all-inclusive time. All living things, all occurring phenomena are time. Each instant, each moment of time embodies all existences, all worlds. Uji is inclusive of all time. All the grasses and everything that occurs are time. All existences, all phenomena are contained in the ever-occurring presence of time. Contemplate deeply as to whether or not there is anything at all outside of the present.

Despite that, ordinarily, people unfamiliar with the Buddhadharma hold onto a fixed idea of uji as signifying that there *was* a time [in the past] when they were three-headed, eight-armed beasts, and *another* time when they were sixteen-foot- or eight-foot-tall buddhas. In a sense, [they believe that] one time is like first crossing a river and, at a later time, climbing a mountain. Even though the rivers and mountains may have existed somewhere else, they think they have left them behind completely and are presently residing in the lofty crimson tower of a gorgeous palace.[162] Such people delude themselves by thinking they are now as far from those rivers and mountains as heaven is from earth.[163]

---

160. "Ten thousand forms and one hundred grasses" (*banshō hyakusō*, 万象百草) refers to temporal phenomena and incalculable circumstances. The overall connotation of the expression includes both physical as well as nonphysical things, such as thoughts, feelings, circumstances, situations—that is, it includes everything.

161. That is, sometimes there is understanding of circumstances, situations, and/or how things function.

162. "Crossing the rivers and mountains" can be taken as a metaphor for practice, while "the lofty crimson tower" might be seen as a metaphor for some imaginary state of realization.

163. That is, they think that who they were when climbing the mountains or crossing

The true actuality of the Buddhadharma teaching, however, is not like this. The time they crossed the aforementioned mountains and rivers, they themselves had to have been present there,[164] and so, they themselves were also time.[165] Without a doubt, they had to have been completely present there; time did not disappear.

If time seems to lack the aspect of coming and going, then time on top of the mountain is uji of the present. If it seems to possess such a characteristic, it is experienced [as the scenery] within the actual living present of self—which is also uji.[166] When climbing those mountains or traversing those rivers, is not the time of being in the crimson tower of the jeweled palace entirely swallowed whole, is it not entirely thrown up?[167]

The three-headed, eight-armed beast is yesterday's time. The sixteen-foot-standing or eight-foot-sitting image is today's time. Still, regarding this working of past and present, both are wholly contained in the present climbing of the mountain. Within that time, the present looks back over the ten thousand peaks; it is not that they [one's experiences] have in any way disappeared. The three-headed, eight-armed beast lives in the totality of the living present; it only seems as though it was in the distant past. The sixteen-foot or eight-foot image, too, lives in the wholeness of the immediate present. Though it appears to be something in the far distant future, it is living right now. Therefore, the pine tree is [all] time, the bamboo is [all] time; do not think of "flying away" as a true

---

the rivers is an entity totally separate from and cut off from the one presently residing in the palace. Professor Mizuno writes, "They think each is a separate existence." Here, Dōgen is explicating the widely held but mistaken linear conception of time.

164. That is, as a presence or as a living reality, they had to have been there.

165. Where they were, time also was there.

166. Sometimes we are so immersed in what we are doing that there is no lingering feeling about the past or sense of anticipation for what is coming; sometimes there is such a feeling or sense. Either way, with or without such a feeling, both are uji. Both the past and the future are living within the present.

167. In other words, facing adversities totally consumes one. There is no room for contemplating one-shot realizations.

quality or functioning of time. Do not imagine that such seeming passing away is real. If time were something that was cut off, there would have to be a gap.[168] People are incapable of experiencing uji, because they are convinced only of the ephemeral appearance of time.[169] The essential characteristic of uji is this: while all existences in all the various worlds are interconnected, each existence is unique in itself, and precisely because of this, we can speak of *personally* experiencing the living quick of time.[170]

Uji possesses the virtuous power[171] of *kyōryaku,* moment-to-moment occurring.[172] What we normally refer to as today becomes tomorrow;

168. That is, if time contained the trait of separation, one time from the next, if this moment of time were actually separated from the next moment of time, there should be a gap between the two. The original Japanese expression is *hiko* or *hikyo* (飛去), meaning, literally, "to fly away and disappear." I have translated it here as "cut off."

169. They fail to experience the wholeness or totality of time, time inclusive of past and future, because it is easier to believe in time as a passing-into-the past.

170. "Personally experiencing the living quick of time" is a translation of the expression *gouji* (吾有時).

171. Nishiari Bokusan Zenji defines *kudoku* (功徳), or "virtuous power" as "the inherent or natural quality or characteristic of a thing." Nishiari Bokusan Zenji Teishō 西有穆山禅師提唱, *Shōbōgenzō Keiteki (jō)* 正法眼蔵啓迪(上巻) (Tokyo: Daihōrinkaku 大法輪閣, 1965), 1972.

172. Traditionally, Buddhism defines *kyōryaku* (経歴) as simply "moment-by-moment change," although in Dōgen, there is an emphasis on the aliveness or vividness of time in every moment rather than on any perceived change or movement.

Translators have variously translated *kyōryaku* as "flowing," "passing," "continuous existence," "changing," "moving," and so forth. However, all these words articulate only the seemingly moving aspect of time. This is why Uchiyama Rōshi uses the term *kokkoku* (刻々), or "moment-by-moment" to express the nuance of *kyōryaku* in ordinary language. Used alone as an adverb or adjective, the word seeks something to attach itself to; hence, I have translated it in places as "moment-by-moment [life]." Readers should be aware, however, that as Dōgen is using the word, he is using it to negate dichotomies prior to the division of movement/nonmovement, change/stagnation, etc.

Nishiari Bokusan writes, "Ordinarily we think that the wind and rain go from east to west, that there is a *passing* from east to west. Or, looked at in terms of human interactions, we might be apt to say, 'That guy *used to be* the head of the village, *but now* he's the county commissioner!' as if the person had changed, or that time had passed. But today, yesterday; yesterday, today; today, today; tomorrow, tomorrow.[173] Since this constant and vivid occurring is the virtuous quality of time, time past does not intrude on time present. Though the former is not linked to the latter, Seigen is time, Ōbaku is time, Daijaku and Sekitō are time, you and others are all time.[174] Consequently, practice/enlightenment is all times; likewise, entering the mud and going into the water is also time.[175]

Further, though the biased views of ordinary people, along with the internal conditions and external influences that affect those views, form people's misunderstanding, the dharmas are not people's possessions; it is simply that all these so-called dharmas[176] temporarily inform the person.[177] Because ordinarily, we take it for granted that living time and all existences do not live within ourselves, we assume that the sixteen-foot-tall golden body cannot reside within us. Consequently, we remain unable to imagine that such a buddha could in any way lie within us. Therefore, those who have not yet made such confirmation should examine carefully each and every living moment of time.

Dōgen Zenji's *kyōryaku* here should be understood to mean that as the village head, the fellow was the village head completely—that was everything he was. And, as the county commissioner, that is who he is totally." Nishiari, *Shōbōgenzō Keiteki*, 1: 476.

173. That is, the scenery or content of our thoughts can be of yesterday or today or tomorrow.

174. Seigen Gyōshi (青原 行思; Chi: Qingyuan Xingsi; ?–740); Ōbaku Kiun (黄檗 希運; Chi: Huangbo Xiyuan, ?–?); Daijaku of Mount Kōzei, or Baso Dōitsu; and Sekitō Kisen, or Musai Daishi (石頭 希遷; Chi: Shitou Xiqian; 700–790). These are all famous Zen teachers.

175. "Entering the mud and going into the water" means choosing to live and function in the world with compassion as a bodhisattva.

176. In this case, *dharmas* simply mean entities or things or phenomena.

177. Mizuno Yaoko comments, "All the dharmas (entities, phenomena) are the Buddhadharma. [In this passage] the Buddhadharma simply appears as an ordinary person." Mizuno Yaoko, *Shōbōgenzō*, 2:51.

III.

That which has been mutually agreed on as the hour of the horse and sheep is inclusive of the rising and setting, the greater and lesser aspects of the naturally residing dharmas, all of which are as they are—living time. The hours of the rat and the tiger are living time.[178] Sentient beings and buddhas are also living time. The three-headed, eight-armed beast affirms[179] living time through its functioning throughout all realms. The sixteen-foot golden body does the same. Since both contain all worlds, each and every world functions completely in all worlds.[180] This is referred to as thoroughly penetrating.[181] The golden body penetrates the golden body thoroughly in manifesting its totality by arousing the attitude of a bodhisattva, practicing, functioning as a bodhisattva, entering nirvana. The golden body is living presence, living time. All times totally penetrate all existences with nothing left over. This is because

178. Each hour of the day. Nishiari Bokusan Zenji comments, "*Rising* and *setting* means to show that there are no dichotomies—no subject-object, and so forth. . . . Each time is independently uji." Nishiari Bokusan, *Shōbōgenzō Keiteki* (Tokyo: Daihorinkaku, 1965), 1:470.

179. In Japanese, *shōsuru* (証する), or "affirms," is being used not in the abstract sense of say, realizing an idea, but rather in the sense of bringing into concrete existence. This is the same sense that Dōgen gives to it in *Shōbōgenzō* "Genjō Kōan": "To practice the refined way of life of the Buddha entails the functioning of jiko. The functioning of jiko means the letting go of one's ego [the narrow self-identity that pits oneself against others]. Letting go of [conceptualizing] jiko manifests through the realization [concretization] of all things. For this *realization* to come about, one must cast aside all conceptions that divide *self* from *other*." Obviously, if there is no "other," "self" must be all-inclusive.

180. The Japanese expression here is *jinkai wo mote jinkai wo kaijin suru* (尽界をもて 尽界を界尽する). Dōgen is using the same word for the subject and object, and reversing the order of the Chinese characters as the verb. It is the same idea behind Sawaki Rōshi's "self selfs the self." Such expressions obviously don't make common sense in any language. That is, they do not fit into any widely accepted formula for using language; they aren't rational expressions in the conventional sense of our being able to *reason out* or pull out a meaning that makes sense. Such expressions are meant to encourage us to give up trying to fit reality into reasonable (but lifeless) categories.

181. In Japanese, "to thoroughly penetrate" is *gūjin suru* (究尽する).

whatever might remain, remains totally.[182] Even that living presence that has not been fully penetrated[183] is penetrated thoroughly as unfulfilled living presence. Even if something appears to be a mistake or misguided intention, we are still living out moment-by-moment living time. Further, from the viewpoint of uji, the mistake (or misguided intention), inclusive of before and after, resides in living time; it is contained within the vivid actuality of where all existences naturally reside—this is uji, living time! Do not be deluded into nonexistence, nor fanatically insist on existence.[184]

People stubbornly take it into their heads that time passes away, with no comprehension that that which has not yet arrived is also uji. Even though such misunderstanding itself is also uji, living time itself is unaffected by such mistaken views. People unquestioningly believe time comes and goes, but no human being[185] has ever realized exactly where the living quick of time resides. Much less has any human being ever been liberated from time.[186] Even though there might be someone who

182. In the *Shōbōgenzō Keiteki*, Nishiari Zenji defines *jōhō* (剩法) or, literally, "remaining" dharmas as delusion; "whatever might remain, remains totally" refers to times when we are confused or deluded.

183. By "not fully penetrated," Dōgen Zenji means "incomplete" and, therefore, that even when we harbor doubts or feelings of unfulfillment or incompleteness, this has nothing to do with the deeper truth of our always living fully in the present.

184. There is a parallel passage in Dōgen Zenji's *Gakudō Yōjinshū* (学道用心集, *Points to Watch in Practicing the Way*): "One can never come into harmony with Buddhadharma clinging to an attitude of accumulating gain nor with an attitude of seeking extinction." By "accumulating gain," he is referring to the idea of materialism, and by "extinction" he is referring to the small-vehicle attitude of striving never to be reborn.

185. The expression Dōgen Zenji uses here, in reference to the human body, is *hitai* (皮袋), literally, "skinbag," or *shūhitai* (臭皮袋), "stinking skin bag."

186. The Japanese expression *tōkan* (透関) has been used to describe the so-called gate or border of "seeing through," i.e., satori, or realization of time. Because of the nature of what the expression is pointing toward, there is really no single way to express it in language. "To be liberated from time" might be one way to express it, or "to transcend the limitless border of time" might be another.

intellectually grasps where uji resides, who can possibly express living time itself? Or even if someone in the past were said to have expressed it, there is no one alive who would not continue groping to see whatever is eminently presenting itself before their very eyes.[187]

IV.

If [the idea of] uji were left to the fancies of human imagination, the actual wisdom of enlightenment and the emancipation of nirvana would amount to little more than ephemeral comings and goings. However, the living presence of enlightenment and nirvana can never be ensnared[188] by human speculation or conjecture; all there is, is the living manifestation of uji.

The functioning presence of the guardian deities and the other myriad protectors in all worlds and directions is the manifesting of our personal life experience as living time. This living time in all creatures both in the water and on the land, of the infinite situations and existences both visible and invisible,[189] is the wholly personal manifesting of the entire power of uji, the entire power of kyōryaku. Sit and practice[190] until it is thor-

---

187. Since *uji* is living time, that is, since it is fresh and alive, moment-to-moment, even the wisest or most practiced teacher must face the next moment by him- or herself—earnestly seeking to see how everything is in its original state.

188. The original Chinese characters *rarō* (羅籠) represent a net for catching rabbits or birds (or fish, according to Yaoko Mizuno) and a cage to keep or imprison birds or other small animals. Either way, the *nets* and *cages* are our very own thoughts and emotions, used to try to catch and encase or categorize the actuality of life.

189. In Japanese, the expression for "visible and invisible" is *myōyō* (冥陽) where *myō* means invisible, or sometimes, ignorant, and *yō* means visible or knowledgeable. Some scholars see the expression as a shortened form for *myōkai* (冥界), the worlds of the dead and living. Nakamura Gen says, "In the broader sense, *myōkai* refers to the lowest three worlds of hell, insatiable spirits, and domesticated animals; in the narrow sense, however, it refers only to hell." Nakamura Gen, *Bukkyōgo Daijiten*, 1309.

190. The original term *sangaku* (参学) derives from the four-character Chinese expression *sanzen gakudō* (参禅学道). This expression was often used by Dōgen as a sort of signal or signpost that the following sentence is very important. The English word "study" doesn't convey the impact of the original which means, literally, to sit zazen and practice the Way.

oughly clear that if uji were not all the power of kyōryaku, not a single thing would manifest, nor would there be any moment-by-moment [life].

By *kyōryaku*—the living quick of moment-by-moment—I do not mean the way the wind and rain seem to blow from east to west as has been taught in the past. *Kyōryaku* does not imply immobility; neither does it imply progress or regression.

Moment-by-moment [life] is like spring; spring unfolds the myriad forms of spring—*that* is moment-by-moment. Investigate and look carefully at how moment-by-moment [life] is not influenced by anything outside of you. For instance, the moment-by-moment of spring brings forth the multifarious spring appearances in every moment. Look closely at how moment-by-moment, though not itself spring, is entirely complete at springtime, since each and every moment, each and every thing fully expresses spring.

If we understand kyōryaku as all things going on outside of ourselves, and that only the subject faces east, and we encounter all the myriad worlds that seem to pass through endless expanses of time, we are not yet practicing the Buddha's Way with our whole heart.

V.

At the direction of Master Sekitō Kisen, Yakusan Igen called on Master Daijaku of Kōzei. Yakusan said, "I understand the essence of the teachings of the three vehicles and the teachings of the twelve divisions to a

---

The *san* of *sangaku* can also be read *mairu*, meaning "to go toward or approach something," although it can also mean "to give into or surrender"; Uchiyama Rōshi often defined *sanzen* in this way. "Surrendering to zazen" is the same as Rōshi's "opening the hand of thought." It demonstrates a truly religious attitude toward life as opposed to an attitude that would use zazen as a psychological or self-help tool. The use of zazen in the field of psychotherapy is fine, but then, it should be understood that such a use is only an example of utilitarian zen, not of Zen in the religious sense.

Other examples of surrendering to zazen can be found in Sawaki Rōshi's somewhat shocking expression "Sitting zazen is like climbing in the coffin and pounding down the final nail from the inside," or Uchiyama Rōshi's "kōan" "Who would you be if your mother had aborted you?"

certain extent.[191] Still, I can't say that I have truly grasped the significance of why Bodhidharma came from the west?" Master Daijaku replied, "Śākyamuni's teaching by deliberately raising his eyebrows and blinking is uji; raising them and blinking unintentionally is also uji. Raising them and blinking at the proper time is uji, and doing so inappropriately at the wrong time is also uji." On hearing Daijaku's reply Yakusan had a profound realization. He, in turn, replied, "Although I have been practicing with Sekitō for some time, in trying to understand what is behind his teaching, I've felt like a mosquito trying to climb on the back of an iron ox."[192]

Daijaku's comment is unlike anyone else's. His eyebrows take the form of grand mountains, and his eyes are like the vast oceans, since mountains and oceans are not different from his eyebrows and his eyes. "Deliberately raising the eyebrows" is seeing the mountains; "blinking intentionally" has the same power as the rivers flowing into the oceans.[193] The moun-

191. The "three vehicles" refers to the teachings of the śrāvakas, pratyekabuddhas, and bodhisattvas. The "twelve divisions" refers to the twelve categories into which the Buddha's teachings were divided.

192. *Bunsu, tetsugyū ni noboru* (蚊子、鉄牛に上る). This kōan is the same in meaning as the more famous *Bunsu, tetsugyū wo kamu* (蚊子、鉄牛を咬む): "There is no way for a tiny mosquito to penetrate the hide of an iron bull." This is a metaphor for expressing the impossibility of penetrating the truth of life merely through rational thought.

193. Through this metaphorical passage, Dōgen is expressing the transcendence of dichotomies and the all-inclusivity of uji, suggesting that human intention is not separate from the life force.

The equation or identity of mountains and oceans with eyes and eyebrows, of something big and small, is common with Dōgen to connote the importance of all our actions, regardless of whether we are personally able to see or believe in their value or not. Dōgen expresses this same attitude in the *Instructions to the Cook*: "When you prepare food, never view the ingredients from some commonly held perspective, nor think about them only with your emotions. Maintain an attitude that tries to build great temples from ordinary greens, that expounds the Buddhadharma through the most trivial activity.... Handle even a single leaf of a green in such a way that it manifests the body of the Buddha. This in turn allows the Buddha to manifest through the leaf. This is a power which you cannot grasp with your rational mind." Kōshō Uchiyama, *How to Cook Your Life*, 7–8.

tains and oceans become one with us. We become led by the power of the mountains and oceans: uji. Never assume that what is inappropriate has no power to move us, nor that unintentional actions are necessarily untrue; that is not uji. Mistaken actions as well as unintentional ones are the living quick of time. The mountains are living time; the rivers and

---

In Masunaga Reiho's commentary on *Shōbōgenzō* "Uji," he writes that the term *jinchi* usually refers to the environment, while *jiko* refers to the subject, but that for Dōgen, *jinchi* and *jiko* are actually synonymous. They can't be separated. There is also reference to *senga* in the expression *senga jiko* (山河自己), referring to sentient and nonsentient things. The expression is inclusive of and, at the same time, transcendent of dichotomies.

In the *Zengaku Daijiten,* under *yōbi shunmoku* (揚眉瞬目), we find, "'Raising the eyebrows and blinking the eyes' is a suggestive metaphor for carrying out the most natural actions in everyday life. Daijaku's words derive from the *kōan* [of Śākyamuni Buddha's turning the flower, smiling, and blinking, the significance of which his disciple Mahākāśyapa alone was able to catch]. The expression has also been used to indicate, in a broader sense, the function of a teacher to guide the student." Komazawa University Publications Committee, ed., *Zengaku Daijiten,* 1252.

The original kōan refers to Śākyamuni Buddha, but also broadly speaking, to any enlightened being. As Dōgen breaks down this kōan, who or what is the prime mover of the eyes and eyebrows is ambiguous. He would seem to have done this (as he has done throughout *Shōbōgenzō*) in order to give the fullest play possible to the written language.

Nishiari Bokusan Zenji's commentary: "The text reads something or someone had someone raise their eyebrows and blink. But just who made who raise their eyebrows and blink? Or, who did not have someone raise their eyebrows and blink? The command or *cause* of raising or not raising, blinking or not blinking, derives from uji itself. So it is actually uji that causes the raising or blinking. It is we who raise our eyebrows and blink, but it is uji that brings this about. . . . Eyebrows and eyes are 'mountains and rivers' is a reference to all phenomena. So the eyes and eyebrows in Baso's kōan means the *sengadaichi* (山河大地)—the mountains, rivers, and land—or, in the widest sense, the entire cosmos. But here, 'his eyes and eyebrows' (which have somehow become mountains and rivers) 'raise mountains or become rivers,' respectively, does not mean that these things now move his eyes or his nose. He's talking about the scenery of *jinkai,* all inclusive world(s); the appearance of the *Dharma* world, *hokkai* (法界). He's saying that what moves and what is moved are not separate. Concretely speaking, [we can look at this passage in the light of] *fukimon* (扶起門) and *sōtōmon* (掃蕩門)—the leadership methods of a teacher, the former totally supporting the practitioner; the latter, teaching by pulling away any support the practitioner might cling to." Nishiari, *Shōbōgenzō Keiteki,* 1: 479–80.

oceans are living time.[194] If they were not, there would be no mountains or oceans. Never think that the very presence of these mountains and oceans is not time. If time collapses, the mountains and oceans also die. If time is indestructible, so, too, are the mountains and oceans.[195] The appearance of the morning star, the Tathāgata, the enlightened eye of wisdom, the turning of the flower[196]—all of them are possible because of the undeniable living presence of uji. If time were not living presence, nothing would be as it is.

VI.

Kisei Zenji[197] of Sekken was of the Rinzai lineage and a Dharma heir of Shuzan Shōnen.[198] While instructing his disciples one day, he pointed out:

[Within uji, the living present]
Though the aim hits the mark, the expression may fall short.
Though the expression hits the mark, the aim may be off.
Aim and expression sometimes both hit the mark;
Sometimes both fall short.

194. In Buddhism, to speak of mountains or oceans and rivers may sound very "back to nature," but the parameters of these words go beyond the physical environment. This passage should be read over and over, bearing in mind that "mountains and oceans" refers to all phenomena or to the entire cosmos.

195. Nishiari Bokusan interprets the syntax of this sentence slightly differently. He understands it to read, "*Since* time collapses and is destroyed, the mountains and oceans also die." Hence his comment, "Destruction is time. No destruction is also time!" Nishiari, *Shōbōgenzō Keiteki*, 1:480.

196. "The Tathāgata, the enlightened eye of wisdom, the turning of the flower" is a reference to the time of the awakening of Śākyamuni Buddha, his (and later descendants') deep wisdom, and the transmission of that wisdom.

197. Kisei Zenji (帰省禅師; Chi: Shexian Guixing) lived in the tenth century, though exact dates are unknown.

198. Shuzan Shōnen (首山省念; Chi: Shoushan Xingnian; 926–93) was also known as Shōnen of Mt. Shuzan.

Aim and expression are both uji, living presence; hitting the mark and falling short are both uji, too. Although hitting the mark[199] may seem incomplete, falling short is entirely complete.[200] While aim is the same as Reiun's donkey, expression is like his horse.[201] The "horse"—hitting the mark—is the expression, the "donkey"—falling short—is the aim. Hitting the mark, having arrived, has no connection with still coming from somewhere else. Likewise, not yet having hit the mark is not the same as having not yet come to some imaginary future.[202] Uji can be expressed in these ways and more. Hitting the mark obstructs[203] hitting

199. The word Dōgen Zenji uses in the text is "having arrived," but the implications are difficult to discern. "Having arrived" or "hitting the mark" here are used in the sense of being enlightened.

200. The actual manifestation of falling short, because it is a manifestation of the reality of life, is a total or complete manifestation. While "having arrived" or "hitting the mark" is incomplete, not having arrived [missing the mark] is totally complete.

Although it seems like a contradiction, it is only natural to feel a sense of incompleteness even though we are complete. This is because the reality of any completeness or enlightenment, precisely because it is a *living presence*, has to include a component of incompleteness or insufficiency or of something lacking.

201. The metaphorical use of donkey and horse in Zen goes back at least to Reiun Shigon (霊雲志勤; Chi: Lingyun Zhiqin; dates unknown). One day a monk asked Reiun, "What is the grand design or overall aim of the Buddhadharma?" Reiun replied, "The horse has arrived before the donkey has left." *Keitoku Dentōroku,* Vol. 2. There are various ways to look at Reiun's response. The most straightforward one would be to understand the donkey and horse simply as metaphors for all the various aspects of day-to-day life. That is, the day-to-day workings of practice continue one after another without any gap. In other words, Buddhist practice has no end, and that is the grand design.

Some interpreters of "donkey and horse" suggest that the donkey is a symbol of immaturity or not yet enlightened—i.e., a young monk, not yet "arrived"—while the horse represents a person of maturity or realization, perhaps a teacher. In this sense, all people would embody both the donkey and the horse, with aspects of both undevelopment or unrefinement and aspects of maturity or refinement.

202. This is the same idea as in Dōgen's *Fukanzazengi* (普勧坐禅儀), or *Universal Recommendation for Zazen*, that one's treasure does not come from outside.

203. Here "obstructs" has no special meaning. Dōgen is simply trying to express the

the mark; it cannot be obstructed by having not yet hit it. Not having hit the mark is obstructed by itself—there is no obstruction from having already hit the mark. Aim obstructs aim, thereby seeing [being] totally itself. Expression obstructs expression and becomes itself. Obstruction obstructs itself, therein seeing [being] totally itself alone.[204] Obstruction obstructs obstruction—this is uji, living presence.

Although it is commonly taken for granted that obstructions hinder other dharmas, there has never existed anything that has obstructed anything else. "I meet another person, another person meets their self, I meet myself, going out meets going out."[205] If these things were not living time, there would be no living presence of all things being what they are—*immo* (恁麼).

Moreover, aim is the same as the vital and living manifestation [genjō] of the present encounter [kōan]; expression is the key to the gate of supreme enlightenment. Hitting the mark is the casting off of body and mind, and not yet hitting the mark is separating upon arrival.[206] It is in this way that we should practice diligently and actualize the living quick of time.

Our Buddhist ancestors have expressed their living presence in these various ways. Is there nothing further that I might say? I would add that aim and expression only *partially* hitting the mark are uji. And aim and expression only *partially* not hitting the mark are also uji. Study and practice diligently in this way.

fact that every action is complete in itself and not balanced against something else. A young monk is complete as a young monk, and an older experienced one is complete as an experienced one. There should be no comparison made between the two.

204. This is similar to the idea expressed in "thoroughly penetrating."

205. This is a kōan from Sanshō Enen Zenji (三省慧然禅師; Chi: Sansheng Huinian Shanshi; exact dates unknown). Enen Zenji was of the Rinzai tradition during the Tang dynasty. When he says that "I meet another person," the other person is within or an extension of himself. "Going out meets going out" means that there is no "other" to encounter.

206. "Not yet hitting the mark" or "not yet arriving" might be compared with the spirit of the bodhisattva: separating from or letting go of things as soon as they have been grasped.

Having him partially raise his eyebrows and blink is uji. Not having him do so even partially is uji. Even mistakenly having him not do so time and time again is also uji.[207] In this way, delve deeply into these issues of living time, of coming and going, of hitting the mark and having not yet hit the mark as the truly living issues of uji, living time.

> Written in November, at the start of winter,
> in the first year of Ninji Gannen [1240],
> while residing at Kōshō Hōrinji Temple.
> Later recopied by Ejō during the summer
> practice period, 1243.

---

207. Alternately: "Halfheartedly raising the eyebrows and blinking is uji; blindly doing the same is uji. Halfheartedly not raising the eyebrows and blinking is uji; the same in halfhearted blindness is also uji."

6. Commentary on "Uji"

KŌSHŌ UCHIYAMA

Translated by Daitsū Tom Wright

Moment-by-moment time unfolds each ever-changing world.

It is critical that we are able to clarify for ourselves just what is written in this fascicle. If we miss its point, whatever way we see it, it has no meaning whatsoever in terms of Buddhadharma.

What is most fundamental in Buddhadharma? First of all, most other religions like Christianity or Islam set up a god that human beings must depend or rely on. That is, God is separate from humankind, from ourselves. And this God is given absolute status. In contrast to this religious concept, Śākyamuni Buddha said, "Revere self, revere Dharma, and revere nothing else."

He said this is what should be the foundation of our lives. In the *Dhammapada* we find: "The ground of self is self alone. Only a well-arranged, well-adjusted self can be relied on."

Whole self, jiko, settling into itself is the life-teaching of Buddhadharma, the ultimate foundation for our lives. It comprises the fundamental position of the Buddhist teaching as a religion prior to doctrines and scholarship, and is what makes Buddhism different from other [theistic] religions.

People were sitting in the zazen posture, in full lotus, in India long before Śākyamuni Buddha. However, it wasn't until Śākyamuni that zazen as a singular teaching, where jiko settles into itself, appeared.

This way of doing zazen has been variously described as the "direct transmission from past buddhas and ancestors" or as *jijuyū zanmai,* the samadhi of the freely receiving and functioning self. Needless to say, the word *self* in the expression "freely receiving and functioning self," as found in Dōgen's *Bendōwa,* or in "the ground of self is self alone" or "revere self, revere Dharma, and revere nothing else" should not be taken to mean simply "I" or "me."

What we refer to as "I" or "me" or "myself" is generally set in contrast to other things, people, or worlds. Whole self, or all-inclusive self, or jiko, in the above expressions, however, is not a "self" opposed to an "other." *Jiko* refers to a self prior to the split between self and other, subject and object, seeing and what is seen, thinking (or imagining) and what is thought (or imagined). This is the jiko that is the animate, direct living quick of Buddhadharma. I have sometimes referred to this jiko as *seimei no jitsubutsu* (生命の実物), the true vital reality of life.

Since jiko precedes the duality of an individual ego separate from or independent of other things, people, environment, etc., another way this metaphor might be expressed can be found in Dōgen's *Shōbōgenzō* "Sokushinzebutsu" (即心是仏), "This Very Jiko Is Buddha": "Jiko is inclusive of all Dharmas, all Dharmas are at the same time jiko."

In "Uji," this is expressed as all worlds being embodied in Jiko, and that jiko is not some thing set in opposition to an "other." Since jiko in these examples is the immediate, living, quick-of-life jiko, it is the moment-by-moment constant change that is time. Because of this, Dōgen tells us that all phenomena are unique, different moments of time, and that every moment of time contains all existences, all things, and all circumstances. In other words, when Dōgen uses the term *uji,* it is an *u,* "aliveness," that contains everything, and a *ji,* "a time of moment-by-moment [life]." Finally, that which actually lives these moments-by-moments is jiko. Hence, we get the expression *gouji*—a personal jiko of all-existing, all-inclusive time.

What is crucial here is that, through doing zazen, we personally run smack into the reality we are presently facing, which is, at the same time, the way this reality of life ought to be. Therefore, what we find in this fascicle "Uji" is certainly not anything that is difficult nor something mystically profound. What is written is about nothing other than the most natural scenery of our zazen. This teaching is one that enables us to move that much deeper into our very ordinary way of practice. That is, it is not some ideal or abstract explanation, unrelated to our everyday lives.

"Uji" is moment-by-moment living time.

I.

An ancient buddha has said, "The living quick of time stands on the peak of the highest mountain. The living quick of time moves on the floor of the deepest ocean. It takes the form of the three-headed, eight-armed brutish beast. It appears as the figure measuring sixteen feet tall when standing and eight feet tall when seated. It takes the form of the precautionary staff or a monk's fly chaser; it is a pillar or a lantern. It is the common third or fourth child; it is the earth; it is the heavens."

Normally, we would read these opening lines as "Sometimes [we] stand on the peak of the highest mountain; sometimes [we] move on the floor of the deepest ocean, etc." and actually, the passage would be easier to understand that way. But then the "sometimes this, sometimes that" would seem to imply a succession of times. That isn't what Dōgen is trying to say. "The living quick of time stands on the peak of the highest mountain." Here, the sentence is finished. "The living quick of time moves on the floor of the deepest ocean." Again, here it stops; it's entirely separate from the above sentence. Uji is the moment-by-moment living quick of time. And each separate moment of time "stands on the peak of the highest mountain," or "moves on the floor of the deepest ocean." Each moment itself unfolds all phenomena and all worlds. That is uji, living time.

The three-headed, eight-armed brutish beast is the metaphoric posture of the ashura. For example, someone like [former Prime Minister]

Tanaka Kakuei (田中角栄), an outrageous figure, too, is the unfolding quickness of time.

The figure measuring sixteen feet when standing and eight feet tall when seated is a reference to the Buddha. This is also the unfolding vital life of time.

The precautionary staff and monk's hossu, or flywhisk, are examples of everyday items monks used to carry around. In ancient China, in order to protect themselves when journeying deep into the mountains or forests where there were tigers and wolves, monks would carry one of those staffs *tengu*[208] carry in festivals, the ones with the rings on top. The rings would make a sound, and the animals would know that some human was coming and get out of the way. Even in olden times, the human beast was the most dangerous animal! The hossu, a monk's fly chaser, looks like a horse or cow's tail. It was used as a fly swatter to shoo away flies and mosquitoes. All these things are the unfolding living quick of time.

The pillar refers to the large round pillars that support the roof of the temple. The lanterns are the traditional *tōrō* (灯籠) lanterns that stand on either side of the altar in the main hall of the temple. (Today they're sometimes made of stone and stand at the entrances to temples.) These, too, are the unfolding of living time.

The common third or fourth child refers to the later offspring in Chinese families who, by custom, were not allowed to inherit the family wealth. They were the expendables in the family, or to put it another way, we could say they symbolize the masses of the lower class. They, too, are living time.

And finally, the eighth example, the earth and the heavens are this whole universe. Right at this moment, all existences and all worlds are unfolding.

208. Tengu (天狗), or "heavenly dog," are supernatural creatures of Japanese folk religion with bird-like characteristics.

By *uji* or "living time," I mean that each moment of time reveals all existences, all worlds. All the various phenomena are themselves time. The
sixteen-foot golden body is itself time. Because of that, the radiant light
also manifests as time. Learn and practice the twelve hours in this way.
The three-headed, eight-armed brutish beast is time. Because of that, it
is not different from the twelve hours. Although no one has been able to
measure the length of time, still, we customarily call twelve hours a day.

Each moment of time unfolds all existences, all worlds. All these various
phenomena and circumstances are the scenery of each instantaneous and
separate moment of time. So the sixteen-foot golden body—the standing
posture of the Buddha—is time. This radiant light appearance of the
Buddha, too, is time. Ultimately, these moment-by-moment passings
of time are completely separate. In the same way that we generally live
within twenty-four hours of time, the old counting system had twelve
hours to the day, and this time is constantly changing.

The grotesque multi-headed, multi-armed fearful posture of an ashura
is also time. Because it is living time, it is not different from the twelve
hours of the day. It is constantly in flux. On occasion, former Prime
Minister Tanaka surely turned livid red with anger or pale from loss of
color. Either appearance is time itself. All those appearances are, ultimately, time. We don't bother to measure its length, whether it's long
or short; nor do we consider its urgency. But it is constantly, in each
moment, evolving. Even the tiniest fraction of a second does not rest,
it has a before and an after of which it is totally separate; it is constantly
changing. It never stops. And normally (or out of habit) we call that
twelve hours or a day.

Questioning and doubt also occur as time.

Traces of the past and the direction of the future seem so clear that
no one truly questions these things. However, this is no assurance that

because there is no true questioning, we understand what time actually is. Fundamentally, all the phenomena and experiences we question are themselves not fixed. This time of questioning cannot possibly coincide with that which is being questioned in the very next moment of time. For a while, questioning itself simply exists as time.

"Traces of the past and the direction of the future" refers to the imprint of change, that is, "Such and such happened this way or that way" or the idea that a particular thing occurs within particular passages of time. Since everyone recognizes such changes, no one ever thinks to question the actual form or nature of time. But just because no one questions what time is, doesn't mean we understand what it is. This time of questioning refers to that which the questioner is facing: in other words, time. However, it's not only time that is being questioned—it's everything. As sentient beings, we don't even know how to doubt or question properly. We aren't even in possession of an eye capable of seeing reality. No matter how much we sit around thinking this or that, since we can't see straight in the first place, there is no reason to expect to hit the target regarding what the true form of things is.

Nevertheless, "For a while, questioning itself simply exists as time." The questioning is contained in time. The only thing that is unmistakable is that the questioning exists in each moment as time.

Jiko is fully arrayed and manifests as the entire universe. Investigate and winnow through all the individual things, all the various phenomena and circumstances of this universe as particular times.

Ultimately, what we ourselves are [as jiko] is a life force that continuously evolves and manifests as all the particulars of our entire universe. Therefore, Dōgen urges us to continue to question everything around us because everything in and around us is constantly changing. The actual quick of life exists before the division into my own personal life experiences and all the phenomena themselves. Therefore, all existences are constantly changing. And I am living out that constantly changing life.

> No thing interferes with any other thing, in the same way that no two times clash with one another. Therefore, all living things aspire at the same time and, simultaneously, all life is aspiring time.

From the foundation of the actual quick of life, such life exists prior to self and other, I and thou, subject and object; therefore, there is absolutely no relationship to some sort of "other."

There's an old proverb that goes "Shame accumulates with the years." In other words, the longer we live the more times we put ourselves to shame. I was a little special, though, because I was building up failures and shame all over the place long before I started putting on the years. So early on, I resolved just not to fall apart over a little shame.... This may have been my instinctual weapon for survival. Anyhow, the important point is that failing happens even though nothing interferes with any other thing. Despite that, things do clash and interfere [in our day-to-day lives], resulting in some horrible situations.

Many people overact to their mistakes. They become depressed, always carrying it inside themselves. For some people, it gets so bad that they develop full-blown neuroses and become incapable of bouncing back. But even when you're thinking about how you've messed up, as the actual reality of life, the mess is already finished; it's over. You don't have to worry about a thing. It would be far better to think that the whole thing is behind you than to go around belittling yourself.

I was with Sawaki Rōshi for twenty-five years, until his death [in 1965]. During that time, I performed any number of mess-ups right before his eyes. Now let me tell you, Sawaki Rōshi was not one who would ignore a mistake or mince words about it. He'd come down on you with that voice of his. Why, if the building was not very large, the whole thing would begin to shake. At that point, there was nothing to do but be still and listen; if you tried defending yourself, he would just get that much angrier. So you'd try your best to sit there, striking as reverential a pose as possible, as though you were listening to God herself. Then once he'd finished blowing up, you could muse to yourself, "Whew... that's over."

So, no matter how severely I might have been scolded, I always had a place to go [inside myself] for relief. I think that was the only reason I was able to stick with a man like Sawaki Rōshi for all those years. Of all his disciples, I was the only one that stayed. Everyone else left.

No two times clash with one another. Making a mistake is one time; getting bawled out for it is another time. When each of those times is finished, all you need to do is start over and return afresh to the actual quick of your life [as it is] now. This is the idea behind "all living things aspire at the same time and, simultaneously, all life is aspiring time."

Of course, there are always going to be people who will argue, "No, no. Things in life just don't take care of themselves that easily. The results of my mistake are sitting right here in front of my eyes." I can't tell you how many people have come to talk with me recently about some crazy thing their child has done. If the kid is ten or twenty years old, well, you can either be moved or amused by it. But when the parent starts talking about their crazy thirty- or forty-year-old "child," well, then you know the cause right away . . . it's not the child so much as it is the parents who brought him up! Here the parents come wanting to know what they should do about the "mistake" they made that keeps lurking in and around their house. They insist they can't just pack up and start over.

You've got nothing to worry about. All you have to do is think about where you would be today if you had been aborted! At the time, you never would have been able to say, "Hey, why are you aborting me?" Even more so now: whatever the result that might be about to emerge or whichever way you might be thinking of to dodge it—any way is okay; it just doesn't matter—that's where you have to start from.

If my expression "where would you be today if you had been aborted?" doesn't quite hit home, how about Sawaki Rōshi's expression "look at your situation as though you were already lying stiff in the coffin!"

Whatever anyone thinks, the fact is we're all living with at least one leg in [the coffin]. Why, every day there are people who, while wandering around worried about one thing or another, get bumped off in automobile accidents.

The driver from Sōsenji Temple has been driving professionally for thirty-five years. Even he says cars are a frightening thing. Make just one little mistake and anything can happen. In the same breath, he says that taking care of his family is most important to him.

He says getting into the car and driving off right after there's been some problem at home just invites an accident. Your everyday surroundings are terribly important; you've got to take good care of your environment. Of course, on the other hand, even knowing how important it is to take care of our environment, we encounter all kinds of unforeseen scenery. We're not going to get off easily by pleading that the reason we banged up the car was because we'd just had a bad scene with our spouse.

So what it comes down to is that whatever our situation might be like, there has to be some place to just let go. And that place where we start all over again is realizing where we would be now had we been aborted.

The driver I've been talking about says that he gets into his car only after he's lit a votive candle on the family altar every morning. It's important to start out fresh by lighting the candles and thinking about just where we'd be today had we been aborted. That's the foundation on which we have to renew ourselves. This is also called *hosshin* (発心), or arousing the spirit that seeks the Way. Doing this in itself is a way of paying reverence to the Buddha or to God.

Doing zazen is opening the hand of thought.

The same holds true for practice and attainment of the Way.

In regard to "practice" as well as "attaining the Way," this means simply to return to just aspiring. That is when we completely live out our life on the foundation of the very quick of life.

This is true of the zazen we do as well. While sitting, various feelings and ideas arise. The sudden appearance of a thought indicates that somewhere in our heads, our "hand" is holding on to some idea. But if we open that hand, the idea we were holding on to falls away; it disappears. Every time we open that hand of thought, zazen returns to zazen. In other words, it's only natural that as living human beings, thoughts and feelings are going to arise while doing zazen. But if we start pursuing those thoughts and feelings, then we are no longer just doing zazen. So realizing that this isn't the time to be sitting and thinking, we have to correct our posture and return to just doing zazen. That is a time when we are sitting with an open hand.

As we sit zazen, the formerly crystal clear image that was in our minds falls away, leaving us just facing the wall. Just facing the wall is what is so wonderful about zazen.

Even at a time when some troubling thing at home continues to arise in our heads, the moment we return to just doing zazen, the whole matter simply disappears and there is only the wall in front of us. Then, out of nowhere, the thought comes back. Again we let go and again, there is just the wall.

Doing zazen is to return again and again to where only the wall is before us—we do this one hundred million times! In *Shōbōgenzō* "Hotsu-mujōshin," or "Arousing the Supreme Mind" (発無上心), there is a passage: "Arouse that spirit of the bodhisattva over and over—millions of times. Arousing the spirit of practice-enlightenment is the same."

Doing zazen is nothing other than returning again and again to the very quick of jiko. We have to do this one hundred thousand times. This is the true meaning of practice. Sawaki Rōshi harped on this all the time: "Satori is satorizing that satori is practice." Ultimately, practice is nothing but returning to the actual quick of jiko—to viewing our life from the position of where or who we would be today had we been aborted, or from the position of realizing who we would be were we already in the coffin. You have to know and believe that there just isn't any one thing that you have to do. Anyone is capable of returning right now to the actuality of jiko.

Living out ever-changing life.

This principle of universal identity as time means to recognize one's total identity as it manifests through the myriad of phenomena and circumstances.

Regardless of phenomena and circumstances, there is nothing outside of jiko that lives out this jiko. We live out jiko whether we are in heaven or have fallen into the deepest hell. Failing, making mistakes, is jiko; being deeply disappointed is jiko. Dying, too, is jiko. All these phenomena or circumstances are examples of jiko living out itself as the vital quick of life.

This sort of self, jiko, is not some prescribed, hard-and-fast entity. It's constantly changing! Since it is the animated quick of moment-by-moment life, it is always a fully present presence. Therefore, what is wholly jiko is also wholly present.

Still, people persist in thinking that they are living out the same continuous life from the moment they were born. But that is a mistake. We need to realize that what we are living out is the ever-changing life force. By "life force" here I mean world-encompassing jiko. There is no world separate from or outside of myself. Because I am alive, my world exists.

Jiko, in the Buddhist sense, is the birth of jiko [self] simultaneously with the birth of the world; the living out of jiko is the living out of that world, and the demise of jiko is the demise of jiko's world. Jiko, living as animated presence, is the simultaneous presence of world—phenomena, circumstances, situations—everything! So jiko is inclusive of all things, all circumstances. "I" and "all-inclusive world" are not entities separate from ever-changing. There is just one life of jiko—whole self.

Everything we encounter is our life.

II.

Because of this underlying principle [of all things being precisely what they are], the whole world appears in its ten thousand forms and one hundred grasses. Learn to appreciate each and every grass and each and every circumstance; strive to enable all these things to manifest in the deepest [and fullest] way. Viewing all things in this way is the first step of practice.

It is this kind of principle, "of all things being precisely what they are," that Dōgen Zenji admonishes us to realize when he says that "the whole world appears in its ten thousand forms and one hundred grasses" and that every blade of grass, every situation, contains the whole world. "The ten thousand forms and one hundred grasses" refers to all things that take a form. As for the expression "whole world," or in Japanese, *jinchi*, in Senne Zenji's *Gokikigakishō* there's this passage; "Jinchi corresponds to jiko. It is similar to saying that all phenomena appear on the ground of jiko. *Jinchi*, 'whole world,' here is pointing to the immediate presence of all things."

In other words, everything that exists does so on the ground of the very life of jiko. Regardless of what we try to look at, or what realm we wish to experience, everything exists on the ground of the very life of this jiko. This is the same as saying that all things are the content of the very life of jiko. So there is nothing—no blade of grass, no phenomenon—that does not unfold within the life of a world inclusive of me.

And a way or view of life that sees all things as the content of the life of jiko is the initial step in practicing the Buddha's Way. To express this more simply, this is what I mean by my expression "everything I encounter is my life." That is, all things should be considered as being a part of oneself.

For instance, sometimes people come to visit and confide their troubles to me. Those aren't the times to think of them as someone else's problems. All of them are my life problems. Or take someone who wants to drive a car. When she takes hold of the steering wheel, for her, she's literally taking her life in her hands. That's the Buddhist practitioner's approach toward their life.

> When all things arrive in their most settled place, a blade of grass is just what it is; a situation or circumstance is just what it is.

Through practice, a blade of grass, some situation, settles by being just what it is. So when the tenzo, the monastery cook, is cooking the rice that is all he or she is doing.

During the period just after Japan lost the war in the Pacific, everyone was always hungry. In such times, if your turn came around to be tenzo, it meant you would be around food in the kitchen. And when the sugar ration came around, you just might dip your finger in for a lick. Why, everyone was doing it when their turn came around, so the sugar would mysteriously disappear before anyone knew it. However, when you work as a tenzo with that sort of servile bent of a petty thief, then you're not encountering everything as your life. You're evading the work of the tenzo, and your actions are empty of seeing your work as your very own lifeblood.

Of course, throwing off that sort of petty disposition and practicing wholeheartedly to settle everything doesn't mean that, in doing so, something special is awaiting you. It's simply that each and every thing or situation settles as it truly is.

> Sometimes there is understanding [of a situation], sometimes there isn't. At times we comprehend what a blade of grass is, at other times, we don't.

Whether we seek to comprehend some situation or not, ultimately, since everything is the content of jiko, it's all the same. In Menzan Zuihō Zenji's commentary on *Shōbōgenzō* entitled *Monge*, he writes, "Understanding or not understanding—both are uji."

In Zōkai Zenji's *Shiki*, we find, "This is not limited to understanding or lack of it. Sometimes there is delusion, sometimes there is none. Sometimes we have true realization, at other times, we have none." Delusion and realization are not separate categories. Both are simply different scenery on the ground of jiko.

As I have been saying for years, in Buddhism, we don't throw away delusion only to pick up satori. Delusion and satori, the ordinary and the sage, understanding or not understanding—all are the scenery of the life of jiko. We look at the contents of such a jiko as the contents of our life. When we return to that ground of the reality of the life of such a jiko, we can look at everything in a completely fresh light.

All things and all worlds lie within time present.

> Because there is only time present, uji is all-inclusive time. All living things, all occurring phenomena are time. Each instant, each moment of time embodies all existences, all worlds. Uji is inclusive of all time. All the grasses and everything that occurs are time. All existences, all phenomena are contained in the ever-occurring presence of time. Contemplate deeply as to whether or not there is anything at all outside of the present.

What is critical in the first clause is the word "only." He's saying that regardless of whether you're talking about the crude and ignorant person or the saint, delusion or realization, because every human being is nothing other than the time of the true reality of the life of jiko, delusion or realization are simply different ways of looking. This uji, this time of ever-changing actuality of life, is a moment-by-moment time. Using my mathematical formula, however, one time is also all times / all times. When I say that we are living out one jiko, that one is also one/one. And, of course, one/one = two/two = three/three. Ultimately, one/one = all/all. The principle of "one time" equaling all times / all times is the same.

For example, let's say someone comes to see me to talk about something troubling them. So now there is a person right in front of me and that makes two of us. However, for me, since everything I encounter is my life, I exist as two/two. Your suffering is my suffering; your problem is my problem.

Further, all the problems I see and hear about that are going on around me—social problems, environmental problems, or whatever—they're all my problems. That's what is behind my expression "all/all."

"Uji is inclusive of all time" means that one moment of time is not simply an isolated entity. Rather, one moment of time equals all times / all times. And "All the grasses and everything that occurs" means that everything is time or the unfolding of time. Next: "All existences, all phenomena are contained in the ever-occurring presence of time." Here, Dōgen is saying to us that everything in this world is embodied within the constantly changing moment-by-moment of the present.

For instance, let's take a person who was born a long time ago, deep in the mountains of Tamba. If he lived his whole life just there, in those recesses, then that would have been the extent of the world he knew. In the current age, however, we have access to all forms of transportation and communication; the conveniences of television and computers are in our homes, and we're virtually bombarded with information from all over the world, whether we want it or not. All of that is a part of our personal life experience of jiko. Our present time contains all things, all worlds.

Despite that, ordinarily, people unfamiliar with the Buddhadharma hold on to a fixed idea of uji as signifying that there *was* a time [in the past] when they were three-headed, eight-armed beasts, and *another* time when they were sixteen-foot- or eight-foot-tall buddhas. In a sense, [they believe that] one time is like first crossing a river and, at a later time, climbing a mountain. Even though the rivers and mountains may have existed somewhere else, they think they have left them behind completely and are presently residing in the lofty crimson tower of a gorgeous palace. Such people delude themselves by thinking they are now as far from those rivers and mountains as heaven is from earth. The true actuality of the Buddhadharma teaching, however, is not like this.

The two Chinese characters 有時 are read *uji*, in the Chinese style, although they can also be read in Japanese as *arutoki*, meaning "a certain time" or "on one occasion." But if the characters are simply arutoki, a certain time or on one occasion, the discussion shifts from all/all to one/all.

People think that at one time they crossed many rivers and then later, at another time, climbed many mountains. They imagine that even though the rivers and mountains may have existed at one time, they have left them behind completely and are presently residing in the lofty crimson tower of a gorgeous palace. Such people think they are now as far from those rivers and mountains as heaven is from earth. All of this is our ordinary way of thinking about time.

Dōgen came from a very noble background so he wrote very poetically about mountains or rivers or soaring towers inside grand palaces. In more earthy language, people think that over many years they have undergone the hardships—crossed over the mountains and rivers—of practice, and are now dwelling in the fine "palace" called enlightenment.

Again in *Monge*, however, Menzan Zenji aptly comments, "They think they've donned different faces, but that is a mistake." In other words, we think that our situation has completely changed, but in actuality, Menzan is saying that it hasn't. Such people think that the person who crossed the mountains and rivers and the one who is now in the palace are totally different entities—so different that the contrast is as far as heaven is from earth. It's sort of like recollecting how poor and down and out we once were compared to how rich we are today.

> The time they crossed the aforementioned mountains and rivers, they themselves had to have been present there, and so, they themselves were also time. Without a doubt, they had to have been completely present there; time did not disappear.

When you climb a mountain or cross a river, what is alive is none other than you yourself. Where you *were*, time *was* also. Ultimately, we live in the ever-changing moment of the present. "Without a doubt they had to have been completely present there; time did not disappear." As long as we exist, this ever-changing moment of the present does not end. This is because we ourselves are always living out what I have referred to mathematically as all times / all times.

> If time seems to lack the aspect of coming and going, then time on top of the mountain is uji of the present. If it seems to possess such a characteristic, it is experienced [as the scenery] within the actual living present of self—which is also uji.

We can say that time has no *appearance* of coming or going, and we can also say that time possesses such a characteristic. We can say it either way. If we say that time has no appearance of coming or going that would be "time on top of the mountain is uji." "Time on top of the mountain" refers to the actual reality of the present. However, looking at it from the view of time having the appearance of coming and going, "it is experienced [as the scenery] within the actual living present of (one) self—which is also uji."

To put it a little differently, precisely because we look from the view of having a fixed self, we are led to believe that our circumstances of when we were climbing the mountains and crossing the rivers have changed now that we are in the crimson tower of a gorgeous palace. But that's just not the case. If from the viewpoint of time we look at the entire reality of our personal life experience, yesterday was yesterday as all times / all times. The now of the present is all times / all times. To the extent we talk about all times / all times, we can say that there is no appearance of time coming and going. At the same time, however, from the view of "this moment," there is the constant appearance of change. Time here has a double structure.

> When climbing those mountains or traversing those rivers, is not the time of being in the crimson tower of the jeweled palace entirely swallowed whole, is it not entirely thrown up?

Here Dōgen's "swallowed whole" and "entirely thrown up" mean to be free of any remnant or trace. Climbing the mountains and crossing the rivers are just that—climbing and crossing. And the time of being in the palace tower is just that. There is no balancing, no comparing one against the other. Since this constantly changing singular time is the jiko of all times / all times, there is no "other" to compare it to or balance it against. Or, to put it another way, whether I think so or believe it to be true or not, in actuality, I am doing nothing but living out the present.

In more concrete terms, try thinking about this by applying it to each of the things that distress you or trouble you. Most of what troubles people in the world seems to center around some event that happened to them, or why things are this way, or what should they do about it. Everything is framed in terms of the present situation being a continuation of past events and, therefore, what should be done next? Or else, we want to get to some point in the future, so what should we do now? Actually, if we looked at all these matters from the foundation of where we would be today had we been aborted, everything would be over. All times / all times is the cutting off of comparing and balancing.

There Is Nothing Other Than for Us to Live Out the Present

The three-headed, eight-armed beast is yesterday's time. The sixteen-foot-standing or eight-foot-sitting image is today's time.

Three heads and eight arms—what a grotesque image has been conjured up here. But, in fact, this is simply the animated model of ordinary human beings.

On the New Year's cards I sent out last year, I wrote this poem:

I spent my youth writhing and flailing around
    Then, somewhere, somehow, like a leaf

that has been tossed about in the wind
    and drifted into this quiet sun-dappled
spot near Jizō[209] in the village of Kohata,
    I just live out this present time in all humility
being fully content in the face of my unfulfillment.

In the opening line, the "writhing and flailing around" expresses the same thing as this figure of the three-headed, eight-armed ashura.

> Still, regarding this working of past and present, both are wholly contained in the present climbing of the mountain. Within that time, the present looks back over the ten thousand peaks; it is not that they [one's experiences] have in any way disappeared.

For me, the "past" means when I was struggling and thrashing about. I'm sure I was grabbing onto and striking out here and there much more than are most of the offspring of the worried parents who come to see me. But now I've totally quieted down and am living a very modest life in Kohata. Sometimes I get the feeling that everything I was doing then is now past; it's gone. Nothing is left. But that's just a false assumption, a mistaken feeling. Everything is still very much alive, right now.

The "present looks back over all the peaks" is a metaphor for all one's past experiences. For instance, the period in my life when I went out doing takuhatsu, mendicant begging,[210] for only one or two yen in order to stave off hunger and starvation is not behind me. That period is living right now as my personal experience. I've got no income coming in

---

209. Jizō (地蔵; Skt: Kṣitigarbha) is a bodhisattva who vowed not to reach enlightenment until all beings in all the hells were saved.

210. Uchiyama Rōshi wrote of his experiences of going out on takuhatsu in "Nakiwarai no Takuhatsu," which was cotranslated by Daitsū Tom Wright and Jisho Warner and published in English as "Laughter Through the Tears" in *Buddhadharma: The Practitioner's Quarterly*, spring 2006.

regularly now, but it doesn't faze me in the least, due to those years of going out on takuhatsu—so I don't see living out that life of material poverty as a bad deal at all. No, that past experience of poverty is not dead; it's a part of my present.

I worked as a tenzo in the kitchen for twenty years, and I believe that experience is living in my life today. As I wrote in *How to Cook Your Life*, life is, in a way, similar to a dish to be cooked, and I feel those years have got to be alive and working in my life right now. In other words, the present looks back over all the peaks.

> The three-headed, eight-armed beast lives in the totality of the living present; it only seems as though it was in the distant past. The sixteen-foot or eight-foot image, too, lives in the wholeness of the immediate present. Though it appears to be something in the far distant future, it is living right now.

This flailing, thrashing figure appears to be something in our distant past, but in actuality, this is not so. It is an integral element in our life right now. Similarly, you make a critical mistake if you put the sixteen-foot-standing or eight-foot-sitting image of the Buddha outside of you. Though it appears to be something in the far distant future, it is alive at this very moment. We have to practice that way, here and now.

> Therefore, the pine tree is [all] time, the bamboo is [all] time; do not think of "flying away" as a true quality or functioning of time.

Here again Dōgen chooses expressions of literary beauty, although what he is doing is simply referring to all the dharmas of the universe. Simply put, the pine tree and the bamboo refer to all things, all existences. The cup in front of me is time, so is the light bulb, so is the wind—there is nothing that isn't time. So we shouldn't just think that such and such a time merely flies away or passes away.

Do not imagine that such seeming passing away is real. If time were something that was cut off, there would have to be a gap. People are incapable of experiencing uji, because they are convinced only of the ephemeral appearance of time.

Ordinarily, we conceive of the past as something that has gone by or ended. But if that is so, then there will be a certain space between the past and the following moment. Consequently, we would be incapable of discerning what time truly is. People who conceive of time as being something that goes by do so because they have never had the experience of what uji, living time, actually is.

We ourselves are living out uji. This is called *gouji*— the personal, experiential quick of time.

The essential characteristic of uji is this: while all existences in all the various worlds are interconnected, each existence is unique in itself, and precisely because of this, we can speak of *personally* experiencing the living quick of time.

The overall gist of what I want to say in regard to this fascicle is contained right here. While on the one hand, all things—existences, situations, circumstances, etc.—of all realms are tied together, they are all constantly changing. It is this uji, this living quick of time, that I am personally living out. This is referred to as *gouji*. This was touched on earlier in the passage "This principle of universal identity as time means to recognize one's total identity as it manifests through the myriad of phenomena and circumstances." What is living out right now, in every moment, this living reality of life before the division into self and all phenomena is none other than me! So what is important here is to thoroughly penetrate the reality of this ever-changing world of jiko inclusive of all things.

> Uji possesses the virtuous power of *kyōryaku,* moment-by-moment occur-
> ring. What we normally refer to as today becomes tomorrow; today,
> yesterday; yesterday, today; today, today; tomorrow, tomorrow.

This ever-changing quality is the virtuous power of time.

When we hear an expression such as "time passes," we're apt to presume that it passes in a linear movement. But the Japanese expression *kyōryaku* used in this passage implies a moment-by-moment manifestation; it's always now, now, now. Regardless of what time we might think it is, it is always in the present that we are living. Though we talk about something past, the fact is, we are simply presently recalling something from the past; we are doing it now.

Or if we speak about the future, we are doing nothing other than imagining the future—now! Now is all there really is—the ever-changing now.

"Now" is really a curious thing; it's actually just a point. A point I can draw has a certain diameter to it: ·. But the point "now" takes up no space and has no measurable length of time. Even just one moment ago is past, and the future is that very next moment that isn't here now. We could say that "now" isn't even a moment. Still, contained in this point of now we can have past recollections or future imaginings. Not only that, we can surmise about ages of an infinite past or a timeless future. So all there is, is the infinite point of the present. Take away the point of now, and there can be no infinite or eternal. Passing back and forth freely from yesterday to today, to eternal past, to eternal future, within the now you are presently living is the virtue of uji.

> Since this constant and vivid occurring is the virtuous quality of time, time
> past does not intrude on time present. Though the former is not linked
> to the latter, Seigen is time, Ōbaku is time, Daijaku and Sekitō are time,
> you and others are all time. Consequently, practice/enlightenment is all
> times; likewise, entering into the mud and going into the water is also
> time.

The past and the present neither spill onto each other nor are they connected. Still, Dōgen says that Seigen is time.

Seigen, Ōbaku, Daijaku, Sekitō—these are all famous Zen masters of the past. We learn many things from these ancients. That is, we learn from them within the context of living in the ever-occurring moment of the present. This is because "you and other"—you and those of the past—are all time. When we think of people in the past, we get the feeling that they're something totally outside of our lives, but that's a mistake. In reality, we are right now living the quick of the life of jiko, and that jiko includes both ourselves and "other." That is why he says "practice/enlightenment is all times." Practice/enlightenment is alive and constantly changing within the present, devoid of any comparison.

One inspiration for my becoming a monk was due to my encounter with the following passage from *Shōbōgenzō* "Jishōzanmai" ("Samadhi of Self Affirmation"): "Following an experienced teacher or adhering to the teachings in the scriptures is nothing other than following or adhering to whole self, or jiko." In other words, neither becoming the disciple of some teacher nor studying the sūtras ever means following something outside of oneself. The text goes on: "The sūtras are sūtras of ourselves and experienced teachers teach us of ourselves. Therefore, encountering an experienced teacher is encountering jiko. Applying oneself to the hundred grasses is addressing jiko, devoting oneself to the ten thousand trees is addressing jiko." A monk seeking a teacher or the Dharma means to self-confidently put on the straw hat, the leggings, and the straw sandals [of takuhatsu], because doing so is learning about and experiencing jiko.

So to look lightly on whatever it is that jiko is presently facing is to look lightly on oneself. Conversely, to value whatever we are encountering right now means to value jiko, our whole self.

"Entering into the mud and going into the water is also time" refers to preaching or speaking for the sake of other people. This, too, Dōgen says, is time. It means we are living out our own life force. We should always bear in mind that time is our life force. It is a grave mistake to think that

Dōgen's use of the word is the same as it is normally used. There is no way to comprehend the spin he is giving to it, unless we redefine it as the ever-changing living quick reality of our own life.

When I read the passage I quoted just now from "Jishōzanmai," I realized that if I didn't study and practice with an experienced teacher, I wouldn't be able to clarify my understanding of what this "self" is. So, I became a monk. After all, without that kind of feeling, how could such a strikingly handsome young man as myself ever have conceived of shaving his head, putting on this absurd outfit, and becoming as ridiculous a thing as a Buddhist monk!

Time is our very own life.

> Further, though the biased views of ordinary people, along with the internal conditions and external influences that affect those views, form people's misunderstandings, the dharmas are not people's possessions, it is simply that all these so-called dharmas temporarily inform the person.

Neither the views held by ordinary people nor the conditions and circumstances that appear as such belong to anyone. Rather, it is simply that the dharmas temporarily [in]form the person. That is, in reality, this unadulterated living quick of life of jiko has done nothing more than temporarily take the form of an ordinary person. In other words, all of us are just ordinary human beings, and the pure quick of life has taken on the appearance of an ordinary person.

As I've said many times previously, if we look again at ourselves from the foundation of having been aborted before we were born, we return to that unadulterated freshness. There's no need to worry about a thing.

> Because ordinarily, we take it for granted that living time and all existences do not lie within ourselves, we assume that the sixteen-foot-tall golden

body cannot reside within us. Consequently, we remain unable to imagine that such a buddha could in any way lie within us. Therefore, those who have not yet made such confirmation should examine carefully each and every living moment of time.

To the extent that all of us are living sentient beings, it is the ever-changing life force that we are living out. At the same time, [within that life force] our whole world is unfolding. This is the meaning of living time and all existences in the above passage.

However, as human beings, we get it into our heads that living time and all existences do not reside within ourselves. In other words, we haven't yet truly understood that living time and all existences are the living presence of jiko. So we assume that the Buddha has no connection to us. We assume that any discussion of the Buddha is about someone else.

This whole ball of wax—including our insistence that we are not Buddha, but ordinary human beings—however, is the ever-changing living presence of jiko. So it is no mistake that we return anew to this living reality of life by letting go of such thoughts.

If we haven't yet understood this truth, we should simply open our eyes and look. Every human being without exception is living out this ever-changing living quick of jiko; we needn't harbor any doubts about it.

Living is inclusive of realization and delusion— the ordinary [secular] and the sage [sacred].

III.

That which has been mutually agreed on as the hour of the horse and sheep is inclusive of the rising and setting, of the greater and lesser aspects of the naturally residing dharmas, all of which are as they are— living time. The hours of the rat and the tiger are living time. Sentient beings and buddhas are also living time.

In ancient China, time was divided into twelve hours with each hour being assigned the name of an animal, such as horse, sheep, rat, tiger, and so forth. Residing dharmas, or *jūhōi* [*no immo naru*] (住法位(の恁麼なる), refer to all things being settled in their original form. My expression "the fresh direct reality of the life of jiko" derives from this *jūhōi*. *Immo* is a [Buddhist] expression that means "unspeakable," "unutterable," "not expressible in words"; the actuality behind or referred to by "the reality of the life of jiko" can never be captured by [verbal] articulation. The personal life experience behind utterances like "self that is only self" or "now that is fully now" is, in actuality, inexpressible.

"The rising and setting," "the greater and lesser" refer to movement or change in that reality. And here sentient beings and buddhas are also living time; the two are set in opposition to one another, but both are time.

> The three-headed, eight-armed beast affirms living time through its functioning throughout all realms. The sixteen-foot golden body does the same. Since both contain all worlds, each and every world functions completely in all worlds. This is referred to as thoroughly penetrating. The golden body penetrates the golden body thoroughly in manifesting its totality by arousing the attitude of a bodhisattva, practicing, functioning as a bodhisattva, entering nirvana. This golden body is living presence, living time. All times totally penetrate all existences with nothing left over. This is because whatever might remain, remains totally.

In the secret teachings of Shingon Mikkyō,[211] this three-headed, eight-armed beast is one of a number of figures that form different groups of anti-deities or other higher beings. For example, Acala, one of the deities known in Japanese as *Fudōmyōō* (不動明王), appears in wrathful form to utterly defeat all the various evil spirits. But conjuring up such images

211. Also known as Japanese Esoteric Buddhism, this is a Vajrayāna school of Buddhism popular in Japan.

in our age doesn't say much to people; that's why I'm always picking on Tanaka Kakuei to illustrate this image. On the one hand, having to uphold the dignity of the office of prime minister, he waves suavely, gesturing to cameras and people as he passes by. On the other hand, in the courtroom where he sits as one of the accused in the Lockheed scandal,[212] he has to sit quietly wearing that awful scowl on his face. And then at rallies for the Tanaka faction of the Liberal Democratic Party, he talks big about all the great changes he's going to bring about next. Right there you've got three different poses. And if we're going to talk about hands and arms, he's got one or two hands filled with money, one that spreads the money around, one offering bribes, and so forth. There's no question that someone as active as Mr. Tanaka has at least three heads and eight arms. And when you think about how he keeps on going despite all of the chiding by the press, you have to admit that he's got to have tremendous appeal or charisma or whatever. He certainly has a lot of supporters who feel he's really a great man.

But you know, when the topic of some person being "great" comes up, I can't help recalling a remark Sawaki Rōshi often made: "They all think the leader of their gang is 'great'—all the weak punks working under him. . . ."

Anyway, all people—even people like Tanaka—affirm living time through functioning throughout all realms. There is absolutely no one who is not living the reality of their own life—everyone actualizes their own world, whatever it might be. Even a person suffering from a severe neurosis fully affirms all the realms of that world. However, from a Buddhist standpoint, all the realms of people like Tanaka are nothing more than the realms of struggling for existence, worlds where trading through language is possible. Worlds, therefore, of giving and

212. The U.S. aerospace company Lockheed made a series of bribes in the 1950s through the 1970s to a number of foreign officials, including the Japanese prime minister Kakuei Tanaka.

taking, borrowing and lending. Worlds in which we are nothing more than individual members of the society. That is, one/all humanity! It's just a matter of course that feelings of "who's greater than whom" will arise, success and failure, good and evil, pushing and shoving each other around, or struggling desperately only to end up dead.

Speaking of inflated ideas of greatness, recall the Chinese mythological tale of Songoku. Using his magical powers, this simian hero flew several million *ri*[213] in a single leap! Then, turning around to admire how great his leap had been, he saw that he was still sitting inside the Buddha's palm. In this same sense, regardless of how powerfully Tanaka functions as a three-headed, eight-armed beast in that world of self-preservation, from the viewpoint of Buddhadharma, all his activity amounts to little more than struggle for survival, because there's no life aim or direction.

The "sixteen-foot golden body" is a reference to Śākyamuni Buddha, who lived out the most refined, settled way of life of jiko. So "the sixteen-foot golden body does the same" means that Śākyamuni had his way of living out or concretizing his life. It should be understood here that Dōgen is not passing down some moral judgment that people like Tanaka with all their fighting and pushing people around are evil and that enlightened people like Śākyamuni are good. His point is simply that we live out our own lives inclusive of whether we're enlightened or deluded, ordinary or saintly, failures or successes. Since uji is moment-by-moment time of all-inclusive jiko—self and all worlds—it's enough just to return to the fundamental reality of our life. In doing so, jiko—whole self inclusive of all worlds—returns concretely, moment-by-moment to all-inclusive jiko. This concrete returning is the meaning of "thoroughly penetrating."

Sawaki Rōshi used to say, "Stalin, Mao Zedong, and Truman should all join hands and sit zazen." In other words, all these people who are pushing and shoving others around, making a lot of noise—they all ought to sit down and do zazen together. Some people want to just go off in the

213. One *ri* equals about 2.4 miles.

mountains somewhere to sit zazen by themselves, but that sort of isolationist or escapist zazen is no good. The zazen taught by Dōgen Zenji is sometimes called *jijuyū zanmai*—the samadhi of freely receiving and functioning. Sawaki Rōshi defined *jijuyū zanmai* as "self selfs the self."

By this, he was referring to jiko—all-inclusive self, a jiko that sits all-inclusively. This all-inclusive jiko, however, is not simply one person among the world's population, in the sense of one/humankind. Rather it is a jiko whose contents comprise all humankind, all existences. It is a presence active in the world as a jiko that contains all worlds and all times, and that is the sort of zazen we practice. Further, this jiko containing all worlds and times is the sense of "The golden body penetrates the golden body thoroughly in manifesting its totality by arousing the attitude of a bodhisattva, practicing, functioning as a bodhisattva, entering nirvana."

Conventionally, we might tend to interpret this passage sequentially as firstly arousing the bodhisattva spirit, then practicing, and then becoming an actual bodhisattva. And then finally we would reach nirvana. But that wouldn't be a truly Buddhadharma understanding. Arousing the bodhisattva spirit is, at the same time, the golden body; practice, too, is itself the golden body; functioning as a bodhisattva and entering nirvana, too, are the golden body. Each of these is the golden body as living presence, living time.

I'm going to repeat myself again: jiko—all-inclusive self—is wholly one. That is one/one, two/two, all/all. Jiko is born as wholly one. This wholly one is not simply one human being among all humanity, nor merely one member among all the members of a society—some sort of cog in a wheel. Everything that is seen or heard or felt—everything—forms the content of jiko that is all/all. At the same time, this is also all times/all times. It is the life of all/all, all times / all times that we are actually living out.

Therefore, "All times totally penetrate all existences with nothing left over"; all there is for us to do is thoroughly penetrate our own lives with nothing left over. "This is because whatever might remain, remains totally"; there is nothing extra remaining, since even what might remain exists in its totality within all existences—*jin'u* (尽有).

> Even that living presence that has not been fully penetrated is penetrated thoroughly as unfulfilled living presence.

Here, Dōgen Zenji is talking about *prātimokṣa*, precepts, or, in Japanese, *haradaimokusha* (波羅提木叉). Prātimokṣa is also referred to in Japanese as *betsubetsu gedatsu* (別々解脱)—emancipation one by one. In other words, if we uphold a certain precept, we will be emancipated to that extent.

Naturally, if we fail to scoop up the water from the wellspring of life, we can't say we are holding it. However, failing to uphold a precept is not considered to be the same as breaking the precept. Actions contrary to the precepts do not constitute the eternal breaking of the precepts. Therefore, practitioners must always aim at living out their lives [with the spirit of] keeping the precepts. If they keep even one, then they become emancipated to that extent. This is the sense of prātimokṣa; it must also be the genuine spirit of any Buddhist practitioner.

> Even if something appears to be a mistake or misguided intention, we are still living out moment-by-moment living time.

Since uji is the [unfolding] jiko of all worlds moment-by-moment, whether we aim to live out that life or not, whether we attempt to live up to that life or not, has no bearing here, in the sense that the life of jiko is not controlled by my intentions or attempts. Far too often we gauge and judge things only with our emotions and narrow perspectives. The teaching of the Buddhadharma, however, is about the true reality of life. Whether we believe it is so or not, you and I—everyone—is living out this reality, which in our text is described as the jiko of moment-by-moment time containing all worlds and existences. Therefore, we actually manifest however much of the life we manifest.

Further, from the viewpoint of uji, the mistake (or misguided intention), inclusive of before and after, resides in living time; it is contained within the vivid actuality of where all existences naturally reside—this is uji, living time! Do not be deluded into nonexistence, nor fanatically insist on existence.

Even if we fall down, we are still living that jiko inclusive of all situations, all worlds. And, further, if we consider uji from the standpoint of the Buddhadharma, since we are talking about a jiko that is moment-by-moment all-inclusive worlds, even mistakes, failures, and misguided intentions reside within the reality of life. This sense of aliveness or "vivid actuality" is conveyed in the Japanese Buddhist expression *kappappachi*.

Kappappachi is what you feel when you try and take a big fish off the line—that animation. In other words, living in and through the freshness of each moment is what is referred to as the "reality of life"—*seimei no jitsubutsu*. In this context, there can be no discriminating whether this situation is okay compared to another one, or misguided thoughts of wanting to get out of or away from delusion and bag some sort of grand realization, or dread or anxiety toward "hell" and a passion for or longing to be in "paradise"—these are just some of the suggestive nuances behind "Do not be deluded into nonexistence nor insist fanatically on existence."

Time neither comes nor goes; it is simply the reality of life.

People stubbornly take it into their heads that time passes away, with no comprehension that that which has not yet arrived is also uji. Even though such misunderstanding itself is also uji, living time itself is unaffected by such mistaken views. People unquestioningly believe time comes and goes, but no human being has ever realized exactly where the living quick of time resides. Much less has any human being ever been liberated from time.

Ordinarily we take it for granted that what we call "time" is something that simply passes away, and we remain ignorant that that which has not arrived is also uji, living time. Actually, time neither comes nor goes.

However, even though we might make such an assumption about time, "living time itself is unaffected by such mistaken views." In other words, the fundamental nature of time remains uninfluenced by wrong understanding. Human beings view everything using their own greedy desires and deluded ideas. The actuality of life, however, is always what it is with no connection whatever to human attempts to judge and evaluate it.

As long as we think of time only as something that comes and goes, we will never be able to realize exactly what the actuality of life—time inclusive of all existences, all worlds—is. "Much less has any human being ever been liberated from time." Being liberated from time is the same as *mu no itten* (無の一点)—the point of no space, no time.

Also, in regard to the word *resides*, it would appear that the reality of life or uji would have to live somewhere, but in fact, since uji unfolds moment-by-moment, we can't even say that.

> Even though there might be someone who intellectually grasps where uji resides, who can possibly express living time itself! Or even if someone in the past were said to have expressed it, there is no one alive who would not continue groping to see whatever is eminently presenting itself before their very eyes.

Even if there were someone who was capable of recognizing the significance of uji—living time, time containing all existences and all worlds—there is no human being capable of bringing forth the unbounded, limitless functioning of reality, who can possibly express living time itself! There is no one who is not fumbling to see the way things truly are in their original form.

By the way, it would be way off the mark to assume that "immediately presenting itself before their very eyes" is referring to something "outside" of ourselves. Whatever it is we are presently engaged in is what is immediately presenting itself before our very eyes.

The true reality of life transcends the dichotomy of movement or nonmovement.

IV.

If [the idea of] uji were left to the fancies of human imagination, the actual wisdom of enlightenment and the emancipation of nirvana would amount to little more than ephemeral comings and goings.

Ordinarily, time is thought to be nothing more than a two-dimensional coming and going. Enlightenment or nirvana would be reduced to being mere transitory existences. Nevertheless, even these imaginary ideas cannot be separated from the all-inclusiveness of uji.

However, the living presence of enlightenment and nirvana can never be ensnared by human speculation or conjecture; all there is, is the living manifestation of uji.

The two Chinese characters for "be ensnared," 羅籠 *rarō*, refer to a net for catching rabbits and a cage or trap for catching fish. In this case, rarō are tools or means for bagging "satori." Ordinarily, people often think they practice in order to bag "enlightenment," but that's a mistake. If zazen is nothing more than a means for having some sort of satori experience, it's not true zazen. Hence, the living presence of enlightenment and nirvana can never be ensnared by human speculation or conjecture. The following sentence: "All there [truly is] is the living manifestation of uji" means that there is nothing else for us to do but to live out this very quick of our lives.

The functioning presence of the guardian deities and the other myriad protectors in all worlds and directions is the manifesting of our personal life experience as living time. This living time in all creatures both in the water and on the land, in the infinite situations and existences both visible and invisible, is the wholly personal manifesting of the entire power of uji, the entire power of kyōryaku. Sit and practice until it is thoroughly clear that if uji were not all the power of kyōryaku, not a single thing would manifest, nor would there be any moment-by-moment [life].

When I come across passages in *Shōbōgenzō* like this one, I'm reminded of what Dōgen Zenji said in *Shōbōgenzō Zuimonki* in reference to himself: "One of my greatest faults is that as soon as I pick up a pen, my writing naturally becomes elaborate and florid." Here in his text "Uji," he uses "the guardian deities and other myriad protectors," "all creatures in the water and on the land," "situations and existences both visible and invisible"—all very elliptical, ornate expressions. But what he is referring to is simply everything that exists. All things are the manifesting of uji, living time. Or they manifest the entire power of uji, as the entire power of moment-by-moment.

That is, all things exist precisely because I personally experience them. He's saying that I myself am living through my personal life experience of all these things. The Japanese word *kyōryaku* here in the original text means "moment-by-moment." And further, he adds, "Sit and practice until it is thoroughly clear that if uji were not all the power of kyōryaku, not a single thing would manifest, nor would there be any moment-by-moment [life]." In other words, if I'm not personally experiencing [the manifestation of all things], there is no way to talk of "moment-by-moment." The entire power of moment-by-moment simply means to be alive.

For example, from my vantage point, Tanaka Kakuei lives in such a different world that I can't even imagine what it is like. And, vice versa, from his standpoint, there can be no doubt that he's living his life totally oblivious to my life experience or the living world I conceive of. Every human being is living out their own world totally different from anyone else's. Every person in the world is personally experiencing their own world.

By *kyōryaku*—the living quick of moment-by-moment—I do not mean the way the wind and rain seem to blow from east to west as has been taught in the past. *Kyōryaku* does not imply immobility; neither does it imply progress or regression.

This word *kyōryaku* is usually read *keireki* and employed when you want to talk about someone's background, what schools they attended, what sort of work experiences they've had up to now, and so forth. But in this case, the Buddhist reading for it is *kyōryaku,* and the meaning is different from what we ordinarily think of as change or movement. It should not be understood as being like the wind or rain that blows this way and that way. "*Kyōryaku* does not imply immobility; neither does it imply progress or regression"; in other words, by *kyōryaku,* Dōgen Zenji does not mean movement or change, nor lack of such. All things in all worlds exist moment-by-moment, so if we hypothetically attempt to divide even one second into, say, 1/10,000, the time it takes to divide that second also takes time, so there you have movement or change, and you would have to break that timespan down even further.

Conversely, if you say there is no movement—that is, that the non-moving point of nothingness isn't moving—no matter what you add to it, there would still be nothing moving. We can talk of either movement or nonmovement, but truly, the living quick of the point of nothingness is that which transcends movement or nonmovement.

> Moment-by-moment [life] is like spring; spring unfolds the myriad forms of spring—*that* is moment-by-moment. Investigate and look carefully at how moment-by-moment [life] is not influenced by anything outside of you. For instance, the moment-by-moment of spring brings forth the multifarious spring appearances in every moment.

We receive the impression that in the so-called springtime of the year, first of all, the plum blossoms begin to bloom, next, the peach come into bloom, followed by the cherry blossoms. In a short time, the blossoms fall and the new leaves appear. We see the appearances of change and become convinced that kyōryaku is simply change, but that is not how it should be understood in the Buddhist sense. These multifarious appearances—the blossoming of the plum and the peach and the cherry, and the falling of the blossoms and so forth—are a brocade of scenery. Yet each and every scene occurs moment-by-moment. The plum blossoms as the plum alone; the peach blossoms as the peach alone. The peach doesn't look over at the plum blossoms thinking that, for social appearances, it better start blooming, too. It is not motivated to blossom by comparing itself to something else. In each instance—the temperature, the humidity, the sunlight—none of these are balanced against anything else. Spring is just spring, since moment-by-moment is not influenced by anything outside. When the flowers bloom, they just bloom. "The moment-by-moment of spring brings forth the multifarious spring appearances in every moment." In spring, all the appearances together comprise spring.

> Look closely at how moment-by-moment, though not itself spring, is entirely complete at springtime, since each and every moment, each and every entity fully expresses spring.

Naturally, kyōryaku—moment-by-moment—is not limited to spring. Dōgen is simply saying that in springtime the moment-by-moment immanence of spring that occurs is entirely complete.

> If we understand kyōryaku as all things going on outside of ourselves, and that only the subject faces east, and we encounter all the myriad worlds that seem to pass through endless expanses of time, we are not yet practicing the Buddha's Way with our whole heart.

"East" here is a reference for spring. Holding onto some idea that there is a surrounding environment outside of us, and that there is this evolving subject that changes over a period of time, is not practicing the Way with a Buddhist understanding.

Deliberations and Evaluations are also Uji.

V.

At the direction of Master Sekitō Kisen, Yakusan Igen called on Master Daijaku of Kōzei. Yakusan said, "I understand the essence of the teachings of the three vehicles and the teachings of the twelve divisions to a certain extent. Still, I can't say that I have truly grasped the significance of why Bodhidharma came from the west?"

From here the plot of our text is going to thicken. Yakusan's teacher at the time was Sekitō Kisen, who decided to send his disciple to see Master Daijaku, known more familiarly in Japan by the name Baso Dōitsu. Yakusan Daishi was extremely well versed in all the various Buddhist schools of thought. Still, he asks, "Why [did] Bodhidharma [come] from the west?" In other words, he was asking just what was Bodhidharma's fundamental intention in taking all the trouble to come to China from faraway India? Or, in more readily understandable language, he was asking what the essence of the Buddhadharma as a teaching is.

Master Daijaku replied, "Śākyamuni's teaching by deliberately raising his eyebrows and blinking is uji; raising them and blinking unintentionally is also uji. Raising them and blinking at the proper time is uji, and doing so inappropriately at the wrong time is also uji."

Raising his eyebrows and blinking his eyes are a reference to the legendary tale of Śākyamuni Buddha holding up a flower in front of all his disciples, raising his eyebrows, and then blinking. Master Daijaku, quoting from this ancient story, said that intentional or unintentional, correct or incorrect, are all a part of uji.

To understand what this means, we have to go back to the opening lines of the text in which Dōgen lined up eight phenomena or situations:

The living quick of time stands on the peak of the highest mountain. The living quick of time moves on the floor of the deepest ocean. It takes the form of the three-headed, eight-armed brutish beast. It appears as the figure measuring sixteen feet when standing and eight feet tall when seated. It takes the form of the precautionary staff or a monk's fly chaser; it is a pillar or a lantern. It is the common third or fourth child, it is the earth; it is the heavens.

There, Dōgen said that all things, all situations and circumstances, are uji, living time. In contrast, in the first line of Daijaku's kōan, he's talking about intention, that is, the function of human will or volition. In the latter line, *properly* and *improperly* refer, in a sense, to human value judgments or evaluations. That is, human judgments, too, are nothing other than uji, living time.

Up to this section, Dōgen Zenji has been saying that uji or the living quick of time is the moment-by-moment [life] of all existences, all worlds. And here in this section, he's moving on to say that even human deliberations and judgments, too, must function on this foundation of the moment-by-moment [life] of all things, all situations. That is, it is critical for us to return and function from one moment to the next in our all-inclusive world, without losing sight of the moment-by-moment reality of our lives, and not just pursue one thought after another.

The passage and the discussion here are not so easy to comprehend, so let's look at it from a different perspective. In place of "raising the eyebrows and blinking" let's substitute the word "peace." Now we have a passage something like this: "Deliberately bringing about peace is uji; not enabling peace to come about is also uji. Bringing about peace at the right time is uji; doing so at the wrong time is also uji." Perhaps putting it in this way may be easier to relate to.

Human life is originally, or most fundamentally, the moment-by-moment [life] of all existences, all worlds—uji. If from that fundamental perspective of life we start to talk of peace being more important than anything else, and then proceed to form a peace movement, at some point we are unaware of, that movement begins to split into two or three groups and those groups begin fighting one another! One side argues that we have to fight in order to maintain peace, while the other side stubbornly insists that under no circumstances—even invasion—should we resist and fight. Ultimately, these so-called proponents of peace end up fighting one another, and no one knows any longer which side they're on or what they ought to be doing.

This whole situation reminds me somewhat of a phenomenon that occurs where I live in Kohata. The area around there tends to stay rather warm and the humidity is generally quite high. As the humidity goes up, these column-like swarms of mosquitoes begin whirling around. Watching them dance round and round, I can't help but think how similar, in a way, they are to human societies. With a can of insect repellant, one press of the button—*sshhhh*—and the mosquitoes all drop dead in an instant. In that same way, you ready a few hydrogen bombs and some missiles and push the buttons and—*sshhhh*—in one shot you've just about wiped everyone out. As long as humankind continues to live on the same level as a swarm of mosquitoes, I don't see that anything can be done about it.

To bring about true peace, before we go running around shouting "peace!" or "war!" or "good!" or "evil!" we need to, first of all, return to the moment-by-moment all-inclusive world of our original, fundamental self—and therein sit up straight. I don't see any other way for humankind other than to sit zazen in the spirit of Sawaki Rōshi's "Stalin, Mao Zedong, and Truman should all join hands and sit zazen." I say this because when we're sitting zazen true peace is being manifest. The troubles all begin with the person who starts, "Stalin is evil, Mao alone is truly good." The most fundamental reality is to return to and live out the reality of the life of our whole self—our jiko, which is already living out a moment-by-moment world inclusive of all things and all situations and circumstances.

When I was in high school, I read this passage from the *Dhammapada*: "Hatred/spite/vengeance will never cease as long as we hate or bear a grudge or seek vengeance. Only by letting go of our hatred/spite/vengeance will it settle." At the time, I thought the passage was very simple, just common sense. But I was completely wrong; this is no simple aphorism. These words seem to embody an undeniable truth.

If we apply this passage to the issue of world peace, we see that peace will never come as long as we merely shout about it. Only by personally refraining from fighting can there be peace. "Only by personally refraining from fighting" is simply another way of saying "only by returning to the reality of the life of the moment-by-moment all-inclusive world of jiko" can there be peace.

Here is where we find the depth of the Buddhadharma teaching of Śākyamuni Buddha and of Dōgen Zenji. You'll never find it in the naive simplicity of "choose A or B," peace or war. The Dharma of Dōgen Zenji and Śākyamuni Buddha is one of great subtlety. You'll only find it if you go to a depth beyond choosing, prior to discrimination. But having said that, I don't mean to imply that it is too deep, too subtle, or totally unapproachable. The fact is all of us are right now living this life of all-inclusive jiko, moment-by-moment.

I frequently hear people say that you often see Christians getting involved in various peace movements or relief projects, and so forth, and how come the Buddhists never seem to get involved? Actually, you do see a few priests marching in such demonstrations, but on the whole, there has always been somewhat of a predisposition among Buddhists to stay away from organized peace movements and charity projects. This has been particularly true of the disciples of Bodhidharma.

Bodhidharma climbed mountains and crossed seas over a period of several years, traveling from India to China. So you would assume that having undergone all that trouble, once he got to China, he would have availed himself of the power of the mass media of his times (which meant appealing to the authority of the king or emperor) in order to propagandize the spread of Buddhism, but he didn't. Off in one corner (actually, a cave) on the grounds of Shaolin Temple, he just sat zazen alone by himself for nine years.

Eventually, after quite some time, there showed up one person who responded: Eka Daishi. Eka continued just sitting by himself in the same way Bodhidharma had, and because he was in resonance with Bodhidharma's style, Eka too was completely ignored by the world. Then Sōsan Daishi and, after that, Dōshin Daishi came along—in a sense, like one thin, very delicate strand, this tradition continued down to the Sixth Ancestor, Enō Daishi, when, for the first time, the zazen of Bodhidharma virtually exploded and spread everywhere.[214]

That was Bodhidharma's way. It had to be that way. Rather than running around getting involved in some movement or project, Bodhidharma simply sat still on the foundation of the self of moment-by-moment [life] inclusive of all worlds. This is the same sense that is behind Sawaki Rōshi's statement about Stalin, Mao, and Truman needing to sit down and do zazen together. What we need in the world more than anything else today is living examples or models—people who work, settling within themselves without running around whining and complaining, along with the development and spread of such people. In Zen there's the expression *ikko hanko* (一箇半箇), which means if even one person is grounded in the living present of all things, all worlds, and that gets transmitted to the next person, then at some point, the flower will open, creating the environment for the next generation. We can see ikko hanko in the way Bodhidharma's style was passed down from one person to the next. My aim is exactly the same. I suspect there are a number of people who are tired of hearing me say this, but almost all of my disciples are much more reliable than I am. I can name at least thirty or so. So what will happen when those thirty have thirty disciples of their own and continue the same lifestyle of zazen that I've been living for all

214. Taiso Eka (大祖慧可; Chi: Dazu Huike; 487–593), Kanchi Sōsan, Dōshin (道信; Chi: Dayi Daoxin; 580–651), and Enō (惠能; Chi: Huineng; 638–713) are the second, third, fourth, and sixth Patriarchs of Chinese Zen, respectively.

these years! I can't help but believe that at some point down the line, a renaissance similar to the golden age of Enō Daishi will blossom forth.

So what is most crucial for me is to develop an attitude of cultivating my own personal life on deeper and deeper levels, just sitting steadily and settling on the reality of the life of jiko—self of moment-by-moment, all-inclusive life.

Standing on the foundation of life beyond making comparisons.

> On hearing Daijaku's reply, Yakusan had a profound realization. He, in turn, replied, "Although I have been practicing with Sekitō for some time, in trying to understand what is behind his teaching, I've felt like a mosquito trying to climb on the back of an iron ox."
> Daijaku's comment is unlike anyone else's.

Although the text here reads that Yakusan Zenji had a truly profound realization, this doesn't mean some trivial little enlightenment experience like throwing out illusion and bagging some sort of satori. Yakusan's realization was one inclusive of such opposites as illusion and realization.

Then, he replied to Daijaku, "Although I have been practicing with Sekitō for some time, in trying to understand what is behind his teaching, I've felt like a mosquito trying to climb on the back of an iron ox." Obviously, it's not possible for a mosquito to penetrate the hide of an ox made of iron. In other words, Yakusan came to realize that he was unable to penetrate the Buddhadharma taught by his teacher Master Sekitō. If it's an insignificant matter like discarding some illusion we've been harboring, I suppose some piddling satori experience might work, but when it comes to the reality of life prior to illusion and realization, there is just no way human perceptions can penetrate it.

Human comprehension occurs in the head only after the separation of realization from illusion. However, the reality of life prior to division is not an intellectual problem. It's not something that can be measured by a secretion of the human mind; rather the reality of life is the origin that enables that secretion to spring forth in the first place.

"Daijaku's comment is unlike anyone else's." Dōgen Zenji is saying that Daijaku's reply to Yakusan's question is not to be compared with what typically passes as "Zen enlightenment."

> His eyebrows take the form of grand mountains, and his eyes are like the vast oceans, since mountains and oceans are not different from his eyebrows and his eyes. "Deliberately raising the eyebrows" is seeing the mountains; "blinking intentionally" has the same power as the rivers flowing into the oceans. The mountains and oceans become one with us. We become led by the power of the mountains and oceans: uji.

Even a single hair of one eyebrow is the "mountains and oceans." "Mountains and oceans" is the same as the moment-by-moment [life] of all existences, all worlds. I see no need here to try and justify Daijaku's equating eyes and eyebrows with such enormous phenomena as mountains and seas, but I'll just add this.

When Dōgen Zenji was working on the fascicle in *Shōbōgenzō* called "Sansuikyō" (山水経, "The Mountains and Rivers Sūtra"), he was most likely living at Kōshōji [then located in Fukakusa, south of the city proper] and was surrounded by the mountains and rivers in the area. These mountains are a part of the same group where I live near the small town of Uji.[215] Every day, I walk along the banks of the Uji River enjoying the scenery of the surrounding mountains. Looking at them, however, from the perspective of size, you have to say that as mountains they're pretty pathetic. Compared with the Japanese Alps in Shinshu, the "mountains" around my area are just big hills. But now if you compare

---

215. Our text is written with the characters 有時; the village Uchiyama Rōshi is referring to is written with these characters: 宇治.

the mountains in Shinshu with the Himalayas, *they* would appear as little more than hills. So does that mean only the Himalayas are truly grand mountains? Actually, even the Himalayas are just a wrinkle on the face of the earth. And the earth, compared with the size of the sun, is just a little pea. And our sun is just a pea compared with our neighboring star, Sirius. Astronomers say that a collection of millions of stars forms our galaxy and that there are some hundred billion galaxies! If we're going to talk about small, then we'd have to call mountains and oceans minuscule. So we needn't think so meanly of a single eyebrow. After all, compared with some germ or virus, even a single eyelash is incredibly huge. So just what is big? It's said there is nothing larger than the space of the universe, but that which contemplates the vastness of this universe is the human mind. And the human mind is, ultimately, nothing more than a secretion of the life force.

In brief, what Dōgen Zenji is talking about in this fascicle is the origin or fountainhead of life, and this is expressed as "His eyebrows take the form of grand mountains, his eyes are like the vast oceans, since mountains and oceans are not different from his eyebrows and his eyes." Dōgen is talking about life in a truly grand way, one that totally jumps over any comparison of big and small. Why I call it "truly grand" is because he has carried the discussion as far as language will reach. That's why it is truly grand.

In short, one becomes intimate with a grandness that beggars comparisons. Actually, reading *Shōbōgenzō* is exactly for that purpose—running into discussions where size no longer commands any bearing.

Seeing a mountain upon raising one's eyebrows—that's the "mountain" of all existences, all situations and circumstances, and the river or the sea or the ocean of all things, all encounters—the "sea" of life itself. The mountains and oceans become one with us. We become truly intimate with this raising and blinking—with "mountains and oceans." It is this "becoming intimate" that is so critical here.

In any event, none of them is outside the inclusivity of the moment-by-moment [life] of all phenomena, all situations—uji. It is this life that we grow more and more intimate with, like our second nature, and that actually guides us—not just is *in* our lives, but *is* our life.

> Never assume that what is inappropriate has no power to move us, nor that unintentional actions are necessarily untrue; that is not uji. Mistaken actions as well as unintentional ones are the living quick of time.

"Inappropriate" is of itself. It has no connection to "has no power." They are not the same thing. Each is respectively uji—the living quick of all existences, all spheres.

> The mountains are living time; the rivers and oceans are living time. If they were not, there would be no mountains or oceans. Never think that the very presence of these mountains and oceans is not time. If time collapses, is destroyed, the mountains and oceans also die. If time is indestructible, so, too, are the mountains and oceans.

Mountains and oceans are the very moment-by-moment quick of time; they are nothing other than the unfolding of our all-inclusive world. Therefore, if there were no time, nothing would exist. Conversely, if time doesn't disappear, then neither will all existences.

> The appearance of the morning star, the Tathāgata, the enlightened eye of wisdom, the turning of the flower—all of them are possible because of the undeniable living presence of uji. If time were not living presence, nothing would be as it is.

The "appearance of the morning star" and "the Tathāgata" derive from Śākyamuni Buddha's sitting zazen and his subsequent enlightenment at seeing the planet Venus early one morning. The moment-by-moment life inclusive of all worlds—this is the true satori of life. Therefore, he

wrote of the Tathāgata and the enlightened eye of wisdom. The turning
of the flower is a reference to the transmission of the Buddhadharma
from Śākyamuni Buddha to Mahākāśyapa. And he concludes here: "all
of them are possible because of the undeniable living presence of uji. If
time were not living presence, nothing would be as it is."

Practice Is Carrying Out Actions despite Feelings of Incompleteness

VI.

Kisei Zenji of Sekken was of the Rinzai lineage and a Dharma heir of
Shuzan Shōnen. While instructing his disciples one day, he pointed out:

> [Within uji, the living present]
> Though the aim hits the mark, the expression may fall short.
> Though the expression hits the mark, the aim may be off.
> Aim and expression sometimes both hit the mark;
> Sometimes both fall short.

In this last section, with the verse of Kisei Zenji, our discussion takes yet
another turn. As I mentioned earlier, in the opening verse of our text,
Dōgen Zenji depicts the particular or individual aspect of things. Then,
in the section on the deliberative or nondeliberative aspect of things, the
discussion turns to intention or aim, while "appropriate" or "inappropriate" takes up the issue of value judgments. In this final section on one's
intention or aim hitting the mark, expression falling short, and so forth,
in a sense the discussion is about the apparent resulting arrangement or
look of things.

For example, my sole aim today is to delve as deeply into the text as
possible. Whether my aim is on the mark or not, or whether my words
are sufficient or not, is the issue in this passage. To rephrase Dōgen Zenji's words so that they might be easier to comprehend, we can say that
this cup is uji, my watch is uji, these glasses are uji—all these particular

COMMENTARY ON "UJI" | 251

things or circumstances that have been laid out in front of us. The next step is whether to put on the glasses or not; this involves will or volition. From there, the issue of making a value judgment—by wearing glasses one's looks will be enhanced or not—comes into play. Finally, we arrive at this point in the text where the issue turns on what *kind* of glasses to wear and how to wear them and, in doing so, how much will one's looks improve. This discussion is, in a sense, about the finished appearance.

All of this is uji, living presence. Hence, we have the passage that aim and expression are both uji, and hitting the mark and falling short are both uji. As long as we're talking about uji, we're talking about the very manifestation of the reality of life itself—regardless of what form that might take. Therefore, the whole idea of something being a success or failure due to the finished appearance being either better or worse simply drops off. It has no bearing here whatever.

Earlier I mentioned that my only aim is to probe as deeply as I can into the issues Dōgen Zenji takes up in *Shōbōgenzō*. However, no matter how well I'm able to clarify what is written here, there is no point at which I can say that I've succeeded: "Wow! Today was a success." For instance, this is the season we see hordes of students checking the announcement boards at various schools to see if they've passed the entrance exams; when the students come to their names on the lists on the board, we see them jumping up and down for joy and hugging one another. That part of success or failure has no relevance to my situation. As I put all my energy into a talk, I look around at everyone's face and I see a few people looking like they're dozing off and others who appear to be wide awake, hanging on my every word. But it doesn't make any sense for me to think that, because some people were listening eagerly, I was a success, or because others fell asleep, I failed. I as the reality of life simply aim at throwing myself into, probing into, and clarifying whatever I can—just that.

I think this is true for any pursuit of study and learning. We can hardly call it "academic pursuit" if young people go to school simply to get a degree or some other certificate or license. That kind of attitude is only concerned with passing or failing. It should come as no surprise then that, upon graduation, many students almost seem to vow never to open a book again, selling all their books with little or no compunction whatever and going off in pursuit of a "successful" career and financial security.

My own attitude toward studying and learning was nothing to be proud of. I was admitted into Waseda through the backdoor, and while I was there, it didn't bother me a bit to cheat on tests or pass on a bribe to the leaders of the student movement. Somehow, I was able to graduate. However, in return, I have spent over half a century studying and learning on my own with no connection whatsoever to obtaining a degree or some other qualification or license. And I plan to continue to discover and learn as long as I'm alive.

Anyway, all that is important here is the true actual presence of life. It's not a simple matter of appropriate or inappropriate, right or wrong. Aiming at the actual presence of life is the only way to live life prior to right or wrong—just doing that. "Just aiming" always carries a feeling of being unsatisfied or unfulfilled. If we've got some sort of goal or objective in front of us, we feel there is some value or worthwhileness in going to all the trouble of carrying out some action. But without any sense of weighing ourselves against others, where there is no competition or comparing, then there is little sense of worth, and we simply feel unsatisfied or lose heart. However, precisely therein lies the truth of life.

> Aim and expression are both uji, living presence; hitting the mark and falling short are both uji, too. Although hitting the mark may seem incomplete, falling short is entirely complete.

There are lots of people running around putting all their energy into having some satori experience or into getting a sense of satisfaction in their lives, but that kind of practice is useless. Practice, or *shugyō* (修行) in Japanese, lies in the doing or living through that which is unsatisfying.

That is what is so critical in the passage "Hitting the mark may seem incomplete."

As human beings we may feel unsatisfied or unfulfilled, however, the living reality of life is being actualized inclusive of that feeling of unfulfillment or discontentment.

> While aim is the same as Reiun's donkey, expression is like his horse. The "horse"—hitting the mark—is the expression, the "donkey"—falling short—is the aim.

This passage recalls Reiun Shigon Zenji's reply to a monk's question of "What is the grand design or overall aim of the Buddhadharma?" Reiun replied, "The horse has arrived before the donkey has left." Reiun Zenji calls that which is unfinished a "donkey," while the succeeding circumstance—having arrived—he refers to as a "horse."

Dōgen brought up Reiun's reply because it relates to the discussion at hand of hitting the target, or "having arrived," and falling short, or "having not yet arrived." In other words, we need to look at the donkey and horse—the various aspects of day-to-day life—as the scenery. The actualities of completion or fulfillment and of incompletion, "having arrived" and "having not yet arrived," are both the living quick of all existences and all situations and times. Aim, expression, donkey, horse, having arrived, still coming: these are all included within the one actual reality of jiko, the whole self.

> Hitting the mark, having arrived, has no connection with still coming from somewhere else. Likewise, not yet having hit the mark is not the same as having not yet come to some imaginary future.

Since each is a feature of the contents of this living reality of jiko, they are not all stuck onto one another; this is this, that is that—one must discriminate one thing from another. Though they may look similar, you can't use human feces to make miso soup.

Uji can be expressed in these ways and more.

The reality of uji has this multiplicity of aspects.

> Hitting the mark obstructs hitting the mark; it cannot be obstructed by
> having not yet hit it. Not having hit the mark is obstructed by itself—there
> is no obstruction from having already hit the mark.

Hitting the mark is totally complete in itself. There is no way it can be
hindered by falling short, by having not yet hit it. And in the same way,
falling short is complete in and of itself; there is nothing to obstruct it.

If a person studies hard and passes a school's entrance exams, then
that person's passing has no connection with not having passed, i.e.,
failing. Likewise, not passing is just not passing; it has nothing to do
with passing. It simply means someone ended up with a higher mark
than you did.

> Aim obstructs aim, thereby seeing [being] totally itself. Expression
> obstructs expression and becomes itself.

Here, too, the passage is saying that nothing is balanced against or compared to anything else. Aim is just aim, expression is just expression.

My own personal desire to delve into and address the issues in the
text as deeply as I am able to has nothing to do with anyone else. It is
simply that my life, or the life force flowing through me, seeks to do so.
Moreover, I'm not weighing what words or expressions to use against
what I imagine you might like to hear from me. It is simply that I am
expressing myself with all the energy I can muster. That's all.

> Obstruction obstructs itself, therein seeing [being] totally itself alone.
> Obstruction obstructs obstruction—this is uji, living presence.

The usual use in Japanese of these various forms of *obstruct* assumes that there is some outside entity that can be obstructed; that one thing is being balanced or weighed against something else. But the way Dōgen Zenji is using it here, *obstruct* or *hinder* just means *obstruct* or *hinder*. And the succeeding passage, "Obstruction obstructs obstruction," even furthers this sense of the completeness of things in themselves. "This is uji, living presence," means that obstruction, too, is part of the life force.

> Although it is commonly taken for granted that obstructions hinder other dharmas, there has never existed anything that has obstructed anything else.

The usual meaning or sense of obstruction is that there actually exists some obstructing entity and something that gets obstructed, that entities hinder other entities. But the actuality is that there has never existed anything that has obstructed anything else. Each and every entity or thing, in Buddhism called *dharmas*, is what it is without being weighed against any other dharma. That is why Dōgen said, in effect, that there are no dharmas outside or apart from obstructing. In this same sense, as long as we are living out jiko—self that is all-inclusive—there can be no obstructing!

People who live with the values of balancing one thing against everything else are all driving to succeed in their careers or to make it rich. If it looks to them like someone is trying to advance ahead of them, they get it into their heads that they themselves are being hindered. Or if someone suddenly falls ill and loses out on making some windfall profit, they blame their sickness as the culprit doing the obstructing. But that is not the true state of things. I am who I am, another person is whoever they are, illness is illness, a business is nothing more than a business.

I've never given any thought to furthering my career or salting away a fortune, so I'm completely carefree. Since I don't hold down any post and don't have much money, why even if someone wanted to, there wouldn't be any way for them to get in my way!

All things are provisional forms of the life of jiko.

> "I meet another person, another person meets their self, I meet myself, going out meets going out." If these things were not living time, there would be no living presence of all things being what they are—*immo*.

[The truth of life] is certainly like this kōan of Sanshō Enen Zenji. The actual kōan goes "[When a guest calls on me] I go out to meet them." Still, even though I use the word "guest," since this "guest" is another part of the living body of jiko, I don't go out to meet anyone for the guest's sake. I'm doing nothing more than meeting myself for myself.

In contrast to Sanshō Zenji's kōan, there was a contemporary of his who was also an heir in the Rinzai lineage, Kōke Zenji.[216] Kōke Zenji countered Sanshō's kōan with "[When I meet another,] I never go out. If I were to do so, it would be for the sake of the other."

Now in Zen, it often occurs that when one person says one thing, someone else will immediately counter it with a remark seemingly opposite in meaning. There's an underlying assumption in Zen that the truth can't be fully expressed by pointing out just one side of things. If all things are other aspects of the living self, there's no way to speak of an "other." Therefore, it's not possible to meet "another" person. And therefore, Kōke says he never "goes out." So together these two kōans are expressing both aspects of jiko: all/all and one/all.

In contrast to Sanshō and Kōke's statements, Dōgen Zenji writes, "I meet another person, another person meets their self, I meet myself, going out meets going out." Here Dōgen is further emphasizing the totality or inclusivity of each and every thing as uji. This is why he closes the paragraph with "If these things were not living time, there would be no living presence of all·things being what they are—*immo*."

---

216. Kōke Sonshō (興化存獎; Chi: Xinghua Cunjiang; 830–88) was a Dharma heir of Rinzai Gigen (臨済義玄; Chi: Linji Yixuan; ?–866/7).

Moreover, aim is the same as the vital and living manifestation [genjō] of the present encounter [kōan]; expression is the key to the gate of supreme enlightenment. Hitting the mark is the casting off of body and mind, and not yet hitting the mark is separating upon arrival. It is in this way that we should practice diligently and actualize the living quick of time.

By "moreover" he's emphasizing that aim, expression, hitting the mark, and not hitting it are each uji, the living quick of time.

"Aim," in Japanese *i* (意), is thought to be the same as *dairokuishiki* (第六意識) that is, the sixth "consciousness"; however, in this case, it refers to the overall aim of Buddhadharma. Hence, Dōgen says, "Moreover, aim is the same as the vital and living manifestation [genjō] of the present encounter [kōan]."

In "expression is the key to the gate of supreme enlightenment," expression as the living quick of time is the key.

"Hitting the mark" in the text means to "pass through" or "be delivered from" or "emancipated from" something; this is the same as Dōgen's "casting off of body and mind" or *shinjin datsuraku* (身心脱落). Finally, "not yet hitting the mark" is to arrive here and in the same instant separate, or *sokushi rishi* (即至離至).

For example, when doing zazen, the actuality of that zazen has nothing to do with knowing just where or even if one has hit the mark or not. As soon as you entertain the idea that such and such is the true reality of life, in that very instant, you're floating in air, abstracted from that reality.

So the reason I say "just doing" is practice is that even though seeing—hitting the mark—is the aim of uji, no sooner do we "hit it" than we have to separate from it; we have to let it go.

Our practice must always be like that. In other words, aim, expression, hitting the mark, falling short—each with its own meaning—is an independent uji; they're not balanced against the other. This is why we should practice diligently and actualize the living quick of time, uji.

Our Buddhist ancestors have expressed their living presence in these various ways. Is there nothing further that I might say? I would add that aim and expression only *partially* hitting the mark are uji. And aim and expression only *partially* not hitting the mark are also uji. Study and practice diligently in this way.

Up to this point, Dōgen Zenji has set forth various comments on kōans of past teachers, and here he raises the question of the possibility of carrying the discussion of uji to an even deeper level. He says that we need to study and practice uji as aim and expression only partially hitting the mark as well as only partially falling short of it. This is because the term *partially* here is used as being complete in itself and not in contrast to *complete*. The moment-by-moment of all existences, all worlds—*jin'u jinkai jiji*[217]—is unlimited. Therefore, half or part of unlimited must itself be unlimited. Surely this has to be integral to our delving into and winnowing through the elements of our day-to-day lives.

Having him even partially raise his eyebrows and blink is uji. Not having him do so even partially is uji. Even mistakenly having him not do so time and again is also uji.

The discussion now returns to the kōan on "raising the eyebrows." What we have to remember in this passage is that the use of *partial* is not being dualistically put in opposition to *complete*. As Buddhadharma, *partial* stands totally by itself.

In the next sentence, the Chinese character *saku* (錯) appears, which can mean "mistaken," such as we find in the word *sakugo* (錯誤). Or, combined with the character for *vision*, the word *sakkaku* (錯覚) meaning "delusion." Normally, the implication behind the character is to err or to

217. *Jin'u jinkai jiji* (尽有尽界時々) refers to all existences, circumstances, etc., all worlds, societies, etc., and all times.

make a mistake. But looking at it from the intrinsic quality of uji as all existences, all worlds, regardless of our situation, whether it be through some accident or human fallibility or through some deliberate error or mistaken notion, we are still living within the inclusivity of the reality of jiko, living self. In other words, no matter how or in whatever direction we might have stumbled or fallen, by mistake or by deception, it is no mistake that right there, before us, is the reality of our life.

Any portion of "unlimited" must of necessity also be unlimited, since mistakes, too, lie within the parameters of the life of jiko; there is no necessity to equate "mistaken" with bad or evil. Just think a minute about what is meant by the word *mistaken* and its opposite, *correct*. If we trace our life back to its beginning—our birth—who is to say it wasn't a mistake? Intuitively, I can't believe there was any absolute necessity in my being born. On the contrary, I wonder sometimes if the truth of the matter might not be that perhaps it would have been better had we all been aborted, that the mistake was that we weren't! But even if our birth was wrong or a mistake, it's surely no use to worry about it at this point. We just have to live through the mistake. It is exactly from that point where our life has been a mistake that we have to continue living through it. That is the true function of the life force.

Repeating myself once more, whichever way we might fall, that is, even if a mistake is a mistake, it is included within the life of jiko. However, since *mistaken* is not the same as *not mistaken*, from that point of mistakenness, we have to constantly aim at a living time, uji, that transcends both mistaken and unmistaken. This is a critical point. In other words, the actual functioning of the life force is not a matter of simply accepting ourselves as a mistake and being satisfied with that. As a mistake, we always aim at penetrating wholly uji, living time. As we read earlier in the text, "All worlds penetrate all worlds. This is referred to as thoroughly penetrating." That is, our aim or direction is to enter completely into whatever situation or encounter we are facing. *Living time* does not mean simply being satisfied with living a mistake, but rather to aim at penetrating the living quick of time, uji, as a living mistake. In other words, we need to live out that life that precedes "mistaken" or "unmistaken," "correct" or "incorrect."

As I have explained many times elsewhere, Dōgen Zenji's zazen is very deep, far reaching, and beyond making comparisons. Likewise, so is any discussion of Buddhadharma. Sawaki Rōshi used to summarize this with his expression *yūsui*, or "profound, far reaching, and beyond comparison." But what about Buddhadharma is *yūsui?*

Once more, every human being in the world is living out the moment-by-moment of all worlds, all things. That is all the more reason then that, while living that life, we should aim even further at living it out moment-by-moment. It is in that sense that the life force possesses depth.

Looking at the syntax of the Japanese of the opening lines of the text—"An ancient buddha has said, 'The living quick of time stands on the peak of the highest mountain. The living quick of time moves on the floor of the deepest ocean'"—it is easy to understand why people might misread this as "For the time being…" or "Sometimes…" or "One time . . ." But in this penultimate passage, there can be no mistake; the entire thing clearly modifies uji, living time: "Having him even partially raise his eyebrows and blink is uji. . . . Even mistakenly having him not do so time and again is also uji."

There is nothing excluded from the life of jiko, living self.

In this way, delve deeply into these issues of living time, of coming and going, of hitting the mark and having not yet hit the mark as the truly living issues of uji, living time.

With this concluding remark, Dōgen Zenji is expressing what Sawaki Rōshi referred to as *yūsui*. That is, "delve deeply into these issues of living time" means there is no end as to how deeply we can go. On the one hand, we are always living within the reality of life; still, paradoxically, we have to continue aiming at that reality.

Part IV. Comments by the Translators

7. Connecting "Maka Hannya Haramitsu" to the Pāli Canon

SHŌHAKU OKUMURA

In 1233, Dōgen established his own monastery, Kōshōji, in Fukakusa. During the first summer practice period there, he wrote "Maka Hannya Haramitsu": a declaration, it seems to me, that his zazen practice was based on the teaching of emptiness expressed in the Prajñāpāramitā sūtras. In the fall of the same year he wrote "Genjō Kōan." I think "Maka Hannya Haramitsu" and "Genjō Kōan" are closely connected and form the philosophical foundation of Dōgen's later writings, including "Shoaku Makusa" and "Uji." As a commentary on this fascicle, I would like to consider Dōgen's insight regarding prajñāpāramitā in the context of the history of Buddhist teachings.

These days, I have been thinking of a thread that connects Śākyamuni Buddha's teaching to Mahāyāna Buddhist teachings, to Dōgen's teaching, and to our own practice of zazen.

For instance, the first sentence of "Maka Hannya Haramitsu" is a paraphrase of the first sentence of the *Heart Sūtra*. "Maka Hannya Haramitsu" begins "The time of Avalokiteśvara Bodhisattva practicing profound prajñāpāramitā is the whole body clearly seeing the emptiness of all five aggregates," while the *Heart Sūtra* begins "Avalokiteśvara Bodhisattva, when deeply practicing prajñāpāramitā, clearly saw that all five aggregates are empty and thus relieved all suffering."

If we follow this topic of the five aggregates back, we see that in

Shōbōgenzō "Hotsubodaishin" (發菩提心), "Arousing Awakening Mind,"
Dōgen quoted a discussion of the aggregates from Nāgārjuna's *Mahāprajñāpāramitā Śāstra*, his commentary on the large Prajñāpāramitā
sūtras. Nāgārjuna said that although there are four kinds of "Māra"—
delusions, death, the five aggregates of attachment (Skt: *pañca upādāna
skandha*), and the celestial demon—actually, Māra was only one. There
is no Māra besides the five aggregates.

Māra, of course, is the demon that Śākyamuni Buddha conquered in
order to attain awakening under the bodhi tree, according to one of the
Jātakas, stories of the Buddha's various lives. If we understand what Māra
represents, we might be able to understand the nature of Śākyamuni's
awakening.

A Lump of Foam: The Saṃyutta Nikāya

In the short sūtra titled *Māra* in chapter II, 23 of *Rādhasaṃyutta* (*Connected Discourses with Rādha*) in the Saṃyutta Nikāya, Śākyamuni said
to his disciple Rādha:

> "When there is form, Rādha, there might be Māra, or the killer,
> or the one who is killed. Therefore, Rādha, see form as Māra, see
> it as the killer, see it as the one who is killed. See it as a disease, as
> a tumor, as a dart, as misery, as real misery. Those who see it thus
> see rightly." [218]

"Form" is the first of the five aggregates. Buddha then repeated the same
thing about the other four aggregates: sensation, perception, predilections (or "volitional formations" in the Nikāyas), and consciousness.
Nāgārjuna's definition of the five aggregates as Māra wasn't simply his
personal interpretation, it seems. Then the conversation continued:

218. Bhikkhu Bodhi, trans., *The Connected Discourses of the Buddha: A New Translation of the Saṃyutta Nikāya* (Boston: Wisdom Publications, 2000), 1: 984.

"What, venerable sir, is the purpose of seeing rightly?"

"The purpose of seeing rightly is revulsion."

"And what, venerable sir, is the purpose of revulsion?"

"The purpose of revulsion is dispassion."

"And what, venerable sir, is the purpose of dispassion?"

"The purpose of dispassion is liberation."

"And what, venerable sir, is the purpose of liberation?"

"The purpose of liberation is Nibbāna."

"And what, venerable sir, is the purpose of Nibbāna?"

"You have gone beyond the range of questioning, Rādha. You weren't able to grasp the limit to questioning. For, Rādha, the holy life is lived with Nibbāna as its ground, Nibbāna as its destination, Nibbāna as its final goal."[219]

Śākyamuni said that seeing the five aggregates as Māra was the way to reach nirvana.

In another short sūtra from Saṃyutta Nikāya, *Khandhasaṃyutta* 26 (5), "Gratification," Śākyamuni Buddha talked about the difference before and after his enlightenment:

"Bhikkhus, before my enlightenment, while I was still a bodhisattva, not yet fully enlightened, it occurred to me: 'What is the gratification, what is the danger, what is the escape in the case of form? What is the gratification, what is the danger, what is the escape in the case of feeling ... perception ... volitional formation ... consciousness?'

"Then, bhikkhus, it occurred to me: 'The pleasure and joy that arise in dependence on form: this is the gratification in form. That form is impermanent, suffering, and subject to change: this is the danger in form. The removal and abandonment of desire and lust for form: this is the escape from form.

219. Ibid.

"'The pleasure and joy that arise in dependence on feeling... in dependence on perception ... in dependence on volitional formation ... in dependence on consciousness: this is the gratification in consciousness. That consciousness is impermanent, suffering, and subject to change: this is the danger in consciousness. The removal and abandonment of desire and lust for consciousness: this is the escape from consciousness.'

"So long, bhikkhus, as I did not directly know as they really are the gratification, the danger, and the escape in the case of these five aggregates subject to clinging, I did not claim to have awakened to the unsurpassed perfect enlightenment in this world with its devas, Māra, and Brahma, in this generation with its ascetics and Brahmins, its devas and humans. But when I directly knew all this as it really is, then I claimed to have awakened to the unsurpassed perfect enlightenment in this world with ... its devas and humans.

"The knowledge and vision arose in me: 'Unshakable is my liberation of mind; this is my last birth; now there is no more renewed existence.'"[220]

Direct understanding of the nature of the five aggregates and their gratification, danger, and escape (becoming free from clinging, desire, and lust for them) allowed the *bodhisattva*, or "way seeker," to become the Awakened One, to reach unsurpassed perfect enlightenment.

In *Khandhasaṃyutta* 95 (3), "A Lump of Foam," we read:

"Bhikkhus, suppose that this river Ganges was carrying along a great lump of foam. A man with good sight would inspect it, ponder it, and carefully investigate it, and it would appear to him to be void, hollow, insubstantial. For what substance could there be in a lump of foam? So too, bhikkhus, whatever kind of form there is, whether past, future, or present, internal or external, gross or subtle, inferior

220. Ibid., 873–74.

or superior, far or near: a bhikkhu inspects it, ponders it, and carefully investigates it, and it would appear to him to be void, hollow, insubstantial. For what substance could there be in form?"[221]

Then he continued, saying about the other four aggregates, "Sensation is like a water bubble; perception is like a mirage, formation is like a banana tree, and consciousness is like a magical illusion; they are all void, hollow, and insubstantial." The exact word "emptiness," śūnyatā, is not used, but the meaning is the same as saying the five aggregates are empty. The examples listed here are similar to the examples used in the Mahāyāna sūtras, such as the *Diamond Sūtra*, as examples of emptiness: dream, phantom, bubble, shadow, dewdrop, flash of lightning.

The text continues:

"Seeing thus, bhikkhus, the instructed noble disciple experiences revulsion toward form, revulsion toward feeling, revulsion toward perception, revulsion toward volitional formations, revulsion toward consciousness. Experiencing revulsion, he becomes dispassionate. Through dispassion [his mind] is liberated. When it is liberated there comes the knowledge: 'It's liberated.' He understands: 'Destroyed is birth; the holy life has been lived, what had to be done has been done, there is no more for this state of being.'"[222]

Suffering without Sufferer: Walpola Rahula

In his explanation of the first noble truth, *dukkha* (suffering), Walpola Rahula said in his book *What the Buddha Taught*:

What we call a "being," or an "individual," or "I," according to Buddhist philosophy, is only a combination of ever-changing

221. Ibid., 951.
222. Ibid., 952.

physical and mental forces or energies, which may be divided into five groups or aggregates. The Buddha says: "In short these five aggregates of attachment are dukkha." Elsewhere he distinctly defines dukkha as the five aggregates: "O bhikkhus, what is dukkha? It should be said that it is the five aggregates of attachment." Here it should be clearly understood that dukkha and the five aggregates are not two different things; the five aggregates themselves are dukkha.[223]

He goes on:

One thing disappears, conditioning the appearance of the next in a series of cause and effect. There is no unchanging substance in them. There is nothing behind them that can be called a permanent Self, individuality, or anything that can in reality be called "I." Every one will agree that neither matter, nor sensation, nor perception, nor any one of those mental activities, nor consciousness can really be called "I." But when these five physical and mental aggregates which are interdependent are working together in combination as a physio-psychological machine, we get the idea of "I." But this is only a false idea, a mental formation, which is nothing but one of those fifty-two mental formations of the fourth aggregate which we have just discussed, namely it is the idea of self.

These five Aggregates together, which we popularly call a "being," are *dukkha* itself. There is no other "being," or "I," standing behind these five aggregates, who experiences *dukkha*. As Buddhaghoṣa says: "Mere suffering exists, but no sufferer is found. The deeds are, but no doer is found."

There is no unmoving mover behind the movement. It is only movement. It is not correct to say that life is moving, but life is movement itself. Life and movement are not two different things.

223. Walpola Rahula, *What the Buddha Taught* (New York: Grove Press, 1959), 20.

In other words, there is no thinker behind the thought. Thought itself is the thinker. If you remove the thought, there is no thinker to be found. Here we cannot fail to notice how this Buddhist view is diametrically opposed to the Cartesian *cogito ergo sum*: "I think, therefore I am."

. . . This in short is the meaning of the noble truth of *dukkha*. It is extremely important to understand this first noble truth clearly because, as the Buddha says, "He who sees *dukkha* sees also the arising of *dukkha*, sees also the cessation of *dukkha*, and sees also the path leading to the cessation of *dukkha*."[224]

Seeing without Seer: *The Heart Sūtra*

I don't see any discrepancy between these teachings from the Pāli Nikāya and Theravāda tradition and what the *Heart Sūtra* says: "Avalokiteśvara Bodhisattva, when deeply practicing prajñāpāramitā, clearly saw that all five aggregates are empty and thus relieved all suffering."

When we are not liberated from clinging to the five aggregates, the five aggregates are called *pañca upādāna skandha* (five aggregates of attachment), and that is Māra. When we see the emptiness of the five aggregates and are released from clinging to them, then the five aggregates are *pañca anupādāna skandha*, that is, simply the five aggregates, without clinging. Then, the five aggregates are Avalokiteśvara. Because there is nothing but five aggregates, there is no one who is seeing the emptiness of those five aggregates besides the five aggregates. When the five aggregates cling to themselves, they themselves are suffering, and when the five aggregates see the emptiness of themselves, they function as Avalokiteśvara.

In "Maka Hannya Haramitsu," when Dōgen paraphrased the first sentence of the *Heart Sūtra*, he changed the subject from "Avalokiteś-vara" to "the time of Avalokiteśvara Bodhisattva practicing profound

224. Ibid., 26–27.

prajñāpāramitā." Also, Dōgen added "whole body" to make the sentence "The time of Avalokiteśvara Bodhisattva practicing profound prajñāpāramitā is the whole body clearly seeing the emptiness of all five aggregates." In our common logical way of thinking, it is strange. But I think Dōgen intentionally deconstructed the subject-object relationship to show there is no "person," no subject, outside the five aggregates, and that there is no object. There is nothing besides the five aggregates, and those five aggregates are empty. The five aggregates are seeing the emptiness of the five aggregates. There is no seer besides seeing.

When "I" am sitting zazen, there is no "I" besides sitting. The five aggregates are sitting. Further we should say that, besides sitting, there are no five aggregates. This means the five aggregates are seeing the emptiness of five aggregates. But there is no subject (five aggregates) and object (five aggregates) relationship. The five aggregates are simply being five aggregates without separation between subject and object. Even "seeing" disappears.

Dropping Off Body and Mind

When Dōgen said that zazen is "dropping off body and mind" (*shinjin datsuraku*), body and mind are nothing other than the five aggregates. In his zazen, the five aggregates are simply being the five aggregates that are empty. "I" do nothing but keep an upright posture, breathe deeply and smoothly into my abdomen, keep my eyes open, and let go of whatever is coming and going within my mind. This is when *pañca upādāna skandha* becomes simply *pañca anupādāna skandha*; the five aggregates of attachment become the five aggregates seeing the emptiness of the five aggregates. Thus, Dōgen says that the five aggregates are the fivefold prajñā. This is the transformation of the five aggregates from Māra to prajñā and Avalokiteśvara, and the pivot of this transformation is dropping off body and mind as zazen. *Here* we find a thread between Śākyamuni's teaching of the five aggregates as suffering through Mahāyāna Buddhist teachings of seeing emptiness and relief from suffering to Dōgen's teaching of zazen itself as dropping off body and mind.

In his teishō, Uchiyama Rōshi does not talk so much about Buddhist philosophy. His teaching is very concrete and practical; that is why we appreciate his lectures. But he did not miss the essential points of Śākyamuni's teaching. For example, he offers a quote from Śākyamuni in the Āgama Sūtras that exactly matches what I quoted above from the Pāli Nikāya:

> The Buddha said, "You must see that rūpa, material form, is impermanent." And, "To see things this way is the right way of seeing." Then he continued, "A person who correctly sees forms arouses the mind of departure. A person who arouses the mind of departure extinguishes greed and pleasure. A person who extinguishes greed and pleasure liberates his/her mind. Thus, you should see that sensation, perception, predilection, and consciousness are also impermanent."

Departure here is the same as *revulsion* in the Nikāya I quoted above, and "extinguishes greed and pleasure" is the same as "dispassion."

Uchiyama Rōshi also often quoted Śākyamuni's teaching in the Āgama Sūtras that the Middle Way is the path between the view of being (*u-ken*) and the view of nonbeing (*mu-ken*) to connect Dōgen's interpretation of prajñāpāramitā to the original teaching of Śākyamuni Buddha.[225] This same teaching by Śākyamuni was what Nāgārjuna mentioned as the source of his insight into the Middle Way in chapter 15 of *Mūlamadhyamakakārikā*, verse 7: "According to the Instruction to Kātyāyana, the two views of the world in terms of being and nonbeing were criticized

---

225. This is in Saṃyutta Nikāya 15 (5), "Kaccānagotta." Bhikkhu Bodhi, *The Connected Discourses of the Buddha*, 1: 544.

by the Buddha for similarly admitting the bifurcation of entities into existence and nonexistence."[226]

I think this teaching of the Middle Way is the foundation upon which Dōgen wrote about the being and nonbeing of delusion/realization, life/death, and buddhas/living beings in the first three sentences in "Genjō Kōan."

226. *Nāgārjuna: A Translation of his* Mūlamadhyamakakārikā *with an Introductory Essay* (Kenneth K. Inada, The Hokuseido Press, Tokya, 1978), 99.

8. Looking into Good and Evil in "Shoaku Makusa"

DAITSŪ TOM WRIGHT

How do we define evil?

I think it will be impossible for Westerners to understand the concept of good and evil as Buddhadharma as long as they cling to the idea that there is an absolute substance that exists that is good or that is evil. It is this assumption of the absolute existence of a good or an evil that is at the root of the problem.

A clear illustration would be the Holocaust. The discourse from the late nineteenth century into the early part of the twentieth century purported that Jews did bad things, that those "bad" people could be punished, and that they could eventually be rehabilitated and returned to society. But when the discourse changed from "Jews *do* bad things" to "Jews *are* bad," then there was no hope for reformation or rehabilitation. For people who do bad things, the solution is to punish and rehabilitate them, but for people who *are* evil or who *embody* evil the only "solution" is to purge them from the society forever. I believe this same mentality holds true for those who support the death penalty. That is, the idea is that there are some crimes that are so heinous that the only solution is to execute the perpetrator. This is also behind the false assumption that execution will bring "closure" to the victim or the victim's family.

This has been my thinking behind undertaking a translation of this particular fascicle of Eihei Dōgen Zenji's *Shōbōgenzō*.

I have struggled with how to translate this word *aku* in the title "Shoaku Makusa." To translate it as "evil" is to invite misinterpretation by suggesting an absolute existence of evil that the original word does not seem to have had. "Unwholesome" deeds would be one way to get around that obstacle. On the other hand, I can readily understand why some people would feel outraged at any perceived attempt to belittle the inhumane crimes that human beings have committed against other human beings and against nature—such as by simply calling them "unwholesome deeds." However, as long as we cling to the idea of the substantiality of evil, we must also understand that we consider ourselves to be the righteous judge to administer the punishment.

And who is to be considered a murderer? The one who locked the door of the gas chamber? The one who dropped the Zyclon B into the chamber, or the one who invented Zyclon B, the ones who prepared Zyclon B to be dispatched, the ones who put the Zyclon B on the trains that took it to the death factories, the one who ordered Zyclon B to be used, the millions who elected the one who ordered Zyclon B to be used? How far do we go in punishing the guilty? As one probes further into the horrors of the Holocaust, Pol Pot, Rwanda, Vietnam, the Atlantic slave trade, who are the innocent? To what extent does involvement in the *whole* deed make you one of the executioners? Is complicity by silence in the carrying out of a terrible deed also punishable?

In any case, the definition of "evil," and what is considered fair punishment for committing an "evil" deed, is governed by the society or government concerned. Such actions—evil ones or the carrying out of a punishment for those actions—exist in the realm of bargaining, negotiation, comparison, etc.: the realm of dichotomies. However, this is not how Dōgen Zenji is using the phrase *shoaku makusa shuzen bugyō* (諸悪 莫作 衆善奉行), "refraining from committing various evils and carrying out all sorts of good."

What does Dōgen Zenji want to tell us?

Below is a very brief outline of what I feel are some of the major points that Dōgen Zenji is writing about in "Shoaku Makusa."

1. *Shichi Butsu Tsūkai no Ge* or *The Gāthā of the Commonly Held Precepts of the Seven Buddhas.*
   a. What transmission and reception are, and how they are carried out.
   b. Evil precedes consciousness of it.
   c. Good and evil must be seen with the same impartial eye.
   d. Awakening to the true reality of things is the same as refraining from evil.
   e. When evils can no longer be created, the virtue of practice manifests.
2. When grounded in reality, no evil is ever committed.
   a. Evil does not break the person; the person cannot destroy evil.
   b. Practice is the practice of the totality of body and mind.
   c. When various evils are viewed impartially, all dharmas are viewed impartially.
3. All there is, is *makusa*, "refraining from."
   a. The buddhas neither exist nor are they nonexistent.
   b. Though evil is not created, we feel remorse for our mistakes.
   c. Though evil is not created, it shouldn't be misunderstood.
4. "Carrying out all sorts of good."
   a. Good is not waiting around to be enacted.
   b. The form of the buddhas' appearances vary with the people and the times.
   c. The carrying out of good is carried out devoid of ego.
5. Personally clarifying one's mind.
   a. Refraining from and carrying out are like the horse arriving before the donkey has left.
6. Haku Kyoi's inquiry of Dōrin Choka.
   a. Haku Kyoi's misunderstanding.

7. Buddhadharma heard for the first time will be the same as hearing it after many years.

a. Penetrating the minutest particle, you will penetrate all worlds without exception.

b. For followers of the Buddha, clarifying the direct and indirect causes of life/death is imperative.

c. Clarifying the true form of our fundamental self is crucial.

d. Winnowing through what Buddhadharma is, understanding it, and expressing it must be based on our practice.

How are Dōgen Zenji's writings connected to practice?

Kōdō Sawaki Rōshi often said that all the Buddhist scriptures are footnotes to our zazen. What did he mean by that? First of all, I think it is natural for those new to Buddhism to think that there is this body of scriptures and then, besides that, there are those who practice Buddhism, but the connection between the scriptures and the practice remains a mystery. Some people would first like to read what those Buddhist scriptures say and then decide whether to practice it or not. Uchiyama Rōshi seemed to intuit early on that if one wants to truly understand those scriptures, then practicing it is the only way. Not just that: Soon after becoming a disciple of Sawaki Rōshi, Kōshō Uchiyama the novice seemed to realize that it was not a matter of the scriptures exhorting students to practice, but rather that the scriptures functioned to shed light on the sitting practice of zazen itself. In other words, the scriptures enabled students to clarify and deepen their practice. I believe that is what Sawaki Rōshi meant by saying that the scriptures are the footnotes to our zazen.

What does Dōgen Zenji want to tell us?

What does it mean that evil precedes consciousness? What is the importance of seeing good and evil with an impartial eye? Or, what does it mean that the carrying out of good is devoid of ego? These are just some of the questions that Dōgen Zenji and Uchiyama Rōshi address in their writing on and commentary to "Shoaku Makusa."

Let us pick up just one of these questions and try and look at it from various perspectives: How can carrying out of good be devoid of ego? Let us say we are seated on a train or bus, perhaps enjoying the scenery as the vehicle moves along. Then it stops and an elderly woman bent over with osteoporosis gets on. We immediately get up and motion to the woman to sit down. She then shuffles over to the seat and sits down, while we grab hold of the leather strap to keep us from bumping into the people standing on either side of us. The elderly woman just sits there and says nothing. We're tired as we get off the train, and our mind begins to churn. "Why, that old bat didn't even say thank you for giving her my seat! No sense of gratitude." And on and on. As our mind goes, we get more and more upset that we did such a "good" thing for someone who is so thankless. What a waste of a "good" deed!

So, now we have to ask, what good is it to do a "good" deed if we fix on the idea that we weren't thanked for doing it? For that matter, having worked oneself into such a tizzy, isn't that "good" deed nullified? Doesn't having our ego stroked by words of thanks make the effort worthless? Surely, the tired and bent-over old woman must have been thankful to have been able to sit down, even if she said nothing to the stranger who gave up his seat for her. In this case, perhaps we would have to say yes, a good deed was done, despite someone's wounded ego. In other words, the carrying out of good takes place with no connection to one's intentions.

There is a story about a follower who came to see Shinran Shōnin, founder of Jōdo Shinshū, a new Pure Land school of Buddhism in Japan in the thirteenth century. The follower asked Shinran Shōnin, "Can evil people be saved?" Shinran's reply was "Of course, all evil people will be saved." Then, after a pause, he added, "And even *good* people will be saved." Here, Shinran Shōnin is clearly looking at good and evil with an impartial eye. People who are aware of their mistakes and misdeeds can more easily cross over to the Pure Land than people who presume themselves to be good. We just need to recall the well-known words "the way to Hell is paved with good intentions."

Hopefully, as we read through Dōgen Zenji's explication of good and evil, we can stop and reflect on whatever fixed ideas we have regarding the seeming opposites "good" and "evil." And, hopefully, reading the text over and over, Dōgen Zenji's words, which at first seemed impenetrable, eventually will become our common sense, our second nature. I don't know of any other way, other than a life of sitting, that can truly help us to put ourselves and our species in a wider, saner perspective.

9. The Ramifications of Time in Dōgen's Zen

DAITSŪ TOM WRIGHT

As the research and practice on the writings of Eihei Dōgen Zenji is an ongoing process, how can any interpretation be anything but partial or provisional? Anyone who is reading and practicing Dōgen's teachings on a regular basis can't help but constantly discover broader ramifications. To date, there have been various translations and interpretations of most of Dōgen's works: some of them very philosophical, and some of them in very readable, everyday language.

There has to be room for all kinds, since no one translation is going to resonate with all people. Besides differences in people's abilities to comprehend, there is just as importantly the problem of interpreting the idiom and cultural context of the original language in which Dōgen wrote—and adapting that for the milieu of the reader of the moment.

Most fundamentally, however, we need to understand from the outset that Dōgen is writing from the viewpoint of the Buddhist practitioner, not as a speculator on abstract ideas. In his opening remarks on "Uji," one of the most fascinating fascicles of Dōgen's *Shōbōgenzō*, Kōshō Uchiyama Rōshi points out:

The following article, along with the translation of "Uji," appeared in the volume *Time and Nothingness*, edited by Dr. Michael Lazarin and published by Research Papers of the Institute of Buddhist Cultural Studies, Ryukoku University, 1997. Both the article and the translation have been revised.

[W]hat we find in this fascicle "Uji" is certainly not anything that is difficult nor something mystically profound. What is written is about nothing other than the most natural scenery of our zazen. This teaching is one that enables us to move that much deeper into our very ordinary way of practice. That is, it is not some ideal or abstract explanation, unrelated to our everyday lives.

The "most natural scenery of our zazen": Dōgen himself expressed this same idea in his *Gakudō Yōjinshū* as "The Buddha Way is directly under our feet."[227] So despite the often conundrum-like style of his writings, it is essential to understand Dōgen in the context of our day-to-day actions. This is not only true for *Shōbōgenzo* "Uji"; it is true for any writings by Dōgen.

Kōdō Sawaki Rōshi often remarked that the scriptures—all the Buddhist canon including Dōgen—are the footnotes to our zazen. That is, they are literary explanations of what is directly in front of us.

For both of these highly respected teachers of Zen, it is essential to put the writings into the context of our everyday lives. For me, this is especially true of fascicles in *Shōbōgenzō* posing similar difficulties as "Uji."

There is one more point I would like to make that concerns our attitude when reading Dōgen: no reading should be undertaken with the intention of trying to get some special benefit from the reading, either to impress others with our sagacity or to judge them. That is, it should only be taken up with an attitude of *mushotoku*, of having nothing to gain. And why is this important? As long as we bring our own agenda, our own predisposition and point of view, into our reading of the text,

---

227. From *Eihei Shoso Gakudō Yōjinshū* (永平初祖学道用心集), section 9. The statement of the Buddha Way being "directly under our feet" means that there is no Buddha Way outside of our each and every activity. The original Japanese expression is *kyakkonka* (脚跟下).

then whatever benefit we might truly derive from such reading will be highly limited and questionably beneficial at best.

Sawaki Rōshi used to remark that practicing zazen is useless, and if we don't understand that, then it is truly useless; this is Sawaki Rōshi's very earthy way of expressing the idea of mushotoku. What he was trying to say through such a statement is this: from the standpoint of confused human beings, we read the scriptures or do zazen in order to gain some insight or some grand realization, but from the standpoint of the Buddhist practitioner, this is neither the motivation for reading nor for practicing zazen. Reading should not be carried out in order to learn what one does not yet know but rather to confirm or to discover what is only natural. What he means by saying that "Uji" is "not difficult to comprehend nor mystically profound, but rather the most natural scenery of our zazen" is that it is not difficult *providing* we do not bring our own agenda or predisposition into the text. Rōshi's "not difficult" is in regard to our attitude; it is not about the difficulty of the text. If we read with an open mind, then what appears in the text will be only natural, since the writings can be understood as "footnotes" to our actual practice of zazen. When Sawaki Rōshi says that zazen is useless, he means that if we bring our own predetermined views and expectations to the practice of zazen—that is, if we bring an attitude of trying to prove some point we have previously convinced ourselves is true—ultimately, such practice will be useless.[228]

It is with this understanding that I would like to present my limited understanding and interpretation of a few aspects of Eihei Dōgen Zenji's

228. Dōgen's *Shōbōgenzō Zuimonki* and *Gakudō Yōjinshū* are filled with passages concerning attitude. In *Zuimonki* 1:9, 3:3, 3:10, and 5:23 of the *rufubon*, or popular edition, for example, he talks about the importance of ridding oneself of any expectation of gain. And in sections 1:13, 2:12, 2:19, 2:24, 3:3, 5:2, and 6:17 of *Zuimonki,* and in section 4 of *Gakudō Yōjinshū,* he exhorts us not to bring our own agenda into our study and practice. Actually, any reading of *Shōbōgenzō* should be accompanied by a thorough reading of these important texts.

depiction of time. For the most part, I shall confine my comments to Dōgen's *Shōbōgenzō* "Uji." I will also be drawing on the comments of Kōshō Uchiyama Rōshi, one of the clearest and most prolific religious interpreters of Dōgen.

Time—a phenomenon that has piqued the curiosity of humankind since, well, pardon the cliché, time immemorial. Philosophers have philosophized and pondered the matter for a millennium or two, novelists have novelized innumerable possibilities on the topic, film directors have churned out their ideas from the days of the one- or two-reelers of early silent film to all sorts of science fiction thrillers with special effects. People have mused about time machines into which people would climb aboard and get blasted off into the past or the future. Men and women in business plan their days around the clock—time is money. We feel the pressure of having to make the most of our time; the new product has to come out on time—good or bad timing can make or break the company.

Needless to say, time is one of the key elements we focus on when watching sports, that embodiment of the competitive spirit of the ashura. Was it a fast time, was it a slow time? Were teammates properly synchronized?

Is time a separate, unique, independent entity, or is it an all-inclusive phenomenon? Does it have a power of its own? Or to rephrase the question, does time have its own control center, separate from me? That is, is time a phenomenon entirely separate from myself? And speaking of "self," is time personal or impersonal? Is time an absolute or a relative phenomenon or, even more basic, does it exist at all? Does time proceed in a linear fashion, from the past to the present and into an unknown future? These are just a few of the intriguing questions surrounding our interest in time.

The Paradox of Particularity and Inclusivity

Particularity

In the opening passages of "Uji," Dōgen emphasizes the individuality or particularity of time: "All the various phenomena are themselves time.... Investigate and winnow through all the individual things, all the various phenomena and circumstances of this universe as particular times."

He does not say that all things exist *in* time, but rather all things exist *as* time. All entities, conditions, situations, and so forth are each expressions of time. Or, as Uchiyama Rōshi expresses it in his commentary, "All these various phenomena and circumstances are the scenery of each instantaneous and separate moment of time.... Ultimately, these moment-by-moment passings of time are completely separate." This reminds one of another statement illustrating this point from Sawaki Rōshi: "You can't trade so much as a fart with another person." This was his way of explaining the particularity of life. No matter how many no-hitters or strikeouts our favorite baseball hero might have or how proud of him or her we might like to be, the fact is, we have to live out our own life. Life lived vicariously is almost like never experiencing life at all. Or to put it another way, to live one's life constantly being bombarded by our *own* thoughts of what others will think of us is another way *not* to live out one's own life.

In the succeeding paragraph, Dōgen raises the question of whether we actually understand what time is: "Traces of the past and the direction of the future seem so clear; no one truly questions these things. However, this is no assurance that, because there is no true questioning, we understand what time actually is." The sense of particularity comes out in the closing sentences: "This time of questioning cannot possibly coincide with that which is being questioned in the very next moment of time. For a while, questioning itself simply exists as time." In other words, time itself takes the form of questioning. What this also shows us is that because the reality of life occurs from one moment to the next, the questioning is one time, and realizing the question is another.

Inclusivity

On the other hand, Dōgen also writes in "Uji" of the inclusivity of time: "Each instant, each moment of time embodies all existences, all worlds." In other words, there is no particular moment or thing that exists that is not connected to every other moment or thing. In Buddhism, this connection of all things is also expressed as the "interdependent origination of all things," or *engi* (縁起); because this exists, that exists.

What is the significance of this idea of inclusivity? Within the moment presently occurring, all the moments extending into the infinite past and infinite future are also included. Additionally, what we call the "past" is not some sort of cut-and-dried event or sequence of events separate from the actuality of the present moment. Rather, even though it might be invisible, there is an inexplicable or incomprehensible reality wherein a skill learned in the past become inseparable from the present.

Really, there is nothing unusual about this, but rarely do we look at the past in that way. Ordinarily, we assume that the past has only a linear sense, that it is an account of events that occurred only in time already gone by, events that occurred—like the American Civil War, or the Crusades, or the Great Flood and Noah's ark, or even the creation of the universe—long before we were born. Understanding the past in a Buddhist sense, however, is to understand that it is we ourselves who create in our imaginations the images of these so-called past events. This past, however, is not something that should be understood as a phenomenon isolated and disconnected from the present, meaning, of course, *our* present. This is what is behind Dōgen's "Each instant, each moment of time embodies all existences, all worlds." That is, every moment is all-inclusive. Although I cannot understand why it is so, I do see that the person who practiced and learned how to drive a car more than fifty years ago is not dead; I give life to that learning and practice every time I get behind the wheel of a car.

If we imagine this inclusivity as a kind of physical or visible inclusivity, however, we are apt to come up with some strange conclusions.

For example, astronomers measure time in terms of light years, the distance it takes for light to travel in one year. It is said that the light from the nearest star takes approximately 4.3 light years to reach the earth. This would mean that when we look up into the sky at night, what we are actually seeing is not where or how bright those stars are now, but where and how bright they *were*. What we are looking at is not the present, but the past. This would seem to make common sense.

But if we accept this as an assumption about the physical universe, we would also have to say that, even though the difference pales in comparison to these astronomical measurements, the distance between the official with the starting gun standing at the side of the track and the runner in the inside lane versus the outside lane is different. When the gun goes off, the runner closest to the starter will hear it first and have an advantage, be it ever so slight.

Or take two people carrying on a conversation. Astronomically speaking, the distance from one side of the table to the other side may seem infinitesimal, but since there certainly is a distance, a certain measurable time must pass from the moment the words leave one's mouth until they strike the perceiving ears of the listener. Therefore, strictly speaking, even the words spoken by someone on the other side of the table were uttered in the immediate past. So, does that mean, then, that the person to whom we reply is not even the same person who asked the question? Accepting the idea of a sequential linear flow of time from past to present to future, we would have to say, yes. This idea is also expressed in the previous quote: "This time of questioning cannot possibly coincide with that which is being questioned in the very next moment of time. For a while, questioning itself simply exists as time."

In fact, even the words of affection spoken into the ear of one's lover are already "old"—past, dead—by the time the lover's ear perceives and processes them. Perhaps my final illustration appears a bit absurd—it certainly seems rather absurd to me. Still, if we are to accept the generally assumed argument on time and space as a kind of conventional truth, regardless of its relativity, my illustration of the two lovers must be included as falling within that truth. That is to say, the perceiver is hearing words from the past—however recent that past might be. We have to be careful in not understanding this inclusivity in some naive literal sense.

Dōgen writes further about the way we ordinarily perceive this phenomenon called time, putting the particularity and inclusivity of time into proper context:

> Despite that, ordinarily, people unfamiliar with the Buddhadharma hold on to a fixed idea of uji as signifying that there *was* a time [in the past] when they were three-headed, eight-armed beasts, and *another* time when they were sixteen-foot- or eight-foot-tall buddhas. In a sense, [they believe that] one time is like first crossing a river and, at a later time, climbing a mountain. Even though the rivers and mountains may have existed somewhere else, they think they have left them behind completely and are presently residing in the lofty crimson tower of a gorgeous palace.

The above passage depicts the way we ordinarily think of time: An event that occurred "in the past" is over. It no longer exists today. It is completely disconnected and cut off from the present. The "three-headed, eight-armed beast" is who we were a long time ago when we were struggling with our lives—crossing rivers, climbing mountains. But now, or at least very shortly, we will be living in a "gorgeous palace"—the palace of enlightenment!

Dōgen, however, says this way of looking at time is a distorted one:

Such people delude themselves by thinking they are now as far from those rivers and mountains as heaven is from earth. The true actuality of the Buddhadharma teaching, however, is not like this. The time they crossed the aforementioned mountains and rivers, they themselves had to have been present there, and so, they themselves were also time. Without a doubt, they had to have been completely present there; time did not disappear.

In other words, for Dōgen, presence is an intrinsic quality of time. "[T]hey had to have been completely present" means that since living time is always an all-inclusive present, the mountains and rivers that seem to have been crossed long ago are, in fact, living right now in the present moment. What Dōgen is also alluding to in this passage is that the "climbing of mountains or crossing of rivers," our rigorous training, although no longer visible, are still alive within us today. In this regard, Uchiyama Rōshi comments:

For instance, the period in my life when I went out doing takuhatsu, mendicant begging, for only one or two yen in order to stave off hunger and starvation is not behind me. That period is living right now as my personal experience. I've got no income coming in regularly now, but it doesn't faze me in the least, due to those years of going out on takuhatsu—so I don't see living out that life of material poverty as a bad deal at all. No, that past experience of poverty is not dead; it's a part of my present.

I worked as a tenzo in the kitchen for twenty years [too], and I believe that experience is living in my life today.

Dōgen adds further:

Still, regarding this working of past and present, both are wholly contained in the present climbing of the mountain. Within that time, the present looks back over the ten thousand peaks; it is not that they [one's experiences] have in any way disappeared.

Because of its subtlety, the significance of this might easily elude us. But even a little thought tells us that it must be the truth. If past experiences simply disappeared, how would it be possible to learn anything? If past experiences were simply divorced from the present, then we would never be able to "remember" or "recall" how to drive a car, or how to cook up a particular dish we like, or even how to string a sentence together.

Although we may grant an element of truth to the scientific way of measuring time and space—after all, that measurement works well enough in a practical way, well enough to send rockets to the moon and other planets—there are dimensions of time in a religious or noncalculating sense, which no human or mechanical calculation can measure.

Taking the illustrations of astronomical distance or the distance between lovers, as long as time is intrinsically tied to space, that is, as long as it takes time for a message to go from point A to point B, then we would have to say that all perceptions "external" to us must be perceived as the past, since during the interval of passage, the sender of the message will have had to change.

So what does this tell us about time? It tells us that, for Dōgen, time, in an all-inclusive sense, has a quality of presence, but not one of space. Uchiyama Rōshi refers to this as *mu no itten*: the point of no space, no time. The light of the star we see in the night sky, though having taken light years to reach us, is surely light we are seeing right now, in the present. This is why Dōgen writes:

It only seems as though it was in the distant past, but it's living in the present . . . do not think of "flying away" as the true quality or functioning of time. Do not imagine that such seeming passing away is real.

So, although it may be true that in one sense we can say the perceiver is always perceiving phenomena from the past—whether it be the twinkle of a star billions of miles away or the whisperings of a loved one millimeters (or less) away—from that same perspective, all perceptions are being perceived in the present, right now.

One ramification of the inclusivity of time

Earlier I mentioned how in the beginning of "Uji," Dōgen emphasizes the particularity of all things. However, if time had only an individual, particular aspect, it would be a very easy thing for us to cut off what I will call "responsible reflection" for our actions and assign guilt to others. To cite one example, let us consider the Holocaust. If we see all things only in a particularized way, then it is not so difficult to say the atrocities that occurred at that time were committed by those "other" evil people. "I" didn't do those things. After all, I wasn't even born yet. The Nazis did them. Or, if we happen to have been one of the Nazis, then blame can be put on the officers above us. Anyway, someone else did those things.

To illustrate further, the defense of the judges brought to trial at Nuremberg a few years after the end of the war centered around the appropriateness or inappropriateness of holding only certain Germans responsible for the decisions that directly or indirectly had a bearing on or were related to the "Final Solution." The argument goes: if the judges in the courts of the Third Reich are found guilty, then all the German people must be guilty, since almost everyone went along with what was happening, either by commission or omission. And not the German people alone, but the capitalists in America and Europe who directly or indirectly profited from the actions of the Third Reich must also be held accountable. As loathsome as such an argument might sound to some people, it must be admitted that there is a kernel of truth to such an argument.

If we see all phenomena as being inclusive, and if we see all times—past and future—contained in the present time, then it becomes impossible to view only certain "others of the past" as evil perpetrators. In other words, to understand time as inclusive of all times means that there are no Nazis outside of ourselves. There are no past atrocities committed from which we can in any way excuse ourselves. The horror of the Holocaust is the inability to see the potential within ourselves to commit such deeds. Moreover, it is from seeing that horror that we are able to draw strength not to act in such a way whenever we are confronted with the potential of such a situation occurring (regardless of the scale). This is what I mean by the expression "responsible reflection."

This is true for the Holocaust as well as for the Japanese atrocities committed against the Chinese at Nanking and other places in Asia; it is true for all the atrocities committed by the Americans, whether it be those against Native American peoples during the expansion across the continent between the 1840s and the 1880s or the fire bombings of Tokyo and other Japanese cities during World War II, not to mention Hiroshima or Nagasaki, or the napalming of large parts of Vietnam in the mid-1960s and into the 1970s, or the egregious acts committed by so-called standard bearers for a "pure" (white) America against people of color; it is true for the more recent happenings in North and Central America, Africa, Southeast Asia, and Central Europe. Indeed, can any place in our world be exempt?

On a personal level, as an illustration of the past still functioning in the present—my present—I could point to the years I was involved in the civil rights movement. The lesson I learned then, and which I am still learning, is how not to treat other human beings due to differences in skin color or culture or language. That lesson has continued and still continues to serve me very well.

I strongly feel that, far too often, philosophical concepts have been taken up by scholars as abstract theories with little connection to the scholar's or philosopher's own life, much less to all the social tragedies that often tend to be overlooked. The damage done by such abstraction, for example, is that in the case of depicting Dōgen's view of time, it is too often presented as a generalized theory of being or existence and time, totally disconnected from the everyday life of the person making the depiction or to the surrounding society. In recent years, for example, defenders of a certain philosopher have argued that his ideas had *naively* gotten completely separated from the ramifications of his political actions. Moreover, scholars tend to depict Dōgen as some sort of otherworldly purist, but if we read between the lines in such works as *Gakudō Yōjinshū*, it should be quite clear that Dōgen is no ivory temple purist.

Look at the following passage from the *Gakudō Yōjinshū*:

> Some say that *bodaishin* [bodhisattva spirit] is the mind of unsurpassed and incomparable wisdom having no connection with fame or personal benefit. Others say that it [bodhisattva spirit] is the mind that comprehends the "three thousand worlds in a single moment," while others suggest that "*bodaishin* is the reality wherein no delusion arises." Still others say that "*bodaishin* is that which enters into the realm of Buddha." People who speak like this are wantonly slandering it! Though being right in the middle of it [the Buddha Way], they are as far from it as they could be. They have no comprehension of the bodhisattva spirit![229]

Dōgen isn't questioning the validity of the Buddhist passages that have been quoted by various well-known priests of that day; he is questioning the sincerity of the priests themselves, saying they slander the teachings due to their overt desire for fame and political power. Dōgen, otherworldly? Hardly.

One significance of seeing both the particularity and the inclusivity of time is that the former encourages us to take stock of our own personal

229. Kishizawa Ian 岸沢惟安老師編輯, ed., *(Eihei Shoso) Dōgen Zenji Gakudō Yojinshū Teijiroku* (永平初祖)道元禅師学道用心衆提耳録 (Daijiji Publications 大慈寺発行, 1979), 2.

actions, to see that our life is not something that we should let others take charge of, and to not be disappointed and blame others if events don't go our way; while an understanding of the latter is essential in encouraging us not to deceive ourselves into thinking that we are somehow superior and exempt from our past actions or the sufferings of those around us. I do not believe that those "three-headed, eight-armed angry beasts" or those "mountains and rivers" of the past that Dōgen mentions in the text are merely the unrefined uncouth actions of "past" lives or the trials and hardships that Zen monks have undergone on their climb toward the peak of some fantastic enlightenment. I believe those "beasts" and those "mountains and rivers" are closely linked to Dōgen's personalization of time. That is, there was no way Dōgen could divorce who he himself was from all the havoc and chaos of his times in Kamakura-period Japan. This personalization of time is expressed later in the text as *gouji*, or "the personal experiencing of living time." Inhuman actions committed at any time in any age must be reflected on by all people in a personal way and seen as a part of one's larger self-identity.[230]

230. In 2001, I had the privilege of giving a talk at an international conference on the legacy of the Holocaust. Before I presented my talk, a copanelist, Eva Mozes Kor, spoke. Eva and her sister Miriam were among the many sets of twins who had been the victims of the deadly and terrible experiments conducted by Nazi SS officer and pseudo-physician Josef Mengele at Auschwitz. After the war, Eva and Miriam were freed from the camp but neither of them ever forgot their experiences there, and for many years they suffered with that burden.

At the conference, Eva explained why she had to forgive Mengele for the deadly and demonic experiments performed on her and her sister. As Eva stated during her talk, as long as she was unable to forgive Mengele, she could never be free. And that is exactly what Eva did in 1995. She wrote and signed a document forgiving Mengele. Sitting right next to Eva, I could see that there were a number of people in the audience who were shaking their heads, thinking "No, never, how could you ever forgive such a monster?" However, Eva said, "I felt a burden of pain was lifted from my shoulders."

From a Buddhist perspective, I have long felt that the problem centered on the issue of reconciliation. However, the reconciliation I am referring to is not some general reconciliation between Jews and Poles. Rather it is reconciliation within *each* Jewish survivor

Although I have outlined the aspect of inclusivity by writing about the many human atrocities of the "past," I do so not because I wish to write about horror or the morbidity of life. I do so rather because few Buddhists seem to write about these connections. Of course, seeing the past within the present through the illustration of human tragedy or through one's own personal tragedy is just one side. Dōgen writes of the future within the present as well:

> Because ordinarily, we take it for granted that living time and all existences do not live within ourselves, we assume that the sixteen-foot-tall golden body cannot reside within us. Consequently, we remain unable to imagine that such a Buddha could in any way lie within us.

First of all, Dōgen is criticizing in this passage a prevalent belief of his time that people were living in the *mappō* (末法) or final, most unenlightened stage. The belief was that there was little hope for gaining enlightenment even in several lifetimes, let alone in one lifetime. Any sort of salvation was possible only through belief in Amida Buddha, whose power to save all beings was referred to as *tariki* (他力), or "other-power." If this idea of other-power were interpreted dualistically, then it would be only natural for Dōgen to regard it as a heresy.[231] If the future

---

(and within *each* Pole) of the person who experienced the camp life of Auschwitz and that person's postcamp life. That is why Eva said, "I was no longer a victim of Auschwitz. I was no longer a prisoner of my tragic past. So I say to everybody, *Forgive your worst enemy. It will heal your soul and set you free.*" Eva didn't say *forget*, she said *forgive*. From a Buddhist perspective, Eva's forgiveness was also a total acknowledgment of her camp life; it was an internal reconciliation. From a Buddhist perspective, the Mengele she forgave was the Mengele that had existed inside Eva's mind all these years.

231. The key word here is "dualistically." From our understanding of Buddhadharma as a teaching, Dōgen's *jin issai jiko* (尽一切自己) is no different from Shinran's *zettai tariki* (絶対他力). That is, the reality behind both expressions is the same when we view them from a nondual perspective.

were not included in the living present, then how would it be possible for anyone to recognize what a buddha or the Buddha is?

Perhaps the following example will help to elucidate my point. Several years ago, people from all over the world gathered in Kyoto to study and practice Buddhism. Some would go from one temple to another; we used to call it "temple hopping." One could often hear conversations like the following.

"I just visited Zenzenji Temple and Akuzenji Temple. The abbot at Zenzenji is worthless. He eats meat and criticizes the monks too much. He surely can't be enlightened."

"Yeah, man. I know what you mean. That guy at Akuzenji isn't any good either. He keeps asking me stupid questions like why I want to practice Zen! He's no Buddha. But that abbot at Nozenji must be enlightened. He served me some wonderful *matcha* (powdered tea)."

The question one has to ask here is how do these two people determine who is or is not enlightened? What do they use as a measure? If any of the abbots at any of the temples these people visited actually were enlightened, then how could they know the abbots' enlightenment unless they themselves were already enlightened and could recognize it? In other words, if one is not innately enlightened, then how could you recognize it if it actually appeared? It doesn't make sense. That is why Dōgen writes that the future (read "enlightenment" here) must lie within the present.

In summary, regarding the aspects of the particularity and inclusivity of time, although the former may seem to be easier to articulate, since in our everyday lives particular things seem so visible, both aspects are indispensable in understanding Dōgen's view of time. The former is stressed for those who have difficulty appreciating their own uniqueness, while the latter is emphasized for those who have difficulty seeing the connections between themselves and all other people, things, and events going on around them. I think it is because of this difficulty in seeing the interconnectedness of all things that the aspect of inclusivity tends to be emphasized more.

Living time as whole self, or jiko.

The relationship between the particularity and inclusivity of the phenomenon of time can be expressed in other ways. For example, Dōgen writes:

> Jiko is fully arrayed and manifests as the entire universe. . . . This principle of universal identity as time means to recognize one's total identity as it manifests through the myriad of phenomena and circumstances.

Here, Dōgen speaks of jiko and inclusivity, but he also advises us to examine particularity and "investigate and winnow through all the individual things, all the various phenomena and circumstances of this universe."

Uchiyama Rōshi elucidates self as jiko and self as an individual entity in the following way:

$$\text{All} = 1 = 1/1 = 2/2 = \text{all/all}$$

In other words, jiko is all-inclusive. Or, as Uchiyama Rōshi also puts it, everything we encounter is our life—*deau tokoro waga seimei*.

We often confuse our uniqueness as individuals to mean some sort of self that is opposed to other people, or perhaps we interpret the idea of our own uniqueness to mean that we also have control or possession over other people or things. This is what I believe Dōgen is addressing here:

> Further, though the biased views of ordinary people, along with the internal conditions and external influences that affect those views, form people's misunderstanding, the dharmas are not people's possessions; it is simply that all these so-called dharmas temporarily inform the person.

Uchiyama Rōshi describes this illusory self as "one over all of humankind": one/all.

This way of looking at oneself is sometimes referred to in Buddhism as "the conditioned self." That is, our self-image or self-identity is formed by our language, culture, environment, anatomy, and so forth. Identity of self as an entity separate from other people or from our environment arises with thought. As soon as the thought of "I" forms, there has to be an opposing entity with which to contrast it. This process is not in itself good or bad. It just occurs. Later in "Uji," Dōgen explains further the connection between this all-inclusive self or whole self and this individual or particular self.

This inclusivity and particularity of things must not be taken in a physical or literal sense. This concept should always be applied to our everyday attitude. Or, to put in another way, it is a quality of mind.

Gouji: The personal experiencing of living time, or living the time of your life.

Gouji, the personal experiencing of time, is the aspect of time that, for Dōgen, takes the discussion out of abstract theory. Time cannot be separated from one's own personal life experience. On this point, Dōgen writes:

> The essential characteristic of uji is this: while all existences in all the various worlds are interconnected, each existence is unique in itself, and precisely because of this, we can speak of *personally* experiencing the living quick of time.

This personal experiencing of the living quick of time is precisely what separates religious experience from generalized speculative thinking.

On the one hand, while all existences are interconnected, each existence occurs moment-by-moment. Dōgen clarifies the significance of this a few lines later:

Because ordinarily, we take it for granted that living time and all existences do not live within ourselves, we assume that the sixteen-foot-tall golden body cannot reside within us. Consequently, we remain unable to imagine that such a buddha could in any way lie within us.

This is Dōgen's way of saying that people become confused about what Buddha is because they posit an absolute that is somewhere in the future and outside of themselves. This becomes crystal clear in the following passage:

> The functioning presence of the guardian deities and the other myriad protectors in all worlds and directions is the manifesting of our personal life experience as living time. This living time in all creatures both in the water and on the land, of the infinite situations and existences both visible and invisible, is the wholly personal manifesting of the entire power of uji.

The confusion regarding Buddha as being external to ourselves is a tragic one that sometimes leads to disastrous results. When Dōgen writes that Buddha is not external to ourselves, he is not attempting to set up the equation "I am the Enlightened One as opposed to all you other lost souls." This is, in fact, the error that those who would call themselves "gurus" make. What Dōgen means by provisionally writing of Buddha residing within us is nothing other than an identification of the life force with our own personal life. In the same sense, there is no difference between Dōgen's way of thinking and Jesus' statement that the Kingdom of Heaven lies within us.

Time neither "flies away" nor "resides" in some fixed place.

We often hear the clichéd expressions "time waits for no one" or "time flies like an arrow." Such expressions work fine as proverbs about general existence, but they make for poor Buddhadharma. The reason for this is because such expressions seem to inherently endow time with an existence separate from ourselves. But there is no person Time, who stands around on some corner, pacing back and forth, looking at his or her watch, waiting for our arrival.

Since Dōgen writes that entities and all phenomena are themselves time, he is giving a quality or definition to it far afield from the ordinary proverb, as likeable as these proverbs might be. Therefore, he writes:

> Do not think of "flying away" as a true quality or functioning of time.... If time were something that was cut off, there would have to be a gap. People are incapable of experiencing uji, because they are convinced only of the ephemeral appearance of time *uji*, because they are convinced only of [the reality of] the ephemeral appearance of time.

Well, if time is not some objective entity and does not fly away, then does that mean it exists or resides in some one place? Dōgen writes,

> People unquestioningly believe time comes and goes, but no human being has ever realized exactly where the living quick of time resides. Much less has any human being ever been liberated from time. Even though there might be someone who intellectually grasps where uji resides, who can possibly express living time itself?

All of this is simply Dōgen's way of trying to cut through any fixed definition of time as either an entity that passes—"flies away"—or resides in some specific place. It is his way of cutting through the seeming dualities of time. And this brings us to the next point in Dōgen's view of time, that of kyōryaku: moment-by-moment.

Kyōryaku is neither change nor stasis.

If particularity and inclusivity are both aspects or characteristics of time, then what is the true actuality of time? Dōgen uses various words to describe uji in the text: for example, *immo* or *jiko*. Another word he uses to refer to that reality prior to such distinctions as existence or non-existence, passing away or residing, particular or inclusive is *kyōryaku*. Translators often use words like "change" or "movement" to refer to *kyōryaku*, but first let's look again at the text.

> This living time in all creatures both in the water and on the land, of the infinite situations and existences both visible and invisible, is the wholly personal manifesting of the entire power of uji, the entire power of kyōryaku. Sit and practice until it is thoroughly clear that if uji were not all the power of kyōryaku, not a single thing would manifest, nor would there be any moment-by-moment [life].
>
> By kyōryaku—the living quick of moment-by-moment—I do not mean the way the wind and rain seem to blow from east to west as has been taught in the past. Kyōryaku does not imply immobility; neither does it imply progress or regression.

Uchiyama Rōshi's comment regarding the definition of *kyōryaku* is that "By *kyōryaku*, Dōgen Zenji does not mean movement or change, nor lack of such.... Truly, the living quick of the point of nothingness is that which transcends movement or nonmovement.... We see the appearances of change and become convinced that *kyōryaku* simply means change, but that is not how it should be understood in the Buddhist sense."

The basis in Buddhist thought for Uchiyama Rōshi's statement concerning kyōryaku not being change (nor no-change) centers on the concept of shohō jissō—all things are what they are. In other words, saying that things change or do not change, reside or pass away, exist or do not exist is to grasp one aspect of the tiger and declare that one has caught the whole tiger.

In the remainder of the text "Uji," Dōgen illustrates in various ways the identity of the interconnectedness or inclusivity of all things and the particularity or uniqueness of all things.

Through the limited examples I have given so far, I hope it is clear that we have to *wear* Dōgen like a loose garment, and not cherry-pick and use those passages that seem to conform with our own fixed, dualistic ideas. Finally, it is my sincerest hope that whatever we learn from Dōgen and our other ancestors, both male and female, we can manifest in our practice as compassion to relieve the suffering of all sentient beings. After all, isn't this what our vow as bodhisattvas is, to enable all beings to cross to the other shore?

Translators' Acknowledgments

There are many people I would like to thank for making this book possible. First of all, I want to thank Shōhaku Okumura for his translation of "Maka Hannya Haramitsu," but even more so for his friendship and advice. Next, I would like to thank Unzan Pfennig for going over both "Shoaku Makusa" and "Uji" line by line, paragraph by paragraph, offering insights and suggestions as to how to improve the clarity of the texts. Whenever I got stuck, it was Unzan who offered another perspective from which to view things. He also reminded me of the importance of living undefended. I also want to thank Jisho Warner for her tough love and for lending me her intellect and encouragement in trying to keep me focused. My living Dharma teacher, Takamine Dōyu Rōshi, also taught and supported me in various ways during the last ten years. Aoyama Shundō Rōshi has been and still is an inspiration to me to do my best and keep my antenna up. Morita Mihoko's always upbeat attitude and knowledge of Buddhism and Michael Lazarin's criticism and advice as a dear friend have both helped me to reflect on what is important to me. I cannot forget Miyo Harumi, Jeanne Beers, Hiromi Beck, Jun Ishimine, Jim Johnson, and Steve and Nobuko Yoshida for keeping me on my toes and challenging me to clarify the relevance of these two difficult fascicles written by a thirteenth-century Japanese Zen monk. They challenged me to clarify how a monk who lived over 750 years ago, coming from a totally different culture, society, social position, and country, could possibly have something to say to twenty-first-century Americans. And, without the encouragement, suggestions, and advice of my editor, Laura Cunningham, this book would never have taken the shape it has. Laura was far more than an editor. Her understanding of Buddhadharma also contributed much to this book. Finally, I want to thank my wife, Yuko, who has encouraged and supported me to continue my work over these many years, despite my shortcomings, stubbornness, and occasional lack of patience. Lest I forget, I also want to thank all the bodhisattvas and deities, visible and invisible, who continually support my life and without whom I would not be the person I am.

DAITSŪ TOM WRIGHT

While I taught at the Minnesota Zen Meditation Center from 1993 to 1996, we had a translation workshop. The first text I worked on with the group was *Shōbōgenzō* "Maka Hannya Haramitsu" and Uchiyama Rōshi's teishō on it. We usually had six or seven people. I made the first draft of a translation and explained the meaning of each word and each sentence and asked people to give me suggestions to make my "unique" English more readable and understandable. This study group was very interesting, because as I offered my translation and understanding, and those in the workshop offered their suggestions regarding the English, we studied and taught each other. It took about three years to complete "Maka Hannya Haramitsu." Then we began to work on "Genjō Kōan" and Uchiyama Rōshi's teishō on it. Unfortunately, my term as interim head teacher at MZMC was terminated before we completed "Genjō Kōan." I moved to California to teach at the Sōtō Zen Education Center in 1997 and became very busy. So I did not have time to finalize the translation of "Maka Hannya Haramitsu" and Uchiyama Rōshi's teishō and publish it until today. I deeply appreciate the assistance from all the participants of the translation workshop. This translation is the fruit of the mutual study of the Buddhadharma and English.

I also appreciate Rev. Daitsū Tom Wright's kindness for accepting this translation as a part of his book on translations of "Uji" and "Shoaku Makusa" along with Uchiyama Rōshi's teishōs on those fascicles. I first met Tom when I sat my initial five-day sesshin at Antaiji in January

1969, when I was a twenty-year-old university student. Since then, for almost fifty years, we have been Dharma brothers. We worked together on translations of *Tenzo Kyōkun* and Uchiyama Rōshi's commentary, which later became *Refining Your Life*; *Bendōwa* and Uchiyama Rōshi's commentary, published as *Wholehearted Way*; and *Opening the Hand of Thought,* Uchiyama Rōshi's own writing. He was my English teacher for my translations in 1980s. Without his help and support, I could not be doing what I am doing now.

SHŌHAKU OKUMURA

Bibliography

Bodhi, Bhikkhu, trans. *The Connected Discourses of the Buddha: A New Translation of the* Samyutta Nikāya. Boston: Wisdom Publications, 2000.

Frederic, Louis. *Buddhism: Flammarion Iconographic Guides*. Paris: Flammarion Press, 1995.

Hakeda, Yoshito S., trans. *The Awakening of Faith*. New York: Columbia University Press, 1967.

Kyōji Ishii, trans. *Shōbōgenzō*. 5 vols. Tokyo: Kawade Shobō Shinsha, 1998.

Kishizawa Ian 岸沢惟安. *Shōbōgenzō Zenkō* 正法眼蔵全講 [Lectures on the *Shōbōgenzō*]. 24 vols. Tokyo: Daihōrinkaku, 1972.

Komazawa University 駒澤大学内 Publications Committee 禅学大辞典編纂所, ed. *Zengaku Daijiten* 禅学大辞典. Tokyo: Daishukan Shoten, 大修館書店, 1985.

Leighton, Taigen Dan, and Shōhaku Okumura, trans. *Dōgen's Extensive Record*. Boston: Wisdom Publications, 2010.

Mizuno Yaoko, ed. 水野弥穂子. *Shōbōgenzō* 正法眼蔵. 4 vols. Tokyo: Iwanami Shoten, 1993.

Nakamura Gen 中村元. *Bukkyōgo Daijiten* 仏教語大辞典, Tokyo Shoseki, 東京書籍, 1983.

Nishiari Bokusan Zenji. *Shōbōgenzō Keiteki*. Tokyo: Daihorinkaku, 1965.

Okumura, Shōhaku, et al. *Dōgen's Genjō Kōan: Three Commentaries*. Berkeley, CA: Counterpoint, 2011.

Rahula, Walpola. *What the Buddha Taught*. New York: Grove Press, 1959.

Uchiyama, Kōshō. *How to Cook Your Life: From the Zen Kitchen to Enlightenment*. Trans. by Thomas Wright. Boston: Shambhala Publications, 2005.

Uchiyama, Kōshō. *Opening the Hand of Thought*. Trans. and ed. by Thomas Wright, Jisho Warner, and Shōhaku Okumura. Boston: Wisdom Publications, 2015.

Uchiyama, Kōshō. *Shōbōgenzō: Uji-Shoaku Makusa wo Ajiwau* 正法眼蔵：有

時・諸悪莫作を味わう (*Shōbōgenzō: Appreciating Uji and Shoaku Makusa*). Tokyo: Hakujusha Publishers, 1984.

Uchiyama, Kōshō. *The Wholehearted Way: A Translation of Eihei Dōgen's Bendōwa*. Trans. by Shōhaku Okumura and Taigen Daniel Leighton. Rutland, VT: Tuttle, 1970.

Watson, Burton, trans. *The Lotus Sutra*. New York: Columbia University Press, 1993.

Index

About the Contributors

KŌSHŌ UCHIYAMA was born in Tokyo in 1912. He received a master's degree in Western philosophy at Waseda University in 1937 and became a Zen priest four years later under Kōdō Sawaki Rōshi. Upon Sawaki's death in 1965, he became abbot of Antaiji, a temple and monastery then located on the outskirts of Kyoto. Uchiyama Rōshi developed the practice at Antaiji until his retirement in 1975. After retiring, he lived with his wife at Nōke-in, a small temple outside Kyoto, where he continued to write, publish, and meet with the many people who found their way to his door, until his death in March 1998. He wrote over twenty books on Zen, including translations of Dōgen Zenji in modern Japanese with commentaries, as well as various shorter essays. His *Opening the Hand of Thought: Foundations of Zen Buddhist Practice* is available in English from Wisdom Publications, as is *The Zen Teaching of Homeless Kodo*, with Shōhaku Okumura. He was an origami master as well as a Zen master and published several books on origami.

About the Translators

DAITSŪ TOM WRIGHT, born and raised in Wisconsin, lived in Japan for over forty years. He practiced and studied under Uchiyama Rōshi from 1968 until the latter's death and was ordained as a priest in 1974. A graduate of the University of Wisconsin, he taught as a professor in the English Language and Culture Program at Ryukoku University in Kyoto. He was a teacher for the Kyoto Sōtō Zen Center until 1995, and then conducted zazen gatherings with Rev. Dōyu Takamine in Kyoto and Tamba.

Rev. Wright has worked on the translation and editing of several works on Zen, as well as writing on Zen, the Holocaust from a Buddhist perspective, and Japanese gardens (*Samadhi on Zen Gardens—Dynamism and Tranquility*, with Katsuhiko Mizuno, Suiko Books, Mitsumura Suiko Shoin, 2010). Retiring from the university in 2010, he now lives with his wife in Hilo, Hawaii.

SHŌHAKU OKUMURA is a Sōtō Zen priest and Dharma successor of Kōshō Uchiyama Rōshi. He is a graduate of Komazawa University and has practiced in Japan at Antaiji, Zuioji, and the Kyoto Sōtō Zen Center, and in Massachusetts at the Pioneer Valley Zendo. He is the former director of the Sōtō Zen Buddhism International Center in San Francisco. His previously published books include *Dōgen's Extensive Record: A Translation of the Eihei Kōroku* with Taigen Dan Leighton, *Living by Vow: A Practical Introduction to Eight Essential Zen Chants and Text*, *The Zen Teachings of Homeless Kodo* with Kōshō Uchiyama, and *Realizing Genjōkōan: The Key to Dōgen's Shōbō-genzō*. He is the founding teacher of the Sanshin Zen Community, based in Bloomington, Indiana, where he lives with his family.

What to Read Next
from Wisdom Publications

Opening the Hand of Thought
Foundations of Zen Buddhist Practice
Kōshō Uchiyama
Translated and edited by Tom Wright, Jisho Warner, and Shōhaku Okumura

"If you read one book on Zen this year, this should be that book."—James Ishmael Ford, head teacher, Boundless Way Zen, and author of *If You're Lucky, Your Heart Will Break*

Dōgen's Extensive Record
A Translation of the Eihei Kōroku
Taigen Dan Leighton and Shōhaku Okumura

"Taigen and Shōhaku are national treasures."—Norman Fischer, author of *Sailing Home*

Realizing Genjōkōan
The Key to Dōgen's Shōbōgenzō
Shōhaku Okumura
Foreword by Taigen Dan Leighton

"A stunning commentary. Like all masterful commentaries, this one finds in the few short lines of the text the entire span of the Buddhist teachings."—*Buddhadharma: The Buddhist Review*

The Zen Teaching of Homeless Kōdō
Kōshō Uchiyama and Shōhaku Okumura

"Kōdō Sawaki was straight to the point, irreverent, and deeply insightful —and one of the most influential Zen teachers for us in the West. I'm very happy to see this book."—Brad Warner, author of *Hardcore Zen*

Living by Vow
A Practical Introduction to Eight Essential Zen Chants and Texts
Shōhaku Okumura

"An essential resource for students and teachers alike."—Dosho Port, author of *Keep Me in Your Heart a While*

Wisdom

About Wisdom Publications

Wisdom Publications is the leading publisher of classic and contemporary Buddhist books and practical works on mindfulness. To learn more about us or to explore our other books, please visit our website at wisdompubs .org or contact us at the address below.

Wisdom Publications
199 Elm Street
Somerville, MA 02144 USA

We are a 501(c)(3) organization, and donations in support of our mission are tax deductible.

Wisdom Publications is affiliated with the Foundation for the Preservation of the Mahayana Tradition (FPMT).

Thank you for buying this book!

Visit wisdompubs.org/deepest
for an interview with Kosho Uchiyama:
"Life Is Not Just Winning or Losing"